THE HIDING PLACES OF GOD

also by the author

A Thief in the Night
The Spoiled Priest
Seven Other Demons
Coleridge: Poet and Revolutionary
Earth to Earth

THE HIDING PLACES OF GOD

JOHN CORNWELL

WARNER BOOKS

A Time Warner Company

Warner Books, Inc., 666 Fifth Avenue, New York, NY 10103

W A Time Warner Company

Printed in the United States of America

First printing: October 1991

10 9 8 7 6 5 4 3 2 1

Library of Congress Cataloging-in-Publication Data

Cornwell, John, 1940-
    The hiding places of God : a personal journey into the world of
religious visions, holy objects, and miracles / John Cornwell.
        p.   cm.
    ISBN 0-446-51468-3
    1. Spiritual life—Catholic authors.   2. Experience (Religion)
3. Mysticism—Catholic Church.   4. Visions.   5. Miracles.
6. Cornwell, John, 1940-   I. Title.
BX2350.2.C634   1991
248.2—dc20   91-13911
                                                                              CIP

Book design by H. Roberts

For Tobias Wolff

Acknowledgments

I owe special thanks to Dan Grisewood and Philip Caraman, who encouraged me to write this book from the outset. My debt to the many people who helped me on my journey will be apparent in the text, and I thank them all.

For their willingness to talk around the topic, I am grateful to Aelred Burrows, Audrey Charlton, Bryan Chestle, Don Cupitt, Eamon Duffy, Jack Finnegan, Charlie Glass, John Heilpern, Dennis Hickley, Jo Klein, Emma Loveridge, Gerald O'Collins, Janet Martin Soskice, Michael Walsh, and John Wilkins.

Cyprian Smith's *The Way of Paradox* and Nicholas Lash's *Easter in Ordinary* were crucial sources of inspiration.

My mother, Kathleen Cornwell, gave invaluable moral support, as did my wife Gabrielle, my daughter Johanna, and my son Jonathan. Thanks are also due to John Harvey, who read the manuscript, and to Clare Bayley and Matthew Lohn, who gave practical assistance.

I am grateful to the rector and staff of the Venerable English College in Rome for hospitality and conversation.

I completed the book in ideal circumstances at Jesus College, Cambridge, under its professional fellow-commoner scheme; I wish to thank the Fellows of Jesus, now my colleagues, for their kindness and generosity.

Finally, I must thank Bob Lescher, Carol Smith, Susan Suffes, Judith Flanders, John Guest, and Peter Carson.

Contents

Preface

Not long before he died I was sent by a newspaper to Antibes to interview Graham Greene.

He greeted me at the door of his apartment with a mischievous smile of anticipation. We had agreed to talk about religious belief.

His living room was modest: just room for a cane sofa with cushions, and matching armchairs; a table covered with a simple cloth served as a desk. There were shelves with rows of meticulously displayed books, many of them theological—among them, the distinctive covers of Father Hans Kung.

Our conversation was to range over a number of religious issues. Greene had often been at variance with his Church on matters such as birth control, papal infallibility, and Liberation Theology; but the longer we talked, the more he surprised me by proving himself a free thinker on every subject that was raised.

At one point we were talking about sin.

"I've always rather disliked the word sin," he said. "It's got a kind of professional, a dogmatic ring about it."

"Do you believe in Satan?" I asked him.

He smiled wanly. "No. I don't think so."

"Do you believe in angels?"

A chuckle. "No, I *don't* really."

This led to the obvious question: "So, *what about a future life?*"
He paused. He was gazing at me; his bright cornflower blue eyes were disconcerting in the light of the morning sun.

"I would love to believe in it," he said. "And one would like to let it be more than this world."

"Do you believe in Hell?"

"I don't believe in Hell. I never *have* believed in Hell. I think it's contradictory. They say that God is mercy . . . so it's contradictory . . . I think there may be *nullity,* and for others something that is conscious. But I don't believe in Hell and I feel that Purgatory may happen in *this* life, not in a future life."

"And Heaven?"

"I couldn't conceive what Heaven could be. If it exists it's an entity I can't visualize in any way. My idea of heaven would be that it would be something active, rather than happiness with people one had loved, a form of activity in which we could influence life on earth . . . perhaps one's prayers in that state could influence somebody on earth."

"What about God?" I said.

He fell silent. He just sat there, his eyes looking strange, shifty, haunted.

"Do you contemplate God in a pure, disembodied way?" I asked.

"I'm afraid I don't," he said flatly.

We moved on, eventually to skirt around the question of rational basis for belief or unbelief.

For a brief moment Greene looked down unsmilingly into his lap. Then he began to chuckle breathily with raised shoulders. "That reminds me of Freddy Ayer," he said, "you know, the atheistic philosopher. He always said that given just half an hour he would convince me that there was absolutely *nothing.*"

"Did you ever take him up on that?"

"No. It would have *bored* me," he answered with some feeling.

"Your faith," I said at last, "is nevertheless tenuous."

"One is attracted to the *faith,*" he said. "Believing is the problem . . . But in a curious way I've always believed that *doubt* was a more important thing for human beings. It's human to doubt."

"So what is it that keeps you within the fold of belief?"

He turned, fixing me with a look that announced an imminent ace.

"I suppose," he chuckled, "that I've been lucky enough to *doubt* my disbelief."

Just as I was wondering where we could go from here, he said: "I am able to doubt my disbelief because I once had a very slight mystical experience. In 1949 I traveled out to Italy to see a famous mystic known as Padre Pio. He lived in a remote monastery in the Gargano Peninsula at a place called San Giovanni Rotondo. He had the stigmata, displaying the wounds of Christ in his hands, feet, and side. At this time my belief in God had been on the ebb; I think I was losing my faith. I went out of curiosity, wondering whether this man, whom I had heard so much of, would impress me. I stopped in Rome on the way and a monsignor from the Vatican came to have a drink with me. 'Oh!' he said, 'that holy fraud! You're wasting your time. He's bogus.' "

Greene looked up at me challengingly.

"But Padre Pio had been examined by doctors of every faith and no faith," he went on. "He'd been examined by Jewish, Protestant, Catholic, and atheist specialists, and baffled them all. He had these wounds on his hands and feet, the size of a twenty pence piece, and because he was not allowed to wear gloves saying Mass he pulled his sleeves down to try and hide them. He'd got a very nice peasant-like face, a little bit on the heavy side. I was warned that his was a very long Mass; so I went with my woman friend of that period to the mass at five-thirty in the morning. He said it in Latin, and I thought that thirty-five minutes had passed. Then when I got outside the Church I looked at my watch and it had been two hours."

Greene stopped for a moment as if to gauge my reaction.

"I couldn't work out where the lost time had gone," he went on. "And this is where I came to a small faith in a mystery. Because that *did* seem an extraordinary thing."

He sat for a while in reverie. Then he took a well-worn wallet from his trouser pocket and fished out two small photographs. They were dog-eared, sepia. As he handed them over I detected a faint air of self-consciousness; as if, English gentleman that he was, he had been caught out in a gesture of Latin superstition.

One depicted Padre Pio in his habit, smiling. The other showed the monk gazing adoringly at the host during Mass.

The possession of the pictures, the gesture of sharing them, seemed a declaration of loyalty to faith.

"Why do you keep them in your wallet like that?" I asked.

"I don't know," he said. He looked a trifle haunted. "I just put them in, and I've never taken them out."

I decided to press him a little further.

"If you hadn't had your mysterious experience with Padre Pio you might possibly have lost your faith?"

"I don't think my belief is very strong; but, yes, perhaps I would have lost it altogether . . ."

"So what, in the final analysis," I said, "does religion mean to you?"

Greene looked at me directly, wonderingly. He seemed at that moment ageless; there was an impression about him of extraordinary tolerance, ripeness.

"I think . . . it's a mystery," he said slowly and with some feeling. "There *is* a mystery. There is something inexplicable in life. And it's important because people are not going to believe in all the explanations given by science or even the Churches . . . It's a mystery which can't be destroyed . . ."

There was a time when Greene's remarks might have struck me as superficial, characteristic of a tendency to settle for a "God of the gaps," a God of missing explanations. For how could anybody propose that a meaningful religious faith could be based on anything so shallow, so haphazardly procurable, and ephemeral, as a sense of time contraction?

As it was, I found the story of his "small faith in a mystery" both moving and deeply significant, and not a little coincidental, for at the time of our meeting I had been traveling for a year or so in search of the scope and meaning of the "paranormal" element in religion. In the course of my journey I had traversed a varied landscape of alleged prodigies, miracles, mysteries, signs, and wonders, and encountered, on the way, many people who had tasted the mysterious in their struggles with belief and unbelief, including, even, the atheist philosopher, Freddy Ayer, and the remarkable, if by then ghostly, Padre Pio.

By the time I met Greene I had learned enough to understand that a "small faith in a mystery" is not the culminating discovery of religious conviction, so much as an unexpected *trigger* for the tussle between doubt and "doubt of doubt," which often runs its course only to return to its starting point. Who could doubt that Graham

Greene of all people was familiar with the restless, circular nature of such a struggle.

In this sense my interview with Greene was both a suitable end to my geographical journey and a fitting prelude to this book, which tells the story of a quest for faith that is both a process of discovery and a returning.

Then my delivered soul herself shall learn
A darker knowledge and in hatred turn
From every thought of God mankind has had.
Thought is a garment and the soul's a bride
That cannot in that trash and tinsel hide:
Hatred of God may bring the soul to God.

W. B. Yeats

PART ONE

SMALL MYSTERIES

1

An American Dream

Several years ago I experienced a small mystery in the form of a religious dream that was fulfilled within a few days in waking reality. Although this event was unnerving, like having someone else's hand thrust in one's pocket, I now realize that there was nothing unique about it. The unusual aspect is that I was an unbeliever as far as religion is concerned (although twenty years earlier I had abandoned, after seven years' study, a vocation to the Roman Catholic priesthood).

So when I decided, as a result of that dream, to explore the incidence and the significance of wider realms of paranormal religious phenomena of this sort, I was able to approach the subject from the standpoint of an agnostic investigator who had once been on intimate terms with a religion rich in supernatural and mystical lore.

Throughout my working life as a newspaper executive, which had involved periods working as a foreign correspondent and foreign editor, I had frequently reflected that religion lent legitimacy to much of the world's violence and misery. It seemed to me that religion would have something to recommend it if only humanity could act upon the belief that we are all equal in the sight of God; but I saw no evidence that religionists *en masse* are capable of putting this crucial profession of faith into practice.

So it never occurred to me that after twenty-odd years of confident agnosticism I could, in the space of several days, become obsessed with a "religious" dream experience. And the reader may wonder what kind of dream it was that could have produced such a reaction.

It all began in New York City where I had arrived from London on a publishing trip that was to take me three thousand miles through the United States. On that first night, in a hotel in midtown Manhattan, I went to bed exhausted with jet lag and fell into a deep sleep. The context of the dream I had that night was remote from any of my professional preoccupations, or my role as a husband and father. And yet, it seemed to illuminate in a mysterious way my entire life:

> *I am walking in the garden of what appears to be a college campus, with a range of low, redbrick buildings in the distance. The sun is shining in a bright, blue sky. The air is clean, cold and sweet. Beyond the buildings the tops of tall trees wave slightly in the breeze, the foliage gold, silver, and scarlet. The place is unfamiliar, and yet there is a sense of sacred presence mixed with nostalgia and melancholy.*
>
> *There is a pathway bordered by recently planted shrubs. Young men dressed in black robes are approaching in twos and threes. They are contemporaries of my seminary days, and yet their faces glow with youth and innocence. This is all the more painful as I am aware that I have aged by comparison; I feel ashamed of my appearance, conscious of my sins, convinced that I will be condemned and rejected.*
>
> *To my relief, however, the first two figures acknowledge me cheerfully. I begin to experience an overwhelming sense of grief, as if for lost happiness; a sense of having returned to where I belong.*

When I awoke the next morning I had the impression that the dream had recurred a number of times during the night. The pillow was wet.

After a morning of business appointments I set out after lunch in a rental car to drive to Philadelphia. That night I had the dream once more, identical in every detail with the one of the previous night: the sense of sacred presence, the young men in black—the apparent contemporaries of my youth—greeting me; the sense of loss.

The dream continued to recur, night after night, as I drove on down through Baltimore, Washington, D.C., and on to Atlanta, a blur of newspaper offices, filling stations, and fast-food restaurants.

The dream sequence finally came to an end in New Orleans. After checking into the Howard Johnson Motel, I went out after dark to look for a restaurant. I walked several blocks, then lost my bearings; the streets were deserted and ill-lit, but as yet I had no sense of danger until I found myself in the open space of a parking lot adjoining the rear of the Hyatt Hotel complex. The building was perhaps two hundred yards away; I began to head briskly across the lot toward the hotel, remembering that I had $2,000 in traveler's checks in my pocket, when I heard a voice somewhere to my left.

"Hey man, can we talk with you?"

Four young men emerged from behind a car about fifty yards away. One appeared to be carrying a wrench. In an instant I took off, sprinting on my toes. As they came after me I could hear their curses, the sound of their soles on the gravel lot. Ahead was a system of wire security cages and a staff entrance.

Convinced I was going to die, I thought: "God, please spare me and I'll believe in you!" The men were no more than a few yards behind me, and one had already punched me in the shoulder, when I seemed to be swept forward and away from them with incredible speed. I stormed through a doorway and collapsed in front of an armed security guard. As I passed out I saw the young men in black in my dream coming toward me with all the vividness of waking reality, as if they were now mixed with my attackers.

I eventually returned to my motel in a taxi and went straight to bed. That night I slept soundly, and for the first time for many nights, dreamlessly.

The next morning I wondered whether the series of dreams had not given me some sort of psychic energy and readiness. This was a vague, illogical feeling, connected not so much with the dream's content as with a sense that during the previous two weeks I had somehow been in an unusual psychic state of expectation, a feeling of being affected by a presence or power.

I did not give my bargain with God another thought.

I flew to St. Louis, where I rented another car and checked into a Holiday Inn on Route 55. On Sunday morning, a week after the mugging attempt in New Orleans, I got up early, planning to spend the day touring some of the townships along the Mississippi. The road was empty, sparkling with ground frost and sunlight. After twenty minutes a white circular church like a stranded spacecraft came into view, and I felt an urge to go inside. I parked the car and entered the building by a long ramp.

A service had been recently performed and shafts of sunlight penetrated the tentacles of incense smoke that lingered above the high altar. The exotic scent was entrancing, but I felt panicky and hot. I went out of the nearest exit, but being a circular church it was not the door by which I had entered. I burst from the building in a state of nervous excitement. Outside the air was cold, fresh, autumnal. I looked about me and my heart was suddenly suspended with terror.

Ahead were pathways and lawns bordered by low redbrick buildings beyond which stirred the tops of tall trees in their autumn glory—silver, gold, and crimson.

I had stepped into my dream, of this I had not the slightest doubt.

Ahead was the door through which the young men in black should emerge. Appalled by a sense of inevitability I stood paralyzed on the pathway for several minutes.

Then the door opened and a small old man with pure white hair came out. Dressed from head to toe in the black habit of a Benedictine monk, he limped very slowly along the path and as he drew level he stopped.

"Where am I?" I asked.

"St. Louis Abbey," he said in a clear English accent. Then he added with a bleak smile: "I have to set off early because I'm so lame. I'd stop for a chat, but I mustn't be late for prayers."

He made a gesture of farewell and shuffled away. As he entered the church, a bell rang somewhere in the building ahead, and I continued to stand on the pathway.

After a minute or two the door opened once more; then, first one monk, then two, then three, began to spill out of the building to hurry along the pathway on their way to the church. They came in order of age, the youngest first. With their shorn heads and ascetic features they had a common stamp of appearance. As they passed by none spoke, but they all gave a brief nod, as if of recognition.

A dozen or so monks passed along the pathway, and after the

last one had gone I followed them to the door of the church. I did not enter; I stood outside listening to the sound of Gregorian chant echoing in that strange space-age building.

The serenity and healing quality of Benedictine hospitality is indescribable. I spent a day and a night with the monks of St. Louis Abbey, eating with them as a guest in their refectory and enjoying their company in the common room. This small monastery was founded in the mid-1960s by the English Benedictines of Ampleforth Abbey in Yorkshire and, as if to further confirm the prognostication of the dream, I was to find among them several contemporaries of my student days who had been transplanted from England permanently to America's Midwest.

It seemed clear to me as I sat among them that I had been confronted with a peculiar intellectual and emotional challenge. The million-to-one coincidence with my past in a suburb of St. Louis would have been extraordinary enough, but the foreshadowing dreams gave the episode a "miraculous" quality.

As I drove away from the monastery the next day I continued to sense something of an indefinable longing for a presence associated both with the nostalgia of the dream and with St. Louis Abbey. It was a feeling that never left me during the rest of my journey to Chicago, Cleveland, Pittsburgh, and beyond. I was in a state of obsession, constantly mulling over the implications of the dream experience and its fulfillment.

Back in New York I had an oddly appropriate encounter for somebody in need of an antidote to mystical experience. I went out to dinner in Greenwich Village with a party of friends and found myself squeezed into a corner with the world-famous atheist, Professor Freddy Ayer, who was the stepfather of our host.

The professor, who was in his late seventies, looked spry for his years, although he had recently suffered a bout of pneumonia which had put him in the hospital. His hooded eyes, hook nose, and slightly drooping, sardonic lips gave an impression of sensuality, an air of fastidious disdain. He looked rakish in a well-cut English suit and a floral patterned silk tie.

When he laid down the menu, I asked him what brought him to America.

"My pension is worthless," he said, "so I am obliged to spend my declining years debating the existence of God with Bible Belt Christians. I take on five hundred of them at a time."

I was wondering how his audiences coped with his logical positivism, the view that all propositions are nonsense except those of mathematics and the natural sciences, and those that can be verified, directly or indirectly, by sense experience.

"Were the debates worthwhile?" I asked him.

"If you mean was I paid well, the answer is yes," he said. "From an intellectual point of view, though, hardly so; the debate about God is long dead."

"Have you never had a mystical experience?" I asked him, hoping to draw him out further.

"The ghost-hunter Brian Inglis once invited me to witness him levitating," he sniffed. "Well, I went along to his house and watched him with considerable patience as he shook and heaved about on the carpet; but he failed to get airborne."

"What surprises me about your story," I said, "is that you should have taken the bother to walk five yards to witness such a thing."

"Not a bit of it," he snapped. "I'm a follower of David Hume. I'll believe anything if you show me the evidence. And you'll remember that Hume said that the difficulty with miracles is deciding between the likelihood that they have occurred, and the veracity of the report of them."

"Are you still a logical positivist?" I asked him. I was wondering if I could needle him a little. "I'm no philosopher," I went on, "but people tell me that it's logical positivism that is dead."

"It may well be that the principle of empirical verification is open to criticism," he said airily. "But perhaps you would like to suggest a better way in which propositions about God and the mystical could be said to be meaningful?"

I pointed out (I was getting, perhaps, a little overconfident) that Wittgenstein seemed content to say that the mystical simply *manifests* itself and therefore requires no other proof, or verification, other than its sheer impressiveness.

Ayer took a swig from his glass.

"Yes, indeed. Wittgenstein believed in the mystical," he chuckled, "and he believed in *sin;* but this was because he was a homosexual and suffered guilt. Belief in mysticism made him feel better. I do not believe in shame, guilt, unworthiness, punishment. I do not accept the concept of *deserving;* and yet we behave in life as if these things are a reality."

He paused for a moment as if waiting to see whether I would come back at him.

I was in no position to bandy further words on the question of Wittgenstein, but I thought I would draw him out a little more on verification.

"In 1916," I said, "more than a hundred thousand people claim that they saw the sun spinning and falling to the earth at Fatima in Portugal after a claimed apparition of the Virgin Mary. I've read newspaper accounts of this phenomenon. Would this satisfy your Humean criterion of evidence for the truth of such a statement of fact?"

"No it would not," said Ayer, "for the simple reason that the phenomenon was reported nowhere else in the world, so we must conclude that the sun stayed in its proper place and that these hundred thousand people were subject to some sort of mass hallucination."

Ayer sat back in his seat and cocked his head at me. "After all," he went on, "how do we know whether *anything* is real or purely an illusion? I learn that I've had a hallucination because the further course of my experience assures me that the object that I thought I saw does not exist. Simple as that."

By this time he had gained the attention of the rest of the party. He seemed to be perking up with the prospect of contention; although he was clearly aware that I was no match for him.

"The only people who have ever given me a decent argument on God's existence are the Jesuits," he went on. "I once took on all the Jesuits at Campion Hall in Oxford. I think I converted a few of them to atheism."

This got a laugh.

Then he said: "I upset them by working out how far the Virgin Mary must have traveled into space from earth after her Assumption … but you know, I don't think any of those Jesuits believed in a personal God."

I asked him whether he ever had a sense of religious experience in music.

"No such experience can ever be regarded as a source of knowledge about reality other than the purely subjective experiences of the so-called mystic in question," said Ayer. "So it tells us nothing about the real world. In any case we'll soon be building computers that can compose music as well as Mozart or Bach. What I mean is that there is no mysterious transcendental quality beyond the computable activity of the brain. The brain is just a very clever computer. . . ."

I objected that perhaps the special quality of a work of art had something to do with the fact that it was created within a purely human and precise context: the artist or composer was a particular age; in love or out of love; in sickness or in health; it would be a particular season of the year, and the subject would be aware of his or her mortality. This might be difficult for a machine.

"And if you can describe those factors, then you could download them into a computer," he stated flatly.

After our food arrived he continued to range over the stock objections to arguments for the existence of God. And the more we talked the more I realized that he would be impervious to any propositions that failed the stringent test of his principle of sense-experience verifiability.

Eventually we moved on to other subjects; but later in the evening he stopped in mid-flight.

"If I've trimmed on a philosophical principle in my life it's in the area of ethics," he said suddenly. "I have a problem. I don't accept the notion of public morality, so I would be logically encouraged to accept Huxley's *Brave New World:* the idea of us all taking happy drugs. Life, after all, comes down to our needs and their fulfillment, and provided it does not offend against another's—why not do anything you want? My problem is this: I can see this argument intellectually but I know in an instinctive way that Huxley's vision is wrong."

As we were walking away from the restaurant, he suddenly clutched me by the arm and shouted: "Hey! What's that drogolus behind you?"

I looked behind me and saw nothing but the railings.

"You see!" cried the professor with glee. "It's there; but I can't see it, or smell it, or taste it . . . Just the same as God."

As I set off for my hotel I reflected that Ayer's opinions, which were familiar to me, might have constituted a serious opposition to the reality of a mystical element in the world. That night, however, in the light of my dream, his opinions struck me as superficial and altogether unconvincing.

2

Accounting for It

As I returned across the Atlantic on a night flight I found myself thinking about my dream. I usually spent such flights writing up business reports and hatching private schemes of profit and advancement while listening to music on my Walkman; there was something about the isolation of long night flights home that stimulated reveries of material optimism. My dream, I realized, was intruding on the satisfaction I usually derived from making all those plans for myself and for my family that were to do with money-making, vacations, possessions, enjoyment. I had tried to relegate the dream to where I thought it belonged—the realm of executive stress; but it seemed to offer confirmation that I was being challenged to review my whole way of life. The significance of dreams in the religious traditions of Jews, Christians, Muslims, and Hindus is widely considered to be a crucial element of spiritual growth and revelation, just as it is in the lives of American Indians and many other old cultures. Religious dreams are widely associated as a cultural phenomenon with an individual's rediscovery of an inner self, a conversion process, or even a spontaneous, ecstatic experience that leads to dramatic deliverance.

After returning to London I began to research them. In an article by Lloyd Siegel in *Jewish Contemporary Psychotherapy* (11: 1980) I found descriptions of the "miraculous dreams" of Holocaust survivors who claimed that their dreams, which often came when they were at the brink of despair, gave them strength and courage to overcome extraordinary obstacles.

There is plentiful evidence, it seems, that we are capable of making contact through our dreams with a wider sense of self and belonging. In a contribution to the *Mental Health Society* (2: 1975) I found a report by Mirjam Viterbi which told of the unconscious Jewish content of dreams of Roman Catholic patients of Hebrew descent, despite the fact that the patients were completely unaware of their ancestry: of a young man, for example, who dreamed continually of a ceremonial kiddush cup and only later discovered that his mother was Jewish and had converted to Catholicism prior to her marriage. Later he established a relationship with the Jewish psyche that his mother had discarded, and a trip to Israel became a decisive experience in his self-discovery.

Among all of my reading I was especially impressed with Carl Jung's autobiography, *Memories, Dreams, Reflections*. Jung's father was a skeptical theologian whose doubts had driven him to "irritability and discontent." Jung commented: "He had to quarrel with somebody, so he did it with his family and himself. Why didn't he do it with God, the dark author of all created things, who alone was responsible for the sufferings of the world? God would assuredly have sent him by way of an answer one of those magically, infinitely profound dreams which he had sent to me even without being asked, and which had sealed my fate."

Had *I* been sent, I wondered, such a magical and infinitely profound dream?

According to Jung, the supplanting of mystical and spiritual realities with materialist values has created a deep hunger which is frequently manifested in our dreams, when our conscious lives attempt to connect with reconciling symbols of inner wholeness. Writing in the *American Journal of Psychotherapy* (37: 1983), a Jungian psychiatrist, Richard Gunter, makes the following huge claim: "Dreams, I believe, lead us to symbols that enhance personal growth and health. It can be comforting to know that religious symbols in their varied expression of the divine live in our dreams ... God is alive and well, living in the unconscious, and is sending us nocturnal messages for inspiration, growth, and health."

My first instinct was to reject this sort of stuff as simplistic nonsense and get back to my normal life, which for so many years had been both healthy and fulfilled *without* religion. Yet the power of my dream and its intrusion in waking reality continued to obsess me. Soon after arriving home, I went to see a Jungian analyst friend and told him the dream story.

"It's hazardous to attempt to interpret a dream outside of therapy," he said. "But I'll say one thing: you can always tell an anxiety dream because it's recurrent and you sweat."

After some hesitation, he continued: "Mind you, the blackness of the robes is interesting. That might be indicative of the *shadow*. In Jungian terms that signifies an unacceptable part of yourself that you need to come to terms with. That's a crucial process Jungians call individuation. And the trees are interesting, too . . . the tree of life. . . . It sounds to me as if you are entering something of a crisis. Perhaps your younger self is trying to get in touch with your mature self; or perhaps it's the other way round. And it's difficult to tell which self is finding it more difficult to forgive and make friends."

I next told him about the dream's fulfillment.

He shook his head and smiled. "People have a way of projecting their waking experiences back onto their dreams, and sometimes the other way round. On the other hand, it could be pure coincidence, or what Jungians call a synchronicity. . . . If you accept the supernatural route then you're buying into a complete mystical package. You're going to have to decide on the implications of that."

As a result of this conversation I started to extend my interest to parallel areas of the mystical and miraculous. I pored over accounts of prophecy, miracles of healing, apparitions, visions, bilocation, stigmata, out-of-body experiences, and levitation.

I took out stacks of books on mysticism and the supernatural from the London Library. I enrolled in the theology faculty library of London University at Heythrop College in Cavendish Square; plundered the Catholic library at the back of Westminster Cathedral; made contact with a number of organizations, including the Alistair Hardy Centre for the Science of Religion in Oxford and the newly formed Arthur Koestler psychical research foundation in Edinburgh.

Combing the shelves of bookshops along Charing Cross Road I was fascinated by the popularity of extensive sections that lumped religion, philosophy, and the occult all together in a mystical mishmash. Jungian psychology and John of the Cross rubbed spines with New Ageism, transcendental meditation, Zen, Gaia ecology, witchcraft, Satanism, UFOs, and ley-lines. The great Christian mystics, the understanding of any one of whom would take a lifetime, were given a voguish equivalence with the vast ephemera of parapsy-chology, self-help, and horoscopes. The idea of reading John of the Cross or Teresa of Avila in order to procure some self-help and uplift struck me as very funny. But looking through these shelves helped me concentrate my mind.

What, after all, did I think I was up to?

Was I asking myself whether I was prepared, in mid-life, to subscribe once again to a belief in an alternative world beyond the veil of appearances? Or was I asking this: does God give us evidence for his existence? Does he interfere in his own creation in the sense that Jung suggests? I was conscious that such questions were hedged about with a host of further, tricky philosophical and theological questions. What sort of God would it be, after all, that could be conceived of as an object competing among other objects for my attention in the world? I was aware of the endless ramifications of the debates between materialists and vitalists, reductionists and an-imists, empiricists and metaphysicians; but the notion of "direct evidence" of the supernatural had a new and wonderful, outflanking simplicity.

Of all the books I gutted during those first weeks, the most absorbing was a collection of papers entitled *The Physical Phenom-ena of Mysticism* by the late Father Herbert Thurston, S. J., an English Jesuit who had spent fifty years studying evidence for the operation of the Christian supernatural. The scope of his book, which was published in 1952, seemed to establish sensible limits to the broad area of phenomena in which I had an interest. He convinced me that the traditions of Christian mysticism, as opposed to the realms of the nonreligious paranormal or the occult, contained the best documented, the most fascinating, and the most accessible range of "marvels" or "prodigies" available for scrutiny in the Western World.

I had little doubt that I could find parallel prodigies in the experience of the other great world religions, and I had positive confirmation of this one afternoon in Cambridge. At about this time I was having tea with the Indian writer Anita Desai, who was staying at Girton College. I asked her whether Hindus experienced visions and miracles as a rule.

"It would be rare," she said, "to find a single Hindu who had not experienced at least two visions and a miracle at least once in his life. As for holy dreams, they could be counted by the score."

If I were going to embark on a quest for the supernatural made visible, I would restrict myself to Christendom, not out of a prejudiced favor for the religion of my childhood but in the interests of cultural accessibility. This, at least, is what I told myself at the outset.

Thurston's legacy was a crop of superbly researched and analyzed case histories, which seemed to lay the ground rules for procedure and provide an excellent list of precedents. His approach was skeptical and empirical, which suited me, for although I was obsessed with the possibilities, I was in no mood to give the notion of supernatural origins the benefit of the doubt.

All the same, in the midst of my growing absorption with the "supernatural" my friends began to assume worried expressions in my presence, and one or two even intimated that I was perhaps going off my head. It seemed to them *unhealthy* that a journalist would interest himself in anything so intangible and irrelevant as the "mystical element" in life which, as far as most of them were concerned, came under the heading of "freak news." An old friend gave me a cynical smile as he handed over a clipping of a story about a woman who thought she had seen the face of Jesus in one of her pancakes. Another colleague, a practicing Catholic, said to me acidly, "I find your interest in that stuff *distasteful.*"

I was upset and frustrated by this, not so much because it hurt my pride (which it did), but because they were ignoring, just as I had done for years, the fact that a "mystical element" lay behind fanatical religious conflicts the world over. I was beginning to see every reason, both personal and objective, for trying to understand that element.

The tendency on the part of journalists to draw a strong and unquestioning demarcation line between everyday experience and the mystical "freak news" came home to me strongly as a result of a conversation I had at about this time with the newspaper editor, Donald Trelford.

Trelford had recently published an article in the *Spectator* claiming that many years earlier he had seen the mysterious apparition of a school friend one winter's afternoon in Conventry. He and his friend (they were both in their early twenties then) had agreed to meet under the town center clocktower at six in the evening after playing in separate rugby football matches. Trelford was waiting at the appointed hour, and eventually his friend came walking toward him on the crowded pavement. But instead of stopping, he continued to walk and disappeared in the darkness. Baffled by this behavior, Trelford returned home, where he discovered that his friend had been killed in a road accident earlier that afternoon. The article had not been "written up" as a curious, paranormal episode for Halloween or Christmas, but as a deeply felt reminiscence of a sadly missed friend; it was an eloquent, finely observed piece of "unfinished business."

Not long after the publication of this story I had dinner with Trelford and asked him how he accounted for this experience. Had he seen a ghost? "No! I don't believe in ghosts." Had he been mistaken and seen a look-alike? "No! It was definitely my friend."

Eventually I said: "But Donald, if it happened and you're not making it up, you surely have to account for it!"

"Well it definitely happened," he said with finality, "and I *don't* have to account for it, and I *won't.*"

I could sympathize with Trelford's conviction about the vivid reality of his experience, just as I was equally certain of the reality of my own dream's fulfillment. But the major difference between us was that I felt bound to come up with an explanation, even if that explanation turned out to have uncomfortable implications. And the fact that such an explanation might make not just a particular difference to my life (as would be the case if Yuri Geller were to bend one of my spoons), but *all* the difference to my life, was a risk I was prepared to accept.

At about this time I had another boost of much-needed confidence in what I was doing when I traveled up to Nottingham to meet a marine biologist called Dr. David Hay, who was director of the Alistair Hardy Research Centre in Oxford, which seeks links between science and religion.

Hay had been closely involved in work on the relation between statistics and religious experience and showed me some recent national opinion poll figures carried out for the Hardy center by Gallup Poll of London. According to the poll, about 33 percent of all Britons believe that they have had some sort of religious experience, in the sense that they have been "influenced by a presence or a power ..."

More surprising still was the poll's finding that nearly *three quarters* of those who took part in the survey thought nevertheless that spiritual experience was very important in a positively beneficial sense in their lives. The dramatic difference in the two sets of figures seemed to me fascinating for it indicated that it was arguably the norm for people to be open to the idea of the transcendental even though they might not be churchgoers or have had an actual religious experience themselves.

Did this mean that it was "human" to be open to the notion of the transcendental? And was it possible that statistics could be used to tell us about the validity of transcendental experience?

Hay was quick to emphasize that neither the statistics nor people's "experiences" could prove the existence of God (and I needed no reassurance on this point). On the other hand, he insisted that such data should not be ignored if we want to make sense of our world.

"Statistics show that religion is hardly about to die out," Hay said. "But they also indicate, perhaps, that religious awareness is becoming isolated from the mainstream of modern life. Human realities that are resolutely ignored tend, as Freud pointed out, to return in bizarre and fanatical forms."

"That's the negative view," I said, "so what can you, a scientist, say *positively* about the benefits of religious awareness?"

"I'm a biologist," said Hay, "so I'll take a biological perspective. We need to attend more openly to our religious awareness, so that at the very least its constructiveness and creativity can be used for the benefit of the species. People who become religiously aware seem to experience directly their solidarity with their fellow human beings and their responsibility toward them. Tasks which had previously appeared impossible begin to look less formidable. They are less inclined to be seduced into the amassing of goods, because they perceive there are other sources of security. Life gains meaning. In a world threatened by environmental disaster and the depletion of natural resources, these would appear to be advantages of our biological heritage not lightly ignored."

But was this true? Was this contention about the benign consequences of religion as simple as all that? My meeting with Dr. Hay only heightened my curiosity, and served to raise new questions.

Shortly after Christmas I decided that I could not in good conscience both pursue my obsession and continue working on the newspaper. I talked it through with my wife, who was supportive although not a little anxious as to what I was getting myself into, and I eventually applied to the chief executive of the paper for a year's leave of absence without pay. Calculating that I would be of little use to the newspaper enterprise until I had worked out of my system whatever mid-life crisis I seemed to be tangled in, he gave his reluctant blessing to the idea. At one point in our discussion he wondered whether it would not be better for me to apply to my doctor for sick leave, a measure I am glad I rejected.

So it was that for the first time in more than twelve years I found myself a free agent and ready for a journey that seemed on the face of it enticing in its simplicity. I would go in search of the "supernatural made visible" in the world, seeking out current evidence, wherever I could find it, that God intervenes in the affairs of humankind in literal and observable ways, and asking what difference it makes to the lives of those who are prepared to accept the authenticity of such evidence.

Pondering the problem of a starting point, I found myself reflecting, for the first time in many years, on the story of my early faith and on the path toward skepticism and agnosticism that became such a well-trodden highway for so many Catholics of my generation.

3

A Catholic Boyhood

As a boy I carried around a profoundly disturbing memory of an experience I could never quite locate in time, except that it may well have been my very earliest recollection. As I grew up I sometimes thought of this experience as an encounter with Satan; at other times I believed that I had seen the true face of God, and had discovered what no one else knew, that he was entirely, eternally evil.

> *I am lying on a bed in a room high in a building. It is a summer's evening and I am gazing through a deep window out over rooftops and chimneys. Suddenly the door opens and people enter at a rush with masks and scissors. They lean over me and I can hear a sound of sighing and crying as if the trees are calling to the rooftops, and the rooftops to the distant hills, the sounds ever-expanding in the twilight.*
>
> *There is a presence in the waves of sound, like an ageless, all powerful, dark being, and it gathers strength and purpose in a series of sickening, irresistible pulses. I am about to be engulfed by the monotonous rhythm which intends taking me to itself forever.*
>
> *This I know is the only reality, the ultimate and inescapable truth, all powerful, all evil, and without end. As it ebbs away, like a mighty ocean of darkness it lets me understand that its depar-*

ture is only temporary. Finally, inevitably, it will return to take me to itself forever.

This memory, which I later came to call the "Evil Eternity," had much to do with my turning at an early age toward religion and religious things. I felt safe in the presence of holy objects, and reassured that I had glimpsed the devil rather than God. I carried holy water and wore a medal of the Virgin Mary. I felt a sense of security at early morning Mass, and I became a daily communicant from the age of eight.

Through these daily visits to church I met a woman who was to have a considerable influence over my life.

An old lady called Miss Racine used to hang around the church door looking for companionship after Mass. She had whiskers and misshapen feet; people tended to shun her. One day she invited me to her home, a gloomy, unkempt suburban house in which she lived in one cluttered room amid holy pictures, statues, and devotional books. She had an inexhaustible stock of gossip about religious communities, priests, and nuns. I got into the habit of visiting Miss Racine from about the time that I was eleven years of age, drinking her rancid tea and eating her stale biscuits, despite my mother's anxious warnings that she was a "religious maniac."

Miss Racine painted an enticing picture of life in a junior seminary where young boys could start their studies for the priesthood in a monastic routine far away in the countryside. She encouraged me to believe that I had a "vocation" and gave me a relic of Saint Thérèse of Liseux, the modern French saint who was venerated as the patron of priests. She also persuaded me to wear an item of devotional apparel known as a "scapular," two pieces of cloth not much larger than a postage stamp attached to each other by silken threads. The scapular was a symbol of the Virgin Mary's protection and was to be worn around the neck beneath one's clothing. It warded off evil. Those who died wearing this object, she told me, were guaranteed entry into heaven on the first Saturday following their death.

She also said that the scapular had miraculous properties. I was prepared to give it a chance. Wearing the scapular, I knelt before the statue of the Virgin in the Catholic church in Woodford and begged her to make me a priest. The following year the curate took me to see the local bishop, and it was arranged that I would be boarded at St. Wilfred's, a junior seminary in the Midlands.

My mother, who had been oddly tolerant of my religiosity despite her doubts about Miss Racine, took me to St. Pancras Station and installed me on the train. She stood waving to me mournfully from the end of the platform as if knowing that she had lost a son. I was unmoved by my mother's tears; after all, I reasoned, there were three more brothers and a sister back at home. When I could see her no longer I settled myself back into the seat and began reading a mint-new edition of *The Imitation of Christ,* a medieval work of spirituality written specifically for the formation of religious enclosed orders.

I opened the book and read: "It is no small matter to dwell in a religious community, or congregation, to converse therein without complaint, and to persevere therein faithfully unto death. Blessed is he that hath there lived well, and ended happily."

I was thirteen years of age.

The rural setting of the junior seminary in the high moorlands of North Staffordshire seemed the fulfillment of my deepest yearnings and fantasies. I felt safe at last, sleeping beneath the same roof as the Blessed Sacrament.

One hundred and eighty boys, and twelve priests, lived in a sprawl of cloisters, stairways, attics, and garret dormitories. The building was perched on the side of a gorge-like valley with steep woods and waterfalls. Below the college, in the depths of the woods, was a shrine built by Father Faber, the Victorian spiritual writer. Whenever I could get permission to visit "Faber's Retreat" I would spend time there, saying the rosary and listening to the rushing waters and the wind in the larch trees, identifying myself with the romantic figments of my imagination—St. Francis, St. Bernard, St. Anthony.

Our teachers were a team of diocesan priests who put the lid down firmly on anything that smacked of excess, extravagance, or the mystical. They were men of abundant faith, and they were convinced that belief was all that was required to make contact with the supernatural realms. They would have firmly disparaged the idea of more *direct* encounters with the supernatural in the form of miracles, visions, or voices.

I was comfortable with this ethos, but in common, I imagine, with most of my contemporaries I developed a rich fantasy life to lend reality to the propositions of our faith. Ideas of Christ in the sacrament, the presence of angels, demons, Heaven, Hell, the Virgin Mary, grace, and sin were fed by imitations of Pre-Raphaelite art that were depicted in stained glass that filled the church, and in reprints of paintings that lined the walls of the corridors and cloisters. Our role models were the lives of the saints, about whom we read in our daily spiritual reading. The romantic seclusion of the landscape encouraged a picture of reality that bore little relation to the harsh industrial wastelands of Stoke on Trent that began just twenty miles west of us beyond the edge of the moors.

Throughout these years, from thirteen to eighteen, we learned to define our "selves" in terms of monastic regulations and identification with Christ, Mary, and our guardian angels. There was no feminine influence, save for the members of the elusive enclosed order of nuns who cooked our meals. Relationships with "special" friends were discouraged, and we had no notion of being part of the local rural community.

Our doctrinal studies were sustained by a sort of half-baked medieval intellectualism. The main articles of Christian and Catholic dogma—the idea of the soul, the distinction between nature and person expressed in the Holy Trinity, the transubstantiation (the turning of wine into the body and blood of Christ)—these complex and mysterious notions were clarified and explained by a crude version of the thinking of the medieval philosopher and theologian Thomas Aquinas. Philosophy, as we were taught it at St. Wilfred's, treated ideas as if they had the same sort of reality as a child's colored building blocks. It was held that there was a *real* distinction between a thing's substance and its observable appearances of shape, size, and texture; that a thing's essence could be distinguished from its existence; that ideas such as justice, beauty, and truth had a sort of separate existence in a universalized world of pure forms, independent of individual minds and actual objects and actions.

It was thus easy to accept, without the aid of sense experience, that a supernatural realm, far more important and durable, lay beyond the veil of appearances.

I believed that I was happy and that I was enjoying a foretaste of heaven. I can see myself, age fifteen, on the Feast of the Immaculate Conception, coming in from a hard afternoon's manual labor and going into church to pray alone before tea. The sky is cloudless with a rich December light streaming in through the west window; there is a keen wind that can be heard in the lime trees outside. As I kneel before the Blessed Sacrament in the empty church, imagining the real presence of Christ before me, I feel a deep sense of holiness and peace. After tea there will be choir practice, and we will be singing Palestrina, or Vitoria, or Carissimi.

After my eighteenth birthday I was sent to the senior seminary of the archdiocese, at Oscott College, Birmingham, a sooty, red-brick pile with commanding views over an industrialized landscape of chimneys, concrete cooling towers, factories, and housing developments. The routine of the day was much as it had been at junior seminary, although we were now trussed up in black cassocks and Roman collars. The emblematic romanticism, the liturgical formalism, the monastic routine continued; but it had gone sour on me.

In the rural idyll of St. Wilfred's I had managed to linger in a state of late childhood. Now on the grim city's edge, the storms of adolescence, with accompanying ravages of scrupulosity and guilt, were unleashed. I suffered migraines and stomachaches; I lay awake at night and fell asleep in chapel and through lectures in the mornings; I took up smoking and drinking; against the severe rules of the house I escaped whenever I could to the cinemas down in Birmingham. I was desperate for affectionate companionship, wracked with sexual torment.

My fellow students struck me as self-absorbed, sanctimonious, gullible. Most of the teaching staff I considered to be narrow, lost without their course books. I was skeptical about Thomistic philosophy, which I began to see as a precarious building with grand, soaring pillars and buttresses; so much interlacing, so much analogous patterning, without true foundations. Pull away one pillar and the whole edifice would collapse.

I began to read and to be influenced by modern British philosophy, which demonstrated the fallacies of metaphysics and nourished my growing skepticism. I became interested in science, astronomy, and anthropology. One day I read an article in a journal about a tribe in Australia that put its god into a stone in order to control the deity. I saw an exact parallel with the idea of Christian priesthood.

Reading Hegel on the function of the Catholic clergy as keepers of the Eucharist I was deeply impressed by this reflection: "The Holy as a mere thing has the character of being taken possession of by another to my exclusion; it may come into an alien hand, since the process of appropriating it is not one that takes place in the Spirit but is conditioned by its quality as an external object." This comment was responsible for the loss of my belief in the mystery of the real presence of Christ in the Eucharist.

I took delight in attempting to undermine the beliefs of my fellow seminarians with what I regarded as clever arguments; I quarreled with the lecturers in class and flagrantly ignored the rules of the house. At the end of my second year I received a reprimand from the rector: either I must mend my ways or a poor report would be sent to the bishop who sponsored me in the college.

I forestalled further acrimony by slipping away without warning or farewells several days before my twenty-first birthday.

I felt no sense of loss on leaving Oscott, nor was I unhappy about relinquishing a vocation that had begun to fill me with foreboding. But what had happened to all that accumulated "religious experience" at St. Wilfred's? Somehow I had managed to bury it deeply as if it had never been. In the meantime I threw myself into a new life. I was accepted at Oxford University to study English literature. For the first time in my life I felt intellectually and emotionally stretched. I fell in love with a girl who was not a Catholic, and religion began to recede from my conscious everyday life.

I turned to literature and found a new spiritual sustenance, especially in the Romantic poets. Wordsworth's "spots of time" in "Tintern Abbey" and "The Prelude" described a sense of transcendent mystery that was far more impressive, and true, I felt, than any of the the sterile propositions about God composed by the "Angelic Doctor," Thomas Aquinas.

> *And I have felt*
> *A presence that disturbs me with the joy*
> *Of elevated thoughts; a sense sublime*
> *Of something far more deeply interfused,*
> *Whose dwelling is the light of setting suns,*
> *And the round ocean and the living air,*
> *And the blue sky, and in the mind of man:*
> *A motion and a spirit, that impels*

All thinking things, all objects of all thought,
And rolls through all things . . .

This I could feel and understand; it was an acceptable prayer.

After Oxford I went on to Cambridge to do postgraduate work in early nineteenth-century English literature and philosophy. I had stopped going to church, and I knew that I would soon come to a firm decision about Christianity itself.

During a long vacation I went to stay in Maidstone with a doctor named Gabriel Fielding, who happened to be a novelist and a Jungian analyst. He offered to "talk me through" my childhood. With the aid of hypnosis he discovered that my childhood experience of the "Evil Eternity" was nothing more than the confused memory of a badly administered ether anesthetic which I had undergone at the age of three for an operation for tonsilitis.

Back in Cambridge I was walking one afternoon across Parker's Piece, an expanse of open ground close to the center of the city. I could see the huge Gothic tower of the Catholic church in the distance and the very sight of it provoked in me a feeling of unbearable tension. I understood for the first time that I had been striving for several years to live my life with two entirely irreconcilable cosmologies in my head. One picture involved a supernatural realm, just beyond the veil of appearances, in which resided the Holy Trinity, the angels and the saints, the souls of the dead—in purgatory, in Hell, and in Heaven—all of which depended on *belief* rather than knowledge and reason, and which one could only *imagine* inadequately as in a fairy tale.

The other—and it was, admittedly, a vision of youthful optimism—centered on the wonders of the universe: the stupendous fertility of life on the planet; the dignity, the genius, the resourcefulness of humankind—all of which could be ascertained by means of direct knowledge and understood by the light of unaided reason.

How was it possible to hold two such utterly opposed pictures of reality together? And yet, despite its purely speculative, shadowy nature, the "supernatural" realm made outrageous demands, claiming for itself paradoxically an even greater sense of significance, grandeur, and importance, even though it required a greater suspension of *disbelief* and was less reconcilable with life as one had to live it in this world.

I could no longer hold these two worlds together. I would have to choose.

Even as I turned the dilemma over in my mind I knew that I had made my choice. It was a simple decision that brought immediate relief. There were no pangs of conscience, no heart-searching; and I was determined that I would not look back. The transition to agnosticism was painless, guiltless, and immediately rewarding in a psychological sense. I could get on with my life unhampered by scruples of conscience or intellect.

After university I took up journalism. I worked as an investigative reporter and, as a foreign correspondent, traveled the world. I married and raised a family. As the years passed I became increasingly convinced that human beings were morally, psychologically, and materially better off without a belief in God. Morality was the avoidance of actions that might bring painful consequences on our fellows; we owed no duty beyond our obligations to family, community, and society.

As I entered middle age nothing short of a miracle could have shaken these firm convictions.

4

The Jesuits

Ln the weeks before starting my sabbatical leave I had been collecting cuttings from newspapers and microfilm from libraries under the broad category of "miraculous." Two-thirds of this material was about "sightings" of the Virgin Mary and prodigies linked with Marian statues. In the previous four or five years such phenomena had been reported in Burundi, Cameroon, Costa Rica, France, Haiti, Ireland, Japan, Italy, Lithuania, Nigeria, Peru, the Philippines, Poland, Rwanda, the Ukraine, the United States, and Zaire.

The most frequently reported instance was the daily visitation of the Virgin to a group of children in Medjugorje, Yugoslavia; a reported 17 million pilgrims had traveled to the town since 1981. There were also numerous reports of "secondary phenomena": many thousands of people said that they had seen the sun spinning and changing color, and there were stories of various luminous prodigies in the district.

These apparitions of the Virgin, still in progress, seemed to offer the most public and varied examples of alleged supernatural manifestations. What was more, the Catholic Church, normally cautious about such matters in modern times, was encouraging the cult. It seemed inevitable that I should start by attempting to make a firsthand study of this most available token of the supernatural made visible in the world today.

In a bookshop near Westminster Cathedral I picked up a magazine entitled "Medjugorje Messenger" and decided that an appropriate starting point would be a meeting with its editor, who turned out to be a London Jesuit, the Reverend Father Richard Foley, S.J.

So I found myself walking across Berkeley Square and approaching the front door of the Jesuit mother house, known as "Farm Street," an Edwardian orange-red sandstone building opposite the Connaught Hotel. There was a cloister with bikes and a sign announcing "Confessions." A man in a gray suit, who might have been an accountant on his lunch break, passed by and walked purposefully toward the sign, disappearing into the dark interior of a corridor.

As I rang the bell the door was immediately opened by a man in a black zip-up bomber jacket who introduced himself as Father Foley; he had been expecting me. His face was that of a boxer: flattened nose, high cheekbones fiery with broken capillaries, and overhanging eyebrows. He greeted me breathlessly, calling me "my dear."

Talking all the way, he marched on squelching shoes down polished stairs to a self-service cafeteria in the bowels of the building. There were a dozen or so Jesuits eating lunch at hexagonal tables; some looked ceremonially academic in traditional gowns of the society with fussy false sleeves, and others were dressed in dark blue shirts reminiscent of New York policemen in summer garb.

The Jesuits looked lean and studious. There was a hum of machinery in the room, air-conditioning perhaps, lending the atmosphere of a power plant.

Father Foley took his place at a table where there was one other priest, who introduced himself as Father Frederick Copleston. I knew him by repute as the author of a prodigious history of philosophy that had been a staple diet in the seminary. Father Copleston, unlike his companions, was dressed in civilian clothes, brown corduroys and a plaid shirt; his eyes were screwed up myopically and he wore a faintly sardonic grin.

Father Foley launched immediately into the business at hand, while his companion listened in silence.

"If you are setting out on an investigation into current evidence for the Christian supernatural, my dear, you cannot do better than visit Medjugorje." He wagged a finger: "Attend the apparitions! Examine the phenomena! Interview the visionaries!"

Then he related the story of the apparitions.

Walking in a field near the village of Medjugorje in southern Yugoslavia, on June 24, 1981, a fourteen-year-old peasant girl, Ivanka Ivankovic, saw a light which she identified with the Virgin Mary. Ivanka had been in good health and had never suffered any psychological illness; her mother, however, had died eight weeks previously. Within the space of a few hours five other children, three girls and two boys, ages ranging from ten to seventeen, had joined her and claimed to have witnessed the same apparition. They said that they saw a woman with long dark hair wearing a gray gown. All the time she was covering and uncovering something she held in her left hand.

In various combinations the children would continue to "see" and "speak" with the Virgin each day for the next eight years. The visionaries would line up to pray, facing a wall in a room in the parish house. Suddenly they would drop to their knees in perfect coordination while observing and speaking to a presence that remained invisible and silent to others. The apparition normally lasted no more than three to four minutes; afterward a Franciscan priest would debrief them to write down the Virgin's messages.

Within weeks of the commencement of the phenomenon a trickle of pilgrims turned to a flood of hundreds of thousands. The regional Communist government reacted with hostility; the children were interrogated and bullied, the Franciscan parish priest was imprisoned and tortured. The Roman Catholic bishop of Mostar, at the outset sympathetic, was soon to call in question the authenticity of the events, but the phenomena were to achieve worldwide fame and approval among devout Catholics. The impact on the local community was dramatic. The villagers now attended Mass each day, fasted twice a week, and were to be seen walking in the fields and lanes with rosaries in their hands. Men had given up drinking and swearing; enemies had been reconciled.

"Nowhere in the world," said Father Foley, "will you witness so many signs and wonders, spinning suns, moving lights, religious pictures filling the sky, rosaries turning to gold. The phenomena are as plentiful as the rocks that are strewn about the hillsides!"

There had been many claims for miracles of healing, and many answers to prayer; the most impressive evidence for the supernatural authenticity of the happenings, according to Father Foley, were the many thousands of conversions to a devout life.

"My dear," said Father Foley, "it's like a veritable Disneyland of the supernatural. And the world needs it so much. We need a bit of starlight and stardust. But you go there and you'll never see anything like it: it's a cross between a pop festival and the Sermon on the Mount. The fervor, the devotion, the real prayer; the mystical and miraculous events sparking off all over the place."

The priest was red in the face, his forehead glistening with enthusiasm. I looked at his companion, Father Copleston, who continued to eat stolidly as if Father Foley were talking about the weather.

"And what message," I asked, "is the Virgin Mary giving to the children?"

"Pray, say the rosary, fast," said Father Foley, "otherwise there will be a great chastisement. There will be ten signs, terrible scourges to be visited on mankind. One of the visionaries, Myrjana, wept when she was told of the chastisement. She cried out: 'Oh no, does it have to be like that?' There will be a great sign, one of the wonders of the earth, which will appear on the hill of the visions. The visionaries will inform a certain priest when all these things are going to occur, and he will notify the media. Three of the children have now stopped having their visions because they have been told all ten secrets. The remaining active visionaries have their full quota still to come."

As Father Foley was imparting all this, I was conscious of having winced. It had not gone unnoticed. He laid a hand on my arm.

"This shocks some people, John, but you know a religion without Apocalypse is like a dragon without teeth."

With this he trundled off in the direction of the self-service counter.

"What do *you* think?" I asked Father Copleston.

He considered the question for a moment. "I've never had any visions," he said flatly.

"What did Thomas Aquinas have to say about mystical phenomena? Didn't he say that all he had written was straw compared with his mystical revelations?"

"Yes, that's true," replied Father Copleston, "it seems that he had a mystical experience while saying Mass a few months before he died in 1274. As a philosopher, though, he had nothing to say about mysticism."

He seemed to smile inwardly to himself. "There is no distinction," he went on, "between Christian philosophy and good philosophy. Some people believe that mystical experience is problematic, that it calls for an explanation involving the intervention of God. There are plenty of other people around, however, who are prepared to accept that there are alternative explanations . . . You ask about Aquinas: as a philosopher his position was that the transcendent being, or God, is indicated not by mystical experience but by the universal mystery of dependent or contingent being. How can an infinite series of dependent being, which does not contain within itself the reason for its own existence, get started in the first place? That is something we can all ponder, irrespective of our religion or lack of it. And you certainly won't have to go to Medjugorje to think about it."

"But not all philosophers would agree that it is meaningful to talk about the transcendent being in the first place," I said. "Doesn't that indicate that there is a sort of mystical aptitude in some philosophers?"

Copleston shook his head. "There are students of Aquinas who argue that there is a sort of metaphysical *intuition* of being, equal to a privileged mystical experience. I don't think that Aquinas ever accepted this. He was a thoroughly professional philosopher and as such he saw philosophy as the striving of the human mind after truth. This striving can only be fully satisfied in the vision of God, but this does not mean that he approved of substituting mystical experience for proper philosophical inquiry."

At this point Father Foley appeared, carrying our desserts. He appeared a little flustered, as if guessing that Copleston might have been sowing skepticism during his absence.

"At Medjugorje," Father Foley began again, "people look at the sun quite painlessly as if it were in eclipse . . ."

With this Father Copleston rose, made his apologies and walked away, still smiling enigmatically to himself.

Father Foley leaned toward me confidentially. "Of course, John, Medjugorje has its skeptics. The local bishop in Mostar, as you will discover, has turned his back on the events. He's resisting the enormous opportunities Our Lady has given him. He's even accused the saintly parish priest of having fathered a child with a Franciscan nun. Just imagine. Then he accused another priest of having had erotic designs on one of the visionaries. . . . You know, the bishop is looking awfully old for his age."

I felt vaguely uncomfortable; the austere talk of Father Copleston seemed preferable to this sort of cranky gossip.

Before I left Farm Street that afternoon, Father Foley gave me a pile of books, a list of contacts in Medjugorje, and letters of introduction.

"If you go, take plenty of small bottles of whiskey and lots of tea bags," he advised. "You'll find that will soften people up. Take bags of sweets for the children."

As he let me out of the front door he said: "If you get to Medjugorje I hope you have a quiet time; but if you see anything you're going to be very busy."

As I walked back across Berkeley Square I was suddenly overwhelmed with misgivings. I was wondering whether I had not made a huge mistake. Father Copleston had in a few sentences warned me of the danger of deducing a God of the "gaps" from a few allegedly paranormal occurrences. On the other hand, Father Foley's enthusiasm for his spiritual Disneyland had filled me with alarm. And here I was planning an expensive trip to a country I did not like, to a place where people were almost certainly suffering from mass hysteria.

But I had made a start, and there was now no turning back.

PART TWO

A SPIRITUAL
DISNEYLAND

5

Baffled Scientists

left London on a cold and rainy afternoon on a Yugoslav Airlines flight mostly composed of elderly holidaymakers on their way to the Adriatic Riviera. Sitting next to me was a Yugoslav pop singer with dark gypsy looks and an evil-smelling cigarette. Over a meal of unidentifiable meat and cake I told him of my destination.

"Those people up there behind the mountains are the smartest," he said. "They make good business with that Saint Mary—The Gospa [the Virgin], we call her. I just wish I could find something like that in *my* back garden!" He rubbed his thumb and forefinger together earnestly.

I spent the rest of the flight examining a publication Father Foley had given me. It was entitled *Scientific and Medical Studies on the Apparitions at Medjugorje,* the work, principally, of one Professor Henri Joyeux of Montpellier University, described as "hospital surgeon and director of a nutrition and experimental cancer laboratory."

The book began:

Never before in the history of the Church has the phenomenon of ecstasy been subjected to modern scientific tests. The Medjugorje visionaries have undergone electroencephalographs, electrooculographs, eye reflex tests and a study of evoked auditory responses

... These are the "firsts" offered by our book: the tests and their implications.

Joyeux usefully described the various empirical tests that had been applied to the visionaries to date. There had been inconclusive psychiatric interviews, attempts at hypnosis, and several unscheduled tests of an amateurish nature. There had been a horrifying "prick" test, administered by a priest who leapt forward with an unsterilized needle and stabbed one of the girl visionaries, in mid-ecstasy, straight through her clothes. The visionary did not appear to notice anything, although a bloodstain appeared on her dress. On another occasion a zealous cleric had suddenly thrust two fingers at one of the visionary's eyes as if to gouge them out; seeing the girl blink, the perpetrator had lost all faith in the authenticity of the apparition.

Setting aside these crude scrutinies, Professor Joyeux and a half dozen French medical specialists, including a brain surgeon, an ocular surgeon, and an ear-nose-and-throat specialist, had made a new "wholly scientific" start. They had traveled to Medjugorje on five separate occasions with a quantity of electrical contraptions. After consulting their apparition and receiving the go-ahead, the visionaries allowed themselves to be trussed up with wires, headphones, and suction pads while they experienced their visions up against the empty wall of a room in the parish church.

The results, according to the medical team, were as follows:

1. No clinical signs of individual or collective hallucination.
2. No signs of individual or collective hysteria.
3. No neuroses or psychoses.

The team also concluded that the visionaries were not experiencing "pathological" ecstasy, which they defined as the sort of trance suffered by hysterics, the chronically delirious, or those suffering from hallucinations. Pathological ecstasy, declared Joyeux, "is normally accompanied by a web of erotic and religious fantasy in which excesses of exaltation alternate with lewd excitability." He could also definitively exclude the existence of dreams, sleep, or epilepsy during the apparitions. He was convinced, as a result of lie detector tests, that the visionaries were not consciously deceitful.

The electroencephalographic recordings positively indicated

the presence of "alpha" rhythms, which, according to the publication, were consistent with "an attitude of expectation, during relaxation and meditation exercises." Mystics and contemplatives, apparently, are capable of an extensive range and "abundance" of alpha rhythms in meditative states.

In their conclusions the medical men professed themselves baffled by just two phenomena. First, they could not understand how it was that in ecstasy the children managed to use their lips and larynxes as in normal speech while not uttering a sound. Secondly, they were astonished at the way in which all six children, or any lesser numerical combination of the six, managed to coordinate their eye movements in exact synchronicity while observing the arrival and departure of the apparition.

But what had the scientific tests proved? Granting that Professor Joyeux was all that he said he was, assuming he was genuinely unbiased and motivated by genuinely scientific objectives, his testimony was nevertheless purely negative; and yet there was something about the circumstances of the experiments that had moved me.

The medical men had taken a number of photographs of themselves and their electrical devices as they went to work on the visionaries. Coming in to land at Dubrovnik, I was gazing at a particularly poignant picture:

The visionaries were kneeling, looking up in wonder at a blank wall, while the medical men leaned forward in the act of twiddling the knobs of their sinister black machines as if they could capture the Virgin in the dials and printouts. Somehow it exemplified a frantic longing for some degree of certainty about the existence of authentic mystery, and the futility of achieving that certainty by empirical means.

At Dubrovnik I stayed in a state hotel where a desultory band played the theme from *The Godfather* to a scattering of dejected guests in the lobby. In a vast, deserted basement dining room, overseen by a waiter in scarlet dinner jacket with gold epaulettes, I sipped a glass of wine that tasted like cough medicine.

That night I fell asleep over a book about Medjugorje extolling the Virgin's special messages to the children. I dreamed that I was in a church that celebrated the cult of the Virgin as a pagan goddess. Priests with moustaches and wearing scarlet skull caps and gold copes pranced around an altar on which her statue had been erected. They were inviting me to join their rites, and I was fighting to escape. I woke up panic-stricken in the small hours.

The next morning I left the city in a rented car and took the coastal road toward Split. Steep mountains descended abruptly to the sea; there were sudden bays with shingle beaches, and misty islands basked like humpback whales on the horizon. In the peaceful morning sun it was easy to forget that these mountains had been the scene of atrocious acts of inhumanity in the Second World War, some of the worst of them committed by Catholics against their Orthodox brothers. Just a few miles from Medjugorje, I had read, Catholic Fascists had thrown some 500 Orthodox men, women, and children to their deaths over a precipice in 1941.

At length the road descended to a fertile valley where a deep, dark green river flowed swiftly toward the sea. The sun was high as I drove inland to Capiljena, a quiet garrison town where a phalanx of soldiers marched up and down in front of a deserted hotel. The road north, toward Medjugorje, now twisted through undulating country until the fertile uplands gave way to the high plateau encircled by mountains.

To the west was a tawny hill surmounted by a concrete cross; this, I knew from my reading, was the famous Mount Krizevac, which dominated Medjugorje. Nestling at its foot were a series of lower hills, thinly wooded. Why, I wondered, should the people of this remote place receive visions of the Virgin Mary? Was there a connection between the "visitations" and the harsh, desolate landscape, as in other great Marian shrines of Europe—Lourdes, Fatima, Guadaloupe, Rocamadour . . . ?

At the junction for Medjugorje I was stopped by a policeman controlling long lines of traffic coming in from the north. He looked inside the car and asked to see my passport before waving me on. I followed a convoy of air-conditioned German buses toward the village; on either side of the road were box-like chalet houses set on the edge of fertile fields. There were vineyards, tobacco plants, and well-organized market gardening; the soil was a deep, rich red.

The road turned at a primitive bridge running across a dried-up river bed filled with garbage. A white stuccoed church loomed ahead, a concrete block with twin towers that might have been designed by a child. Either side of the approach road was a turmoil of traffic and pedestrians; stalls and booths with festoons of belts, handbags, and religious knick-knacks; luminous statues of the Virgin with garish, blue bottle-stoppers; plaques of the crucifixion; key rings of the Sacred Heart. Groups of gypsy women with peroxided hair were sunning themselves in deck chairs; as each vehicle passed they cried out and gesticulated toward their wares.

I left the car in a makeshift parking lot and went in search of the young visionary Jacov's house, where Father Foley said I might get a bed for the night. I struggled along a narrow lane choked with buses, horse carts, and knots of overheated, sweaty pedestrian pilgrims. Some of the groups were led by priests who were saying the rosary and singing hymns. The devotees, however, were rubbernecking in every direction and chatting among themselves. In the background I could see two policemen lounging against a blue Fiat car.

Jacov's house was at the end of a farm track well off the village lane. It was a white stuccoed house with a rooftop balcony approached by an exterior staircase. A woman, perhaps in her early forties, sat on the doorstep in conversation with an elderly priest in a black beret. As I approached, she stopped talking and looked at me coldly.

"Jacov's aunt? Stoika?" I asked.

She nodded.

As I began to speak, slowly in English, I produced from my shoulder bag a quantity of presents. I handed over two large bags of candies, two cartons of cigarettes, a box of cigars, a box of tea bags, and two bottles of whiskey.

She took them unsmilingly and called to somebody in the kitchen.

An unshaven man of about forty with a cigarette in his mouth came to the door and the woman passed him the gifts. He examined the bottles of whiskey carefully and then, without looking at me, he started to talk with the priest.

"They are saying it is not possible for you to stay here," said the priest.

At that moment I saw somebody moving at the top of the outside flight of stairs that led to the rooftop. It was the visionary Jacov. Prowling nervously, he was looking down and immediately glancing away. He was dressed in a trendy blue denim suit with wide shoulders and a cossack-style front; his collar was turned up stylishly, his hair highlighted and spiked up in punk mode. He looked sickly and the whites of his eyes glistened hare-like.

He persisted with his nervous antics for a minute or so as he came and went and pirouetted on the balcony, tossing his head and flinging his shoulders in strange flicking movements. I was longing to speak to him and gave him a little wave and a smile of encouragement. But this only served to throw him into an even greater display of frantic behavior until I realized to my shame that he was trying to work up courage to come down the steps and pass the doorway without being accosted by me.

I therefore studiously ignored him and looked steadily at Stoika, who seemed to be discussing some sort of deal with her husband and the priest. I sensed a mercenary atmosphere, a certain hardness of heart between them; they were evidently discussing money. Out of the corner of my eye I saw Jacov the visionary flitting down the staircase and flashing past within an inch of me. He looked vulnerable, stricken.

Despite my years of doorstepping as a journalist it made me feel wretched to think people like me had made a freakish curiosity of this simple boy to the point where he was half-crazed with self-consciousness.

I left the problem of a bed for the night to Providence and made my way back to the parish house, where the pilgrims were already flocking for the evening's apparition. At the top of the steps leading to the door a young American priest was leading the rosary in English; immediately beneath him, squeezed in tightly on each of the steps, were priests, friars, and monks of all ages who had formed a ragged queue to gain admittance to the apparitions' room. Many of the priests carried plastic supermarket bags containing religious objects which the faithful had passed to them for the Virgin's blessing. Even as the priests jostled on their uncomfortable perches, the pilgrims continued to approach them with more bags.

The reciting of the rosary seemed to have a mesmerizing effect on the crowd, but there was also an atmosphere of suppressed excitement and restlessness. Here and there a group of women would suddenly gabble in high-pitched voices. Many of the people were squinting up at the sun, which was just dipping below the pine trees next to the church, casting dramatic fingers of light and shade over the pilgrims.

At about six o'clock the door of the parish house opened and a priest appeared on the balcony; he looked pale and he had grown his sideburns long until they almost covered his cheeks. There was a pause in the prayers and a strange murmur, like a low growl, went through the crowd. The priest was choosing the privileged ones who were to be allowed into the apparitions' room. He signaled admittance by laying a hand on each applicant's shoulder; some were firmly rejected by a prod in the chest; others he motioned forward by pointing to an individual and beckoning.

I pushed my way forward holding out my letter of introduction from Father Foley. The priest with the sideburns snatched it and read it almost at a glance. "Yes!" he said. "But not today. You come here tomorrow, understand?" And he retreated.

A few moments after the door had shut behind him the rosary recommenced with even more fervor.

Fifteen more minutes passed, then a shudder went through the crowd and people began to cry out: "The children! The children!" Several strapping young men were approaching, making a way through the throng toward the steps; they passed within a foot of me. Then the "children" came into view: Jacov and two girls whom I recognized from photographs as Vicka and Marija. They were walking at speed, arm in arm, three abreast. Jacov was in the center; the girls were blushing, their eyes aglint, their heads raised high, swaggering as they went; they looked like brides on the eve of their wedding.

Pilgrims were calling out to them and holding up rosaries, crucifixes, devotional medals, and even babies, as if seeking blessings. Several women leapt forward to touch them, and one even managed to grab a lock of Vicka's hair, but they were roughly pushed away by the young men.

As the party reached the steps of the parish house the young men made a way through, pressing the priests up against the wall to enable the visionaries to leap up the steps.

At this point the rosary praying began again, in Italian, while in different parts of the crowd the chanting of *Alleluias* and *Ave Marias* broke out spasmodically. Some people were on their knees, their arms raised above their heads. Those nearest the parish house leaned against the walls, stroking and fondling the stucco as if the very fabric of the house would bestow virtue.

After a few more minutes another cry went up: "Oh! My God!

The sun! Look!" Large sections of the crowd were pointing through the trees; they seemed to be able to gaze directly into the sun's rays. Others were screwing up their eyes and shading their faces with their hands.

Most of the crowd had abandoned their prayers and were trying to observe the sun-visionaries, or were gabbling together with their neighbors. I felt nervous. "What is it?" I said out loud. "What on earth are they seeing?"

An American woman standing next to me held me by the arm. "That's their present from Our Lady," she said. "I saw it yesterday afternoon. After coming out of church I looked into the sun for about four minutes; it was painless." She was looking searchingly into my eyes, pleading with me as if under a strange compulsion. "You see the corona," she went on, "then the disc spinning and shooting out colors. I saw reds and yellows."

She shaded her eyes and gazed up into the sky. "But I can't see anything now."

I looked up toward the sun and was instantly blinded. The woman was moving away from me, sharing her experiences with anybody who would listen.

The young American priest who had led the rosary earlier was taking charge of the crowd once more. "Brothers and sisters, I beg of you," he cried, "be sensible and don't stare directly into the sun. The visionaries in there need your prayers; so let us now pray the rosary all together."

With this he began to intone the prayers and carried the pilgrims with him in a great roar of fervor.

After half-an-hour's prayer the crowd suddenly fell silent. People were pointing at the window that faced out over the yard.

"The light is on!" I heard somebody whisper. "The vision is beginning. Our Lady is here!"

Then, quietly, like a tremor of wind, people were kneeling down where they were in the gravel. An eerie silence descended over the entire village, the only sound a distant murmur of traffic up on the main road.

They knelt statuesque in the silence. Some gazed up toward the parish house window, mumming prayers with their lips. Others were bent down almost to the ground. Those closest to the house itself pressed their foreheads on the walls.

I remembered a phrase I had once read referring to pilgrimage as the "therapy of distance," symbolizing needs and yearnings, satisfied by departure, discomfort, and the rigors of travel. I was conscious of the enormous distances these pilgrims had traveled to be here; I was also aware that these people had made sacrifices, many of them journeying despite sickness and handicaps. But pilgrimage is also arrival, and I felt that in these moments I was witnessing the goal of every pilgrim's journey to Medjugorje: the hoped-for presence they had come to encounter.

The silence, the stillness, lasted for some five minutes. Then, without warning, the door opened and the visionaries came out onto the balcony almost at a run. There was a burst of applause from the pilgrims, who rose in an instant to their feet, clapping and cheering. Marija came first, her hands joined in an attitude of prayer, and then came Vicka and Jacov, attended by two nuns and the young men.

The party turned right at the corner of the parish house and walked quickly toward the church, the rest of the crowd following.

There was a great throng of pilgrims already collecting outside the church in readiness for the evening Mass that was now to follow. As I pushed slowly forward I could see lines of people waiting for confessions in a file next to the church. The priests sat on folding chairs, bent double; some put their hands on the penitents' shoulders or foreheads. I saw a priest dressed in a white robe with "Hi-Tec" sneakers gleaming under the hem; a rascally looking Franciscan in conversation with a beautiful young woman was wearing fashionable blue canvas deck shoes under his habit. Somehow I found myself shocked, quite unreasonably, by the inappropriate footwear, which seemed to me to symbolize unorthodoxy.

By the time I reached the door the building was packed. I wormed my way through and craned my neck. There were thirty or more priests on the altar. The congregation was singing the *Kyrie*—"Lord have mercy"—with a devotion that took me straight back to my childhood, to the parish mission weeks when the powerful preaching of visiting friars had brought about an epidemic of religious fervor, church attendance, and resort to confession.

I made my way out again to the fresh air. Most of the outdoor pilgrims were kneeling in the dust and following the service on loudspeakers, which were attached to the trees; but I saw a young couple smoking cigarettes and several gypsies were wandering among the praying pilgrims attempting to sell crucifixes.

I came away and wandered around the side of the church until I stood on the edge of a field looking toward Mount Krizevac and the setting sun. Halfway up the mountain I could see a gleam of light, as if the rays of the sun were reflecting on a piece of glass or metal. Out of the corner of my eye I saw a small fat man approaching me. He seemed to be covering his mouth with both hands in a gesture of emotion.

He stood right next to me for a while, in silence. Then he spoke, in a clear Scottish accent: "You've seen the light on the hill, have you not!"

I turned toward him. He was balding, sandy-haired and be-spectacled, wearing a worn tweed jacket. Rocking slightly on his toes, he kept taking one hand away from his mouth to point up toward Mount Krizevac.

"Yes, I see the light," I said. "Surely it's a reflection of something on the hill."

"No way!" he said with quiet emphasis. "That there's a special light. Just for us. I saw Jesus on the wall of the church this same day last year: I've got a photo to prove it. I've seen Mary; she appears in all kinds of guises. I've seen Jesus and I've got a photo to prove it. I've seen a massive ring around the sun taking in the whole church."

Moving away from the fat man, I headed for the parking lot. I looked back just once to see him standing still, eating a bar of chocolate straight from the wrapper while squinting up at the sun.

Later, after the Mass had ended, I walked from house to house in the semidarkness looking in vain for a bed for a night. In most of the houses there were bands of pilgrims sitting down to a simple evening meal around a communal table. Their faces glowed in the lamplight; there was an impression of nervous excitement, antici-pation, unaccustomed fellowship. I felt envious of them, disap-pointed that there was no place to welcome me in.

6

Fra Zovko's "Voice"

Unwilling to put Providence to the test any further, I had driven to a town called Libjuski, just ten miles from Medjugorje, and spent the night in an empty, echoing hotel, called the Biggeste. At breakfast I was served hard-boiled eggs while the hotel manager at the next table tucked into a plate of pork chops and pickled gherkins washed down with white wine. He wished me good morning with a blast of wicked breath.

Later that morning I drove out to Tihaljina, twenty miles from Medjugorje, to meet Fra Jozo Zovko, who had been pastor at Medjugorje when the apparitions first occurred, and who had spent almost two years in prison for his part in the promotion of the phenomena.

I found a youthful-looking man in his early forties with an innocent, rounded face and a gentle voice. We sat in the back pew of his empty, whitewashed church, and he immediately launched into his story.

"During the week the apparitions began," he said, "I was absent from Medjugorje. I came back through Mostar and a woman yelled to me from a passing ambulance. It was one of the parishioners, she was swathed in bandages from an accident; something had collapsed on her. She wasn't interested in her injuries; instead she shouted: 'Hey, Father, get back to Medjugorje. Our Lady is appearing to a bunch of our children!' So I raced back to find the village in uproar. People were coming in from all over the region."

Fra Zovko sat with his hands resting in his lap with a diffident, inward-looking expression.

"How did the children strike you?" I asked him.

"They were confused," he said. "Their reactions were childish, and they were quarreling among themselves. I didn't know what to do."

Fra Zovko continued with his story in a quiet voice. The police suspected that the children were on drugs; they also speculated about political motives. At the beginning of the Second World War there had been an attempt to establish a Catholic Fascist state in Bosnia Hercegovina; any kind of Catholic manifestation now made the Communists suspicious. One morning a police car drove up to the church where Fra Zovko was standing with his assistant, Fra Zrinko, after Mass. A man got out and handed them an envelope on which was written: "Monk Number One and Monk Number Two." It was a summons from the local Communist party to attend a special session at Citluk. The priests turned up to find the party officials furious; the priests were told to stop the children and the parishioners from going to the hill.

"I would have been more than happy," said Fra Zovko, "to see all those people in my church rather than on the hillside."

At this point the priest stopped and began to swallow compulsively, as if trying to suppress his emotions.

"The people were abandoning the church," he went on. "They were leaving me, their pastor, and the Mass and the sacraments, to search for some sort of phantasm on the hill. I felt a failure; and I felt terrified, because I didn't know what to make of the apparitions."

One afternoon he was in the church praying. He did not know it at the time, but the police were chasing the children to prevent them from going to the hill. The children had successfully eluded the police and were running through the vineyards toward the church.

"I had my Bible in front of me," he said. "I opened it at random to see if God would send me a word of guidance, and I lighted on the passage in Exodus where Moses stands helpless before the Red Sea. I was crying out to God from the depths of my own darkness; I was placing before God all my doubts and despair; all the broken pieces of my life ..."

Fra Zovko was breathing deeply with emotion. One hand was splayed across his chest.

"In that silent and deserted church," he continued, "I heard a voice, a human voice as real as my own, not a voice in my head. It was a voice that seemed to echo across the whole of my life."

Fra Zovko stopped; he seemed on the point of tears.

Eventually he said: "The voice said 'Go outside and protect the children.' I rose immediately and went quickly to the door of the church. At the very moment the door opened the children came rushing up, crying that the police were after them. I took them straight to the priests' house and hid them. That evening the children had their first visions indoors. They had come in under the protection of the house of God ..."

The priest sat in silence for several minutes. With tears in his eyes he hugged himself.

"You witnessed the children experiencing their visions on many occasions, Father. Did you ever see the vision yourself?"

"Yes," he said, "I did see Our Lady ... but, I have to say that this vision was not really for me ..."

He raised his hand in a gentle gesture, as if to forestall any further questions on the subject.

Eventually I said: "How did you come to be arrested, Father?"

"Communist officials sat in the midst of the congregation and took notes on my sermons," he said. "I had preached about the Israelites in exile in the desert; about one of my parishioners who had been taken in sin for forty years and had recently returned to the Church. One day I spoke about the need for courage, even to the point of shedding our blood ... It was the year of the fortieth anniversary of the founding of the Yugoslav Communist Party; I was arrested and charged with fomenting political violence. They bundled me into a car and I was taken to a jail in Citluk. The place was unknown to me; we went through a tunnel, and there we were. I was thrown in with criminals and drug addicts."

When the case came to trial, he said, they refused to hear the testimonies of his 300 parishioners, who would have spoken on his behalf; nor would they allow him to explain the spiritual significance of his sermons. He was sentenced to three years' imprisonment, but the sentence was later commuted to eighteen months.

The priest's voice trailed to silence. He was unwilling to speak further.

"I have to go," he said, "there are people waiting for me."

As I drove away from Tihaljina I felt curiously saddened and moved by Fra Zovko's story. He had a strong charisma that seemed to transcend the drama of the alleged miraculous events in his former parish. It was one thing to believe in visions and voices and to go in search of them as a pilgrim during one's vacation; it was something else to end up in prison for them. His story about the voice telling him to protect the children seemed to me both impressive and authentic. Impressive because the voice had imparted an accurate message; authentic, for it seemed to me inconceivable that he could be lying.

I returned to Medjugorje the next morning to mingle with the pilgrims. In the church there were about fifty people deep in prayer before the Blessed Sacrament. Many of them were old peasant women in black. As they prayed their beads they seemed to be summoning enormous reserves of concentration. The church had an almost tangible atmosphere of stillness and peace.

But outside I could hear the constant murmur of querulous voices. Curiosity overcame me and I wandered back out and walked into a group of young men who were squabbling heatedly. In their midst was a Swiss youth who was passing around a color photograph. It depicted what looked like a pretty Italian model posing as the Virgin Mary.

"What's the problem?" I asked.

"The problem?" said the young men. "Some priest has been saying that he captured this in his camera while taking a picture of the Krizevac. I don't believe it. Why do these people have to do this? It spoils the truth."

"I believe it!" insisted a young American. "You've got to have faith."

Before I could say anything a man in a red singlet drew me to one side. "My name is Dermot, I'm from Belfast. . . . Where are you from? . . . What's your name? . . . Is this your first time?"

Before I could reply he launched into a testimony: "Before I came here I had just enough religion to put under one fingernail.

I think I've found something here. It's changed my life; I'm praying.
I love to go up on the mountain; the animals and birds up there
never seem to sleep; there is a ceaseless chorus all through the
night. Last week we went up with Marija to the cross—there were
about two thousand of us. She said that we would all receive a kiss
from Our Lady. And sure enough, when we knelt there in the
darkness and prayed each and every one of us felt the firm imprint
of a kiss on the cheek."

Before I could question him more closely, Dermot had vanished from my life only to be replaced by another informant, then
another: a stream of buzzing pilgrims seeking willing ears for their
testimonies.

One of them fished out his rosary. "See this? When I came
here the links between the beads were silver. Now they are gold.
You'll find hundreds of people who've had this happen. A man told
me yesterday that he had his rosary beads assayed and the jeweller
said the gold was of a unique kind only found in the Middle Ages."

During the next hour I wandered slowly through the picnic
area greeting pilgrims who were only too happy to "share" their
witness. Testimonies of curious luminous experiences abounded,
and there were more claims of rosaries "turning to gold." But the
most popular anecdotes featured "coincidences," all of which were
said to be "amazing."

An American man wearing a label that said "Peace Tours" accosted me. He carried an open beach bag in which there were dark
glasses, a camera, suntan lotion, and a crucifix.

"I called the cab service the morning of our departure from
Dulles Airport. Who turns up? A Yugoslav! Can you credit that? You
can't tell me that something like that wasn't *meant.*"

The "witnesses" buzzed about the place, swapping their testimonies. Yet there were many more who remained silent—people
who seemed closed in on themselves, who could be seen sitting
alone looking out toward the mountains.

One such was a middle-aged woman from New York City, who
I found reading a book on a bench near the parish house. I apol-
ogized for disturbing her and invited her to tell me why she had
come to Medjugorje.

Her name was Lois and she was single. She had spent her life
working among addicts in Hell's Kitchen. She looked exhausted.

"I could have gone anywhere for a vacation," she said, "the Caribbean, Florida, California. I came here because I felt empty. I wanted to get *close* to something."

When I asked her whether she had found what she was looking for, she said "Sure!" and left it at that.

There were others whose feelings were more ambivalent, as was the case with a priest I spoke to near the coffee shop.

I had seen him making his way slowly but purposefully toward the church as I arrived that morning. He was tall and stooped with wispy gray hair, and he had a kind, contemplative face. He clutched a plastic supermarket bag that appeared to be stuffed with a white Mass robe. Sitting close to him, I introduced myself, telling him of my experience on the steps of the church. He shook his head.

"There are a lot of people here who need their heads examined. Myself included! Eh? You shouldn't be surprised at that. Almost everyone here, God love them, has brought a problem."

Then he launched at once into the story of his life in a soft Irish brogue.

"I'm a Carmelite. I entered the order in 1960 after being a printer on the *Irish Independent* all my working life from the time I left school. I'm a late vocation. I raise funds for the order. I have to raise one hundred thousand pounds a year, or we're in trouble. Talk about stress . . .

"This is my second visit here. The first time I came just to accompany a friend and it did nothing for me. This time I've come on my own account hoping for something to happen."

"And what have you seen?" I asked. "Anything that's convinced you of the authenticity of the apparitions?"

He gave a short laugh. "God, what am I saying! I'm a firm believer, John, in the principle of Saint Paul's second conversion, where he puts reason and logic and *proof* to one side and goes for the illogical. It's a question of belief, not of proof. I believed deeply in another set of apparitions, at Garabandal in northern Spain; I believed in them because the visionaries were *obedient* to the local pastor, and because of the support of Padre Pio, who was the most powerful saint of his era. But the Church came down against it. Now Medjugorje has been endorsed by Sister Briege McKenna, who is the only equivalent we have to a contemporary Padre Pio. What a wonderful woman. She prophesied the events here several months before they occurred.

"I don't think you can set out to find God as if he's in the bottom drawer," he went on. "He reveals himself *to* you. I can only dispose myself for revelation. That's all I can do, you see. The growth of the spirit is an extraordinary thing; it's the work of a lifetime. Saint John of the Cross said that most of us get stuck less than half-way in our journey to God because we think we've made it. What a man he was! He was a spiritual *mountain climber,* that's what Saint John of the Cross was . . . What on earth did he mean by that thing he said—*nada, nada, nada?* Finding God in the vast emptiness, you see . . ."

He scratched his ear and smiled to himself. "I spoke to Marija outside her house the other day. She said to me: 'How long are you staying, Father, are you staying until Pentecost?' And I said to her, 'Why, Marija, is there to be a sign on that day?' And she just winked at me and said: 'You'll see! You'll see!' "

"You're looking for a personal sign?"

The priest shrugged his shoulders. He looked weary.

"I don't know. I pin everything on the promise that Jesus gave to Peter and his disciples, the promise of Peter's authority. It's the only thing we've got to hang on to, the one little straw. And at the very end of it all, there may be a precious small remnant hanging on. I'll tell you, if the pope says that Medjugorje is false I'll burn my books on the subject and never set foot here again."

With this he collected his things together. As he made ready to leave me, he said: "Remember, John, it's not the big politicians that make the decisions in the world, it's the little people and their little prayers."

As he trundled away with his supermarket bag I felt depressed. Nearly thirty years a monk and the man seemed beset with contradictions: a contemplative religious, harassed by financial problems; hanging on to faith, yet looking for a sign; declaring his trust in Church authority, yet hoping for private revelation; searching for God, yet insisting that God would find *him.* And all the while puzzling over that stark riddle of Saint John of the Cross: *"Nada, nada, nada!"* Nothing, nothing, nothing!

7

In the Apparitions' Room

By 5:30 in the afternoon I was in position once again by the balustrade of the parish house, hoping to gain admittance to the evening's apparition. The huge crowd of pilgrims pressing in on all sides behind me were again being led in prayers and hymn singing from the steps.

At 5:45 the door of the house opened and the pale Franciscan with the sideburns emerged to select those who were to be admitted. The priests went up first, pushing and jostling; so forceful was the crush of people behind that I despaired of being spotted. The priest was looking about in the crowd, while hundreds of devotees, some holding up sick children, cried out, begging to be noticed and admitted.

At last he saw me and shouted: "You! Mister! You come up now quickly." I put my best shoulder forward and squirmed through; as I went, a woman thrust a supermarket bag full of holy objects in my hand.

"Get it as close to the apparitions' wall as you can!" she implored.

Once I was inside, the door was slammed by a young woman.

I was out of breath and perspiring. I turned to her and said: "How do you cope with this?"

"You say '*no*,'" she said grimly, "and you mean it. Otherwise you're dead."

The pale priest introduced himself as Father Slavko and ushered me to the study bedroom, where the apparition was to take place.

Some thirty priests, their faces drenched in sweat, were crammed together in uncomfortable kneeling postures in a space no more than twelve feet by twenty feet; they were praying the rosary in Latin. There was something peculiarly primitive and shamanistic about the scene, as if the clerics were there to ward off evil.

There was only one woman in the room, an elegantly dressed, bejeweled, highly made up lady with false eyelashes, who, it seemed, had been introduced to the room in a more dignified fashion than the rest of us.

The attention of the priests was focused on the wall opposite the window where there was a low bookcase on which stood a vase with a single red rose and a crucifix. There, in the blank space above, the Virgin would appear. I found myself wondering whether one day, like Fatima and Lourdes, this simple room might not be the sight of a vast and ornate basilica.

The priests now began to sing the *Veni Creator Spiritus,* stumbling uncertainly over the words; only one of them appeared to be fully confident—a corpulent Passionist who, despite the heat, was dressed in the full habit of his order: cassock and cloak with various badges, belts, and buckles. Scanning the assembly, I fancied I could see Irish, German, Spanish, Chinese, and Mexican faces. I wondered if they were indeed all priests, or whether some of them might be imposters. One cleric looked particularly suspicious. He was dressed in a cassock with a sash around his middle, his hair was a mass of greasy ringlets, and there was something bogus about his demeanor. His eyes were turned up so that only the whites were visible, but every so often he would come down to earth for a few seconds and take a swift, canny look about him before resuming his ecstatic expression.

In the midst of the hymn there was a sudden commotion at the outer door. Two women and a little boy had somehow gained entrance. One of the women was the mother of the boy, who, she insisted, was suffering from an incurable illness, although the child seemed more likely to die of imminent choking from the scores of rosaries that were hung around his neck.

The doorkeeper managed to eject one of the women, but the

mother had wrapped herself up in a ball, refusing to speak or to budge. She was sitting on the floor of the corridor with her hands overhead, her knees drawn up to her ears.

But the site of the apparitions was spared further disturbance by the arrival of Jacov, Marija, and Vicka. There was an excited hush as the priests stopped their praying to stare at the young people. Jacov was dressed this evening in a fashionable pink linen suit and his hair was freshly spiked up again; scowling and avoiding eye contact, he went down immediately on his knees, attempting to crouch out of sight. Marija, despite the heat, was dressed, for modesty I imagined, in a pale blue sweater, a woolen plaid skirt, and dark woolen stockings. Her oval face glowed in the heat; her nose was longish and strong, and she had a rather pointed jaw. As she looked directly at those about her with tranquil gray eyes, there seemed to be nothing artful about her. She looked a trifle nunnish, in fact guileless. Vicka, who had a wide mouth and slightly crazy eyes set in a Slavonic face, had her hair swept back with an elastic band; she was wearing a simple green dress. Both girls went down on their knees and began to recite the rosary out loud in Croatian while the priests responded in various languages.

Father Slavko, the Franciscan, had joined us now and was squatting next to Marija. I was still standing, no more than a foot away from her, studying her face closely. Once or twice she looked directly back at me and I felt a sense of peculiar, almost erotic, excitation (and therefore tinged with guilt) in the momentary eye contact.

The voice of Marija was dominant; she spoke slowly, enunciating each word clearly. And the longer she prayed the more she drew the attention of everybody in the room. Was it the highly charged intensity of expectation, or the stirring of some barely understood, primitive undercurrent? Whatever the case, with every passing minute this plain girl seemed to me to become more radiant, mysterious, and graceful. I found it impossible to take my eyes off of her.

For much of the time she was kneeling upright; occasionally she would rest back on her heels in a swanlike movement for a few moments before resuming a straight position once again. Jacov was hidden from sight, his head bowed low.

Meanwhile, it was clear that the majority of the priests found the unaided kneeling excruciating; they fidgeted and attempted all sorts of squatting contortions while the perspiration rolled down their faces. Outside the crowd could be heard reciting the rosary and singing, and as time passed the responses became a steady, concerted roar; it was as if they were willing something to happen in the room with their fervent pleading.

When we reached the end of the complete fifteen mysteries of the rosary, Slavko stood up. He pointed to the window and asked the nearest priest to shut it; then he switched on the light, a simple naked bulb hanging from the center of the room. The crowd fell silent.

He said simply: "Let us pray now that the children will receive an apparition."

Jacov, Marija, and Vicka stepped forward, causing the priests to squeeze together even tighter to make room. The three stood before the wall, their hands joined in an attitude of prayer, and began to pray out loud in unison. I was now standing less than a foot away to Marija's left, slightly in front of her so that I could see her full face and profile.

Suddenly, in perfect coordination, they went down on their knees and continued to pray; then, together, their heads rose and they were now speaking silently, their lips and throats moving quite rapidly, gazing intently as if at a real object. They had entered their ecstasy.

It was at this point that I witnessed something truly astonishing, and for which, in principle, I could grasp no ready explanation. For about three minutes I saw Jacov, Marija, and Vicka speaking silently and in turn to the invisible figment that hovered in front of them. The extraordinary fact was that when one of them *stopped* "speaking," the other, in that same split second, would *begin*. Yet they were not uttering a sound, nor were they capable of seeing each other's lips; I could see no bodily movement whatsoever by which they could cue one another in order to achieve such a feat.

Marija, on whom I now began to concentrate, did not appear ecstatic in any melodramatic or histrionic way, but her face radiated a striking loveliness, innocence, and wonder. Her gaze was steady, unblinking, tender; the whites of her eyes seemed to shine with an unearthly light. "Transfiguration" was a word that came at once to mind. And when I focused my attention on Jacov I saw that same transfiguring quality in his face, made all the more poignant because of his youth.

While I stood watching them I became aware of the stunning silence and stillness, both inside and outside the room; momentarily a child cried a long way from the building, and the sound and the distance gave depth and gravity to the quiet. As I watched the visionaries in the deep peace of those few minutes I had an experience that was both fascinating and unexpected.

The cliché about seeing the whole of one's life in an instantaneous panoramic vision on the brink of sudden death was certainly not something that I had ever experienced personally, and I had always thought it an exaggeration; but I now believe that I have an inkling of what such an experience might be like. For as I stood in the apparitions' room I saw in my mind's eye, with great clarity, each and every one of the images of Mary before which I had prayed thoughout my childhood and youth, from the statue of Mary in my mother's bedroom in my infancy to the carved stone Mary Queen of Heaven that adorned the Lady Chapel at Oscott College in my young manhood. And in a mysterious expansion of a single moment I was somehow *aware* of each and every prayer I had prayed, and hymn that I had sung, to Mary, from my earliest Hail Mary's to the poignant *Salve Reginas* at the end of Compline in later years.

As the experience faded, I found myself thinking that these memories gave new meaning to the phrase "full of grace," and for a moment I had the impression of something unblocking inside myself. Somehow, unawares, I found my heart *inclining*.

Then the moment was past.

All this took, I believe, a matter of a few seconds. Then, without warning or any indication of a cue, the three young people whispered something together; they leaned back slightly at the same instant, their faces awestruck; then they gave a little sigh. They were now praying out loud and I noticed that Marija's voice was thick and throaty and full of emotion. Then all three stood up and the ecstasy was over.

Father Slavko led the visionaries from the room as the priests began to chant over and over again: *"Ave, ave, ave Maria . . ."*

The debriefing, which was a strictly private affair in a separate room, took no more than three minutes.

When he reappeared, the priest said: "Let us go now to the church."

Next we were walking out of the apparitions' room and facing the crowds outside, who looked up at us expectantly, enviously, shading their eyes in the rays of the setting sun. A man who was wearing four crucifixes around his neck shook me by the hand. Then the woman came to retrieve her supermarket bag; I was grasping it in my hand with a bloodless grip. I had not noticed it since the moment she handed it to me.

During Mass I went off to sit alone on the edge of a tobacco field to try to get the experience of the apparition into some sort of immediate perspective.

How could one define what was happening to these young people day after day in Medjugorje? To say that it was an "illusion" would imply that they were in some way *mistaken* about a visual stimulus corresponding with an extramental reality. It was quite possible, it seemed to me, that they had indeed been in a state of illusion during the original apparition, when they might have extrapolated a presence around a light in the mountain mist. But in the confines of the parish room it was clear that the young people were now engaged in "perceptions" without a material external stimulus, and from this point of view they were, by any clinical definition at least, in a state of *hallucination,* as opposed to *illusion*. At the same time these hallucinations, to refine their status a little further, were clearly aural and visual and projected an *external* rather than an internal presence.

Clearly they were not asleep and dreaming, nor did they appear to be on drugs (after such a long period that possibility would by now have been exposed). Nor could I accept that all three were suffering from epilepsy or schizophrenia, and suffering identical hallucinations simultaneously.

So what were the remaining possibilities? It seemed to me that they were limited to the following:

1. That they were engaged in a deliberate and sustained hoax. To put it bluntly, that they were lying.
2. That they were affected by hypnosis, either by one or several of their number, by self-hypnosis, or even by hypnosis controlled by somebody outside the group.
3. That they were hallucinating spontaneously in a powerful act of the imagination.
4. That they were "given" the hallucinations by a supernatural agency.

5. That the Virgin was there in reality, and that we ourselves had been deprived of normal sight.

My natural inclination was to discount the latter two possibilities and favor some sort of combination of the second and third. Hypnosis, from my own reading about the subject, was a far more elusive phenomenon than is widely understood. For example, the common notion that people forget their hallucinations or behavior outside hypnosis has long been proved false, as has the idea that one needs to be on a couch and focusing on a hypnotist's eyes. The forces and "laws" of hypnotism are powerful, extraordinarily flexible, and deeply mysterious, although hardly in a mystical sense. The mechanisms of hypnotism undoubtedly involve complex neurological considerations and the explanation as to what is happening, and how, must surely lie at the frontiers of neuroscience; the problem is that we simply do not understand nearly enough about those mechanisms as yet.

All the same, having seen these young people in action, it seemed to me that there was no reason why a Christian believer might not accept the idea of there being no contradiction between the spiritual presence of the Virgin Mary combined with a process of hypnotic or imaginative hallucination. This would come within the Christian idea of "grace building on nature" and would outflank the extreme debunkers and reductionists, while not doing violence to the views of those who sought a rational explanation. Yet even for a believer the question still remained as to whether an authentic spiritual or moral resonance was being exerted at Medjugorje. And was this resonance something that only the "children" were experiencing? Or was it something that the pilgrims were encountering, too?

This reflection brought me to my own reactions during the apparition. In the strange otherworldliness of the place, in the peculiar psychic atmosphere that seemed to attend the behavior of Marija, my imagination and emotions had been stimulated in a quite dramatic fashion. I had felt "touched." I could not deny that the experience had been arresting and even slightly uncomfortable. But had I been in receipt of a genuine moment of what Christians call "grace," or was it something more akin to powerful sentimental emotions?

I believed that I could explain away my experience rationally;

and yet, I did not see any reason why this should exclude the possibility of a supernatural agency if I were inclined to believe in such a thing. My own personal experiences in the room offered no token or "proof" of a supernatural agency beyond the vague (but daunting) conviction that I had felt myself drawn toward some sort of "higher power"; but neither did they *disprove* a supernatural agency.

I felt confused, and restless, even harassed. But these feelings did not amount to any kind of newfound conviction about belief. As for "evidence," there remained only the strange phenomenon of the synchronized behavior of the children; but I was not personally inclined at present to fill the "gap" with a supernatural agency.

I made my way to the foot of Mount Krizevac and began to climb. I had gone no more than twenty yards up the steep rocky path when a little crone leapt out from behind a boulder. She held out her hand for money and mummed something through her toothless gums; as she did this her face almost disappeared like a concertina. I gave her a note and hurried on.

The path twisted upward, marked at intervals by the Stations of the Cross. There were wildflowers, foxglove, purple heather, and brilliant poppies in the rusty soil that clung around the tawny rocks. The scrub resounded with crickets.

I passed a young man who was walking slowly and painfully up the hill on bare feet; his soles were bloody with lacerations. I tried to smile encouragement through my ill-concealed disgust, and he said: "It's tough, but it's good for me!"

Another man passed me on his way down; he was carrying a rock on his shoulder. Shouting with laughter, he cried out: "I'm taking a bit of this little ole mountain with me!"

A man surrounded by several teenage girls was standing by one of the shrines, dressed from head to toe in a sort of pale blue religious habit. He caught my eye. "I'll take my vows," he called out to me, "on the Feast of the Assumption; Our Lady planned it all, a whole host of coincidences; she planned my vocation, everything . . ."

Panting and bathed in sweat, I eventually emerged on the summit, which was still flooded with light from the setting sun. There was a platform of rock into which a huge concrete cross some hundred feet high had been set. A man wearing a combat jacket and dark glasses stood to the side of the cross with a tape player to his ear, and the strains of Gregorian chant could be heard. A dozen or so pilgrims squatted among the rocks, praying in silence.

The stone on the platform had a curiously luminous quality, deformed by scorch marks evidently caused by votive candles. Stuck in the crevices of the rocks were hundreds of wooden crosses to which were attached thousands of rags, gloves, scarves, and handkerchiefs, blowing in the wind like fetishes in a Buddhist graveyard. Pilgrims evidently liked to leave something of themselves behind in the holy place. But what did all these pieces of rag signify? Was it the detritus of their sins, their miseries, their lives?

I sat down and looked out at the vista. Medjugorje lay in the foreground, like a picture of a village in a fairy tale book, its farmhouses spread out in a great loop amid the fertile fields, with a winding road leading to the very doors of the church. It was a landscape of fable.

Here was the home village of the visionary children, living among devout peasants led by the saintly Franciscans. And up there in the north, beyond those snow-clad mountains, dwelt the wicked bishop in his palace, plotting to stop the visions and to persecute the children and the friars.

What was extraordinary about this fairy tale was the fact that it was a living, continuing drama, with the protagonists permanently on stage in a long-running show.

The time had come to hear the bishop's side of the story. I started the descent down the mountain.

8

The Bishop of Mostar

At Hotel Biggeste I telephoned the Bishop of Mostar's secretary to arrange an appointment. Bishop Pavao Zanic was not only eager to speak to an English writer about the Medjugorje apparitions, but there should be no delay, he insisted; and the bishop himself would provide an interpreter.

The next morning I drove to Mostar, a gray, modern town nestling in a valley beyond the mountains north of Medjugorje. The baroque stone episcopal palace on the outskirts of town faced a hulking concrete cathedral across a busy highway. I peered through the glass doors of the cathedral; inside, nuns were polishing the parquet floors.

At the door of the palace I was greeted by a dapper young priest with a halo of curls who ushered me into a parlor; lace curtains were hung across the French windows and a bright modern oil painting of the Assumption of Mary into Heaven was prominently displayed. The interpreter had arrived, a young suntanned Yugoslav in a T-shirt who shook my hand and told me that he had been to California and to Oxford Street.

Bishop Zanic appeared almost instantly, limping a little as if slightly arthritic. He was somewhat overweight, his face puffy and purplish around the jowls. His silvering hair was well trimmed and oiled, and he wore a long, black linen frock coat, but the black stock below his Roman collar was blemished with food stains. He scrutinized me balefully through horn-rimmed spectacles.

We sat at a long polished table on which he drummed his fingers.

"Look here," he began, breathing noisily. "I'd like to say straight off: there's nothing supernatural going on over at Medjugorje. *Nothing!* Understand that and you've grasped everything."

His delivery was explosive, his face bright with emotion.

"In this diocese," he went on, "there are about 180,000 Catholics. We have a difficult enough life under the Communists without a gang of kids saying they see the Virgin Mary every day! These Franciscans have been a nuisance to Rome for generations. They are disobedient. They've been in conflict with me for years because they don't wish to accept my authority over the allocation of parishes. And they're using these so-called apparitions to attempt to get their own way. The Virgin, if you please, is intervening and giving verdicts on the question!"

I said: "Monsignor, in your view are the children lying? Or are they hypnotized, or what?"

As I was having this translated, I could see Bishop Zanic's leg trembling nervously.

"These so-called visionaries," he snapped, "probably experienced something to begin with. I acknowledged that and I said I didn't think they were liars; but the important question is, did they experience something supernatural or was it merely psychological? Most of the reports just take my first words and say that I originally said the children are not lying. You see? They try to make out that I've contradicted myself."

The bishop was now gasping between sentences, holding on to the table as if it would run away from him.

"Now," he went on, "I have a book in French called *True and False Apparitions.* Out of 230 sets of apparitions of the Virgin Mary in this century the Church has only acknowledged two as authentic; so you have to look on these things with a lot of skepticism."

"But what makes you so certain that the Medjugorje apparitions are false?" I intervened.

The bishop pointed at a row of some twenty box files on the sideboard behind him.

"If you could *see,*" he fumed, "all the things the visionaries have said from the very beginning. . . . And they write that the *pope* has said this and that about Medjugorje, and you discover that he's said nothing of the sort ..."

"What sort of things did the visionaries tell you?" I asked.

The bishop clenched his fists and shut his eyes tightly.

"Listen!" he said. "When I spoke to the visionaries I got everything they said down on tape, and I caught them out in *lies*. One minute they're saying one thing; the next minute they're contradicting themselves. It would take *weeks* to demonstrate all their lies and contradictions."

"Anything else?"

"Anything else!" mimicked the bishop. "It's endless! I saw the notebook of one of them, conversations she'd had with the Virgin. And it was just full of ... silliness ... that the blessed Virgin Mary is talking unfavorably of me, the bishop, and on the side of the Franciscans ... that the Virgin Mary is saying that all religions are equal ... then they're saying the Virgin has announced a different date for her birthday. Next, I suppose, they'll want a different date for the Immaculate Conception ..."

The bishop fell silent; he was staring, eyes wide, at the French windows. He looked as if he were about to have a fit of apoplexy.

He leapt up from his chair, then paused for a moment, his head cocked. In the shocked silence I could hear the furious buzzing of a bluebottle fly. Suddenly he lurched across the room toward the windows and began to flail the curtains until, with a grunt of satisfaction, he had destroyed his quarry.

Limping back to the table, he resumed his seat. He took a deep breath and looked at me directly.

"Listen!" he said. "A Jesuit came to see me, and said he'd got hold of this diary of one of the visionaries. It was full of the most complete nonsense that Our Lady was supposed to have said. So I asked to see the diary, and he starts to give me the runaround. First there *was* a diary, then there *wasn't* a diary. Next he's *going* to bring the diary; then he's *not* going to bring the diary ... You see there are so many people playing games!"

"Tell me about the commission of inquiry," I said.

The bishop seemed to calm down a little, putting his hands together and assuming a more moderate, even defensive, expression.

"The commission? Well, it was very *thorough*. I had fifteen experts on it. There were thirteen theologians and two psychiatrists, and over a period of three years they studied everything the children said. And at each meeting a member would receive statements and they would be given the job to study a certain statement and bring the answers back at the next meeting. Then we'd examine the answers, discuss them, and take a vote on them. At the end of the three years, twelve members of the commission voted that there was nothing supernatural going on there, one member abstained. Just two voted that the visions were authentic, and those two members were *Franciscans!* In my opinion all the arguments put forward by those Franciscans were poor."

"Were there any miracles put before the commission?" I asked.

The bishop threw back his head and laughed. "They speak of three hundred miracle cures!" he roared. "They sent documentation on fifty of them to the medical tribunal in Lourdes. Each and every one was turned down."

"So if the happenings at Medjugorje are bogus, my Lord, what is your theory about the children?"

He shifted around uncomfortably in his chair, took off his spectacles and started to wipe them with a handkerchief.

"I was never present at any of the psychiatric examinations," he started cautiously, "because I didn't want to show any interest or give any importance to that. But all the results were brought to me, and it's proved that some of the children are not mentally healthy ..." his voice trailed vaguely.

"You mean one or more of them are mad?"

The bishop raised his hand. "Please. The doctors' ethic does not allow that to be publicly stated. All I will say is that one of the visionaries has been taken to a mental hospital many times under a false name."

"Are you referring to Vicka, the one that has a brain cyst? Surely that's common knowledge."

"No, no, no, no! I'm *not* referring to Vicka. And in any case her cyst is not dangerous."

The bishop was conscious, it seemed to me, of being on shaky ground. Suddenly he started to flutter his fingers in front of his face, as if to ward off a swarm of flies.

"But all this is beside the point," he insisted. "You've heard of the visions at Garabandal in Spain in the sixties? Well, I think those had much more claim to authenticity than these at Medjugorje. But look at the difference between the two cases. The moment the bishop in Spain declared against the visions, everybody accepted his verdict and was obedient to him."

Suddenly the bishop jumped up from his chair and banged his fist on the table. *"Why* do they [the Franciscans] behave toward me in this way?" he cried. "Why do they *hate* me so much? They have written books, and books, and books, and I have only written twenty-five pages. But they are frightened of my criticism. Those people over there, who are misleading the good, ignorant faithful who come here, deserve to be thrown into the deepest pit of *Hell!"*

The bishop was so beside himself with impatience to get the words through the interpreter I thought he would start pummeling the unfortunate young man who was struggling to keep up.

"Now!" The bishop's chest was heaving; there were tears in his eyes. "If Our Lady gives a sign to me of her genuine presence I will be the first to walk all the way to Medjugorje on bare feet! You hear? BARE FEET! But what will those people over there say to the poor faithful when it is finally proved that the visions are false? What will *they* say? Eh? And make no mistake about it, many people will abandon the faith when it becomes apparent that the Medjugorje events were false."

The bishop was beginning to look exhausted.

"One thing seems certain," I said. "There are a lot of conversions over there. Don't you think that counts for something?"

"Ha! Conversions! That's the same propaganda given out by the Adventists, the Jehovah's Witnesses, even the Muslims."

With this the bishop had risen from the table; he was talking to the interpreter. Then he gave me a brief nod and started limping from the room.

The interpreter looked at me a little awkwardly.

"The bishop says he has to go to his lunch now and wishes you good day and *bon voyage.* He says he doubts whether you will be any better than anybody else at explaining his point of view, as nobody wants to hear what he says and report it faithfully. He also says ... that you are to pay my interpreting fee." The young man shrugged and gave a wan smile. "Which is ... ten dollars, please."

On the porch of the church at Medjugorje a group of pilgrims was peering at a bulletin on a red baize notice board. They were reading the message that Our Lady had given the visionaries at the previous evening's apparition; it was typed out in French, German, Italian, and English:

"Dear children! I desire you to be the reflection of Jesus who enlightens this unfaithful world which is walking in darkness. I wish that all of you be a light to all and to witness in the light. Dear children, you are called to darkness, you are called to light. Therefore, live the light with your life. Thank you for your response to my call."

These were the supposed actual words of the Virgin Mary.

But what did they mean: " . . . you are called to darkness, you are called to light . . ."? Was it a riddle to be pondered reverentially? Was it nonsense? The result perhaps of poor translation?

My reverie on the subject was interrupted by Father Svet, a slightly built Franciscan with a huge bald dome of a head, who had run in from the picnic area, his cowl up against the light rain. He had come by arrangement to take me to meet the visionary Marija.

There was a flight of steps to the living quarters of Marija's parents' farmhouse. Svet led the way into the kitchen; the walls were painted bright yellow and there were pictures of the Virgin, the Sacred Heart, and the pope. Marija was standing by the stove; she was wearing blue jeans, a blouse, and sneakers; her hair was tied with a scarf, peasant fashion. She greeted me with a hard handshake and ushered us through to a sitting room.

There was just enough room for two armchairs, a sofa and a coffee table. One whole wall was papered with a lake scene against a backdrop of pine woods. Cutouts of a bumblebee, Saint Francis of Assisi, and the shape of a heart had been pasted onto the side of the lake.

There were statues of two child shepherds on the sideboard, and two stickers in English had been fastened to the curtains: "Praise the Lord," said one. "Try God!" said the other.

No sooner had Marija shut the door behind her than she went straight up to Father Svet and launched into a diatribe in Croatian, eyes blazing, face flushed.

While this tantrum was in progress I sat down, placed my tape recorder on the coffee table and switched it on. She noticed this action and immediately swooped forward; picking up the little machine, she deftly, without a moment's hesitation, pressed the "off" button and continued with her harangue. Then suddenly she stopped and started to laugh, throwing herself into an armchair opposite me.

Svet smiled. "It's nothing," he said to me. "She's overwhelmed with housework, you know, and the demands of the pilgrims. There was a row this afternoon about a pilgrim group."

Marija the visionary now gazed at me with bright eyes. She was wearing a T-shirt with a map of Louisiana printed on the front. Down the side of one of her socks was printed: "MY FRUIT." Her looks were unremarkable but her face had something of that appealing luminous quality I had noticed during the apparition.

As I asked my first question, she leaned over to her side and moved a vase of flowers on a low table to reveal an effigy of the infant Jesus with white spun wool hair.

She fiddled with the effigy as she began to piece together her story, Father Svet translating sentence by sentence.

"They refer to us as 'children' but I'm now twenty-three years of age," she began. "As a child I was maybe more delicate in health than my brothers and sisters and more sensitive in my feelings. They doted on me more when I was small, especially my father.

"Among grandfather's belongings I found a book about the life of Dominic Savio, an Italian child saint. Dominic was one of ten children and he died very young with tuberculosis after a life of great holiness. He once remained in ecstatic prayer for six hours. He died having a vision of Heaven. He is now my saint whom I love more than any other, even more than Saint Francis of Assisi.

"The day of the first apparition I was in Vicka's house with a lot of other people from the village listening to her story. Everybody was arguing and laughing, saying that it was probably a flying saucer or a shepherd's lantern in the mist. But I begged Vicka to call me if the Virgin appeared again. I told her that I didn't mind if I couldn't see the Virgin; I wanted to be there.

"The next day, during the second apparition, she came running down off the hill to fetch me; I was with Jacov and he came along as well. When I got up there I could only see a light about a hundred meters away from where the others were standing. It was like a mist clearing; I gradually saw the shape of a figure in a long gray dress and a white veil. I could see her face quite clearly although she was a long way off at the top of the hill. The Virgin was summoning us and we threw ourselves to the ground. We prayed for a time, then Ivanka asked the Virgin about her mother who had died two months before. Our Lady told Ivanka that her mother was well and happy. After a quarter of an hour Our Lady told us to go in peace. As we came down the hill Ivanka was in floods of tears.

"The visions have changed my life. As I grew up I had a very different future planned for myself than all this. I trained to be a hairdresser, I thought of getting married, having a family, things that every normal little girl thinks about. Now everything has changed. When my visions have finished I plan to go into a convent. It never occurred to me that I might do something like that. For me a convent was just a prison.

"After my visions began I experienced a steady growth in my faith. I began to feel God more like a friend. Before that I feared God, and my religion was an obligation. Now it's what I want to do, the whole purpose and goal of my life. It's been a kind of school. My faith grows not only from the apparitions, but from my prayers and meditations, and the sacraments."

Marija had been talking with great fluency all this time, her face animated, her expressions mobile. She had a very positive, confident personality, and once again I began to be struck by her peculiar beauty, which seemed to bloom the more she became the sole center of attention.

I had felt repulsed by her tendency to see her own life in terms of hagiography, but this was somewhat mitigated by her playfulness with the priest. Frequently she laughed at him; several times she punched him playfully through his habit as he questioned her about a term or phrase she had used. Once or twice she looked at me curiously and winked, as if to say, "I hope you're getting what you want."

It occurred to me that she was the strangest mixture of home-spun vivacity, peasant shrewdness, and priggishness. I wondered, too, whether she might just be capable of fraud, but I rejected the thought even as it came to me.

"People don't understand," she went on. "They think of me as a walking saint, but I have my own feelings. There are times when I find it difficult to restrain myself. But then I say it's all for the greater glory of God, for the conversion of sinners, and at that moment I can cope with it.

"There was an incident just today when somebody accused me of refusing to come out to see pilgrims. This woman had simply made it up. So I said to her: 'Lies are short-lived.' I wanted to show her that I knew she was a liar and that I wasn't some sort of deaf and dumb holy statue. I know what's going on!

"I lead an extremely busy life because of the apparitions and the pilgrims. Sometimes I take a cushion, go to the hill, sit down on a rock where nobody can see me and remain in prayer and silence. That's when I have the best rest, when I pray by myself.

"If you devote more time to your friend, then you will come to know his secrets. It's the same with God. The more time we devote to God the more we shall know him and the easier we shall find it to talk about him because we have experienced him.

"I am conscious that my life may not always be so well protected. Our Lady once said: 'you are in an oasis but Satan is lurking outside.' I'm not afraid because I have a great trust in God. And yet God has given us great freedom. Each of us can decide for or against God."

With this, Marija's story, or homily, had reached a natural conclusion and she stood up, signaling that our meeting was at an end.

She shook me by the hand and looked solemnly into my eyes. "Do you have any special intentions or personal requests," she asked, "to put before Our Lady?"

The question threw me. I knew that for a confirmed believer this might have seemed a wonderful privilege. In my state of complicated skepticism and obsession, it made my blood turn cold. Instead of answering it, I said, a trifle meanly: "Marija, am I right in saying that you think yourself holier than others because of these visions?"

Father Svet was unhappy with the question, but he translated it all the same.

She was unruffled. "Certainly I am not better," she said. "What's more, I could have passed on the messages without keeping them myself. But Our Lady says time and time again: live and testify with your lives."

As I picked up my tape recorder I said, "Marija, when Our Lady speaks does she say the same thing to all of you? Simultaneously?"

"Not necessarily," she said. "She says different things to us at the same time."

"And another thing. Can you describe how Our Lady speaks? I mean, is there anything special about the way she says things that's different from the way ordinary people, like you and I, speak?"

"She speaks in Croatian," said Marija promptly, "and you get the impression that every word is exactly the right word and that it is in exactly the right place."

At the kitchen door she shook me vigorously by the hand.

I said: "I'm very grateful for the time you've given me. I'm sorry if I've added to your troubles."

"It's no extra burden," she said, "and even if it were, I would welcome it, because it means I would get to my Father in Heaven more quickly."

She said this without the slightest hint of playfulness or self-mockery.

As Father Svet and I came out of the house a band of pilgrims had gathered below the balcony hoping for a glimpse of her. Svet stood in the lane looking at me.

"That was remarkable," he said. "Did you hear that? If you devote more time to your friend then you will come to know his secrets. And it's the same with God. That's beautiful."

We walked a little down the lane together. Father Svet still seemed captivated by the interview.

"She's different from the others, you know," he said. "Vicka is ill a lot of the time, and she is a great example of suffering. The other two girls, I believe, have resisted their vocations as seers— they would never have given interviews like that. But Marija has said an unreserved 'yes' to the call; she is cooperating fully with the opportunities God is giving her."

A little further down the road, he stopped and looked about him at the thronging pilgrims on every side. He placed his hand on his chest. "You know," he said, "even if Our Lady is not appearing here in reality, I have to say that the fruits of Medjugorje are good . . . I do not think God will punish us for what we are doing: we do everything in good faith. How can anyone say that this is bad!"

After Svet had gone I went to sit in the church. I was watching the peasant pilgrims kneeling at their long, silent vigils before the statue of the Virgin. I was trying to weigh up in my mind what I thought of Marija.

I found her priggishness distasteful and yet I was impressed by her comments about the vision's mode of speech, which was as close to a definition of poetry as one could wish from a girl of her education and background.

I was convinced that she was not a liar, feeling that she had a strong, charismatic personality, and I wondered if she had taken on the role of a ringleader capable of manipulating the others and engaging in unconscious hypnotic practice.

It occurred to me, too, that in a former age a young woman such as Marija might well have been hauled before the Holy Inquisition to explain and defend her revelations. Historians are only now beginning to discover the extent to which investigations into the religious paranormal were projected substitutes for the clergy's unconscious inclinations toward doubt and apostasy, their deep fear and hatred of the power of women. Having seen Marija in the midst of the priests, it seemed to me that her role was anomalous and fraught with risk. Her status as seer, as prophetess, had raised her above the male-dominant priesthood; but it would be foolish to imagine that they were not ultimately and firmly in control. Her situation, it seemed to me, was precarious and I found it difficult to believe that there might not be a heavy price to be paid in the fullness of time.

9

Satan's Free Hand

As I passed the steps of the parish house I ran into Father Keogh. He was listening to a tall monk who sported a goatee beard which quivered with the vehemence of his utterance.

Father Keogh, who was evidently trying to escape the man's clutches, grabbed me by the wrist.

"You should talk to this fellow here," he said with a wink. "He's an exorcist. When he exorcises people they vomit up the demons."

The monk eyed me speculatively. He was stroking his hairy wrists and forearms as if contemplating a fight.

Before I could say a word, Father Keogh had taken off with a chuckle.

"Does the Virgin speak of Satan?" I asked him politely.

He looked stern.

"Listen!" he said. "In 1890 Pope Leo XIII had a vision that Christ was to give Satan a free hand in the world for exactly one hundred years. This explains many things. The end of Satan's time is near, and he is getting more and more angry and desperate."

The priest spoke rapid English in an American accent.

"The time of Our Lady, she who in the book of the Apocalypse crushes the serpent under her heel, is now coming," he went on. "But the world wars, the rise of Communism, explain Satan's grip over the world in the past one hundred years. You are about to see a vast change in the world as we approach the year two thousand: the demise of world Communism, the reestablishment of the Kingdom of Christ. The day will come when you will see a statue of the Virgin surmounting the Kremlin. Maximillian Kolbe, the Franciscan saint of the death camps, saw this in a vision. And it all links with the Virgin of Medjugorje: AIDS, the disaster at Chernobyl, the Shuttle Disaster, the Armenian earthquake ... these are clearly the chastisements Our Lady refers to in the children's visions. But we see many wonderful signs of conversion and transformation, too, all linked with the warnings. There are wondrous prospects as we turn to the Virgin. On the eve of the Feast of Our Lady of the Immaculate Conception last, President Reagan, President-elect Bush, and Gorbachev stood together at the foot of the Statue of Liberty. President Reagan said: 'Read our smiles!' The very next day Gorbachev flew back to Russia as a result of the earthquake in Armenia. What does it all mean? Who knows! We must ponder these things in our hearts. Our Lady is very busy. Last week she failed to appear to the children on Thursday. We puzzled and prayed over this ... then I read in the *International Herald Tribune* that she had appeared to a nun in the Philippines on that very same evening. . . . We can only ponder these things in our hearts. . . ."

As I drove back to the hotel I remembered a cutting remark of one of my colleagues: "A good journalist doesn't entertain mumbo jumbo, even to debunk it!" I was beginning to feel solidarity with the view.

I went into the restaurant in search of something to eat. After a while a lean, sallow man of about fifty sat down at the next table. He carried a suitcase, from which he removed several books. Beginning a conversation he told me that he was an American, a Catholic publisher and tour operator.

When I told him that I was a writer, he held up a full-color laminated booklet. "See this?" he said. "We're reprinting this thing at the rate of ten thousand every month. Every *month* of the year. I bet you never saw sales like that, buddy."

Between mouthfuls of dubious-looking stew and nervous drags on a Marlboro cigarette, he reeled off facts and figures about back-to-back flights, publishing reprints, and video production. Everything was "looking good!"

"What do you make of the visions?" I asked.

"The most fantastic thing is that they keep *going*," he said. "But I think I know why. Do you realize that this is the first set of apparitions in the modern age of the media? I think that Our Lady is keeping the visions going so that we can get market penetration."

As I began to laugh, he said: "No, I'm not kidding you, buddy. That's what I really think! And I'll tell you one thing, we're worried the pope's going to pronounce against it. If he does, it will show everybody's been taken for a ride and it'll kill the thing stone dead. There are a helluva lot of buildings going up, including a hotel with 500 bedrooms. It's all private money, all private risk."

"You're saying, then, that a lot of people are going to be ruined if the Church says that the visions are false?"

"Actually, if you want my honest opinion—and I wouldn't want you to quote me by name on this—it's a no-win situation no matter what happens. People come here, *I* think, because they like the unspoiled village atmosphere, and that's all disappearing in uncontrolled development. The place is going to lose out eventually whatever happens. That's just my personal opinion. But in the meantime, we're reprinting that thing at the rate of ten thousand a month!"

"But do you believe in the apparitions yourself?"

"I don't know . . ." he said. "I was brought up to believe that it's all about faith, about believing in what you can't see. But this younger generation is different—they need to see and hear. Perhaps it's something to do with the effect of television."

When he had finished his stew he came over to my table to say good-bye. As he shook hands he said: "Mind you, I've seen people witnessing these strange visions of the sun. I've seen more than a hundred people witnessing it spin and change color. I don't know. I just wish I could get it on video."

On the eve of my departure from Medjugorje I went to the parish house to meet Father Svet, who this time had arranged a meeting with the visionary Vicka. He seemed curious about my reactions and eager to discover whether I had formed any strong objections to the cult.

"I suppose," I said mischievously, and without quite understanding what I meant by it, "one of them could be a medium for the others."

Svet looked at me solemnly and shook his head. "Look, there's an Italian priest-sociologist called Gramaglia who suggested this

without ever having been here. How can somebody make pro-
nouncements without studying the phenomenology? Anyway, I think
I can prove that the medium idea is nonsense, because the apparitions have occurred with every combination of the group: one,
three, four, five, and all six together . . . and a problem never arose
because somebody was missing. Unless you are going to say that
they are *all* mediums.

"And if one of them were a medium," he went on a little
heatedly now, "how do you explain that they're doing it at a distance?
If you can't answer that question, what you say makes no sense."

With this Vicka arrived and threw herself into an armchair, as
if feigning exhaustion. She was a sturdy young woman with a wide
face and wild-almond shaped eyes. Her speech was rapid and excited.

Using Father Svet as interpreter, she told me first about the
appearance of the Virgin: her height, her apparel, the texture of her
flesh, the sound of her voice, the manner in which she moved from
place to place. I learned that the Virgin never showed her feet; that
the "cut" of her clothes was always the same, although on special
feast days she wore cloth of gold. She could be touched, and indeed
even kissed. One day a child with dirty fingers left marks on the
Virgin's veil.

I asked her about the manner in which the visions commenced.

"She used to come in the form of a light," said Vicka, "then
we would go to her. We prayed, sang, asked her questions; later,
she would start to appear as soon as we prayed. It was like a light-
picture approaching us, then in a second she was in front of us,
clear, beautiful, smiling; then we would kneel down. Sometimes
she would come the moment we crossed ourselves. At other times
we would pray ten to fifteen Our Fathers before she came. . . . She
eventually got into a routine. She usually left more quickly than she
came."

"Did anybody else appear in these visions?" I asked.

"In Marija's house in 1981 four of us had an apparition: when
Our Lady arrived she was holding in her hand a picture of Pope
John Paul II that had been hanging on the wall in the room. Our
Lady kissed the pope's picture. The picture is still at Marija's; Our
Lady said we should keep it in a safe place."

Vicka went on to describe how she had had visions of Christ,
both as the child in the Holy Family, and in the form of a bust

depicting his wounds during the Passion. She explained how the Virgin had said that the local bishop "made a mistake." She added: "But it's well known that anybody can make mistakes."

"Have you had any other sorts of visions?" I asked her.

"Our Lady showed us Heaven; it's beautiful beyond words, we saw Ivanka's mother there, and another woman we knew. . . . One day Our Lady disappeared and in front of us appeared Hell. Jacov, Marija, and I saw a local woman with blond hair whom we knew, a woman who had died; she had horns, and there were devils jumping sort of sideways toward her."

I stared at Vicka for a few moments in silence. At length I said: "How did it come about that you visited Heaven?"

"I was over at Jacov's house at about 3 o'clock in the afternoon," she said. "His mother was out somewhere. Our Lady appeared and said: 'Glory to Jesus' and told us that she was going to take us to Heaven. We were frightened; Jacov started screaming. He said he didn't want to go because he was an only child and I could go on my own. Our Lady didn't say anything. She took our hands—we were on our knees, me by my right and Jacov by his left—and she stood between us with her face turned toward us, and we started to rise up immediately, right up through the ceiling. The house disappeared and we were going upward. I was afraid but I tried not to think. We reached Heaven quite soon."

"And what is Heaven like?" I asked her.

"It's full of beautiful flowers and angels. Just like people say."

"What else did you see?"

"Purgatory. It's a dark abyss, a dark space between Heaven and Hell. It's full of ashes and it looks horrible."

"Did Our Lady tell you why she had shown it to you?" I asked.

"She wanted us to know that it's the place where souls have to cleanse themselves," said Vicka. "And they are in need of a lot of prayers."

"And how did you return to earth?"

"The same way we went up," said Vicka confidently. "She took us back inside the house and said good-bye and left. We started to adjust slowly; it took us a little time. Jacov's mother saw us first and asked us where we had been hiding. She said she had been looking for us. She started to cry because Jacov was in such a state."

I had heard enough of Vicka's testimony. I turned to Father Svet and told him that I had finished.

With this he said something to Vicka and they both rose and left the room. I sat for a while musing. Up until now most of what I had heard about the visionary content of Medjugorje had kept just on the right side of the traditional expression of pious private revelation on the one hand, and prophetic Marian conventions on the other. Vicka's account, however, went well beyond that pale; all the same, I was intrigued by the psychology of her experience. Assuming for a moment that she was not lying, I could only speculate that she had vividly imagined and acted out the entire episode and related it in turn to Jacov, who had responded to her suggestions as if to a real experience.

After a few moments Father Svet reappeared; he was peering at me owlishly as if expecting a reaction.

"Very interesting," I ventured. "But I must say that I'm worried a bit about Vicka's Hell."

"But all you have to understand," he said, "is that when God reveals a supernatural truth, he does it according to our capacities. Vicka is a simple peasant girl; there is a maxim in scholastic philosophy: 'Quicquid recipitur per modem recipientis recipitur.' Whatever is received is received in the manner of the receiver. Do you understand my meaning?"

I nodded.

"And what are you going to do now?" he asked.

I thought for a moment. I wanted to be truthful with the priest, not merely polite. "I think," I said, "that I am going home to read the gospels again."

The priest smiled and put a gentle hand on my shoulder.

"Wouldn't it be better, Mister John, to go home and read the messages of Our Lady?"

That evening, by the light of a full moon, I made my way to the summit of the hill of the apparitions one last time. The ragged rocks seemed luminous in the pale light and I could make out pilgrims huddled in silence among the primitive wooden crosses and votive candles. As Dermot had promised, the birds were singing in unrestrained chorus in the trees and bushes below, lending an atmosphere of strange excitement to the night vigil.

I looked out on the amphitheater of the mountains: the whitewashed church gleaming in the lunar light, the fertile valley fragrant with night scents.

I felt confused about my experience in Medjugorje. My witnessing of the apparition had somehow opened up my heart ... and yet, I was deeply troubled by many aspects of the shrine.

Huddled up with my back against a rock, I tried to sort out my thoughts about the "children." It occurred to me that whatever their genuine spiritual experience, they were open to considerable manipulation and exploitation on the part of the cult's impresarios and promoters. Their visions now seemed to be structured into a daily routine that had become part of the liturgical ritual. The daily timetable of the visions before Mass every evening had the effect both of creating a daily expectation and of associating the phenomena with the Mass itself, as if the visions were part of the most powerful ceremony in Catholic worship. This seemed to me to provide not only the circumstances of subtle coercion, but to lend liturgical authority to the proceedings in the eyes of the pilgrims.

And the pilgrims at Medjugorje were being told week in, week out, through Our Lady's messages, that things would go well in the world if there were a return to the rosary, but things would go very badly if there were not. To the gullible sensation seekers, who flocked to the place in huge numbers, this was a clear signal that history was merely the capricious plaything of the supernatural. Among these people there was not so much an atmosphere of genuine prayer as a feeling that the Virgin required appeasement.

This fundamentalist tendency in Medjugorje, with its authoritarian and exclusivist program based on primitive fear and propitiation, was clearly at odds with the post-conciliar model of the Catholic Church, which had committed the faithful to a middle ground of pluralism. Nothing so strengthens a strident, fundamentalist agenda as apocalyptic revelation accompanied by evidence of the miraculous.

The principal means of manipulation out of Medjugorje, it seemed to me, involved the amplification of folk religious experience (the ancient Mediterranean tradition of local Marian apparitions), via the skillful use of publishing and the pilgrim-tourist business, into a species of designer pop-religion. The by-products ranged from a type of "Dungeons and Dragons," do-it-yourself "Star Wars" mysticism—spinning suns, sky pictures, and talismanic weapons against the powers of darkness (alchemies to turn rosaries to gold)—to supra-scientific "beam-me-up-Scotty" theories of the supernatural, of which the magic photographs, and the scientists' encephalogram machines, were typical examples.

Father Foley had described the Medjugorje cult, with approval, as a "veritable spiritual Disneyland." The phrase was an accurate, if unconscious, description of the promise of make-believe phenomena that was being peddled worldwide by promoters who were bringing 2 million people there each year.

The tour promotor I had run into in the hotel had boasted that he had a mailing list of more than 100,000 "pilgrims" who had spent an average of $500 each on videos, books, and devotional items connected with the cult. The travel arrangements, moreover, probably involved gross sales amounting to many millions of dollars a year. "We've only scratched the surface," he had told me with satisfaction.

But money alone was clearly not the prime objective. The ultimate goal was an attempt to deal a blow against the perceived enemies of the Christian Right: the specters of liberalism, rationalism, and "secular humanism." The principal casualty, however, was likely to be the tolerant, moderate middle ground.

And yet, I was nevertheless convinced that despite the exploitation on the periphery, Medjugorje was an unusual focus of spirituality in modern times that outweighed the sum of its drawbacks.

The old peasant people who knelt hour after hour in the silent church were a reminder that the shrine was a place of amnesty from the world's doubts and miseries and evils, a deliverance from helplessness.

Against the background of injustice, famine, violence, war, ecological disaster, race hatred, and drug abuse, Medjugorje offered a message of hope. Under its auspices pilgrims could renew their confidence and morale. Here on pilgrimage there were no class or racial distinctions; all were equal in the eyes of the Mother of God; money, clothes, possessions, counted for nothing; few came by car; the lodgings were simple, many people sleeping on the floors; many fasted as often as three days of the week. People who normally saw themselves as powerless, disenfranchised, helpless, weak, now believed that they could do something about the world, about their predicament, and would return to their homes, their communities, and their work strengthened and refreshed.

Medjugorje, then, seemed to me a curious mixture of impressive spiritual drama and obnoxious manipulation. Its negative aspects had by no means encouraged me to dismiss the phenomenon as fraudulent, nor had its positive qualities demonstrated an overwhelming sense of supernatural authenticity.

My principal conviction was that the cult raised far more questions than it answered.

10

Briege McKenna

Father Keogh, Father Foley, and others had told me of the crucial role of a nun called Sister Briege McKenna in the Medjugorje story and had referred to her as one of the most charismatic figures in the Catholic Church: she had, they claimed, astonishing healing powers, as well as gifts of prophecy, bilocation, and the ability to "see into" people's hearts. According to Father Foley, Briege McKenna had foretold the Yugoslav Marian apparitions during a prayer meeting in Rome before a large number of witnesses a month before they had begun.

On my return from Medjugorje I decided that I wanted to meet her, to see whether I would be impressed with her powers. When I called on Father Foley once more at Farm Street, he promptly volunteered to effect the introduction. "Such an extraordinary woman," he said. "She's the successor to the great Padre Pio! You must see her, but you must be prepared; she is a most daunting person."

Father Foley then proceeded to fill me in on her background as a prelude to my meeting her in Dublin.

Sister Briege left school in Northern Ireland at age fifteen to become a member of the Poor Clares, one of the most austere religious orders. Now in her forties, she had an unparalleled reputation in the Catholic Church as a healer; she was, moreover, an outstanding spiritual director of bishops and priests with legendary gifts of discernment.

Sister Briege was currently ministering to many thousands of prelates, priests, and monks on five continents. Her clients included bishops and cardinals and even national leaders. President José Sarney of Brazil had gone on television holding a rosary in his hand to announce that a meeting with Sister Briege had transformed his spiritual life. No one in the contemporary Church, according to Father Foley, could rival this Irish nun for her "supernatural" reputation.

Her ministry had begun from a convent in Tampa, Florida, fifteen years earlier. Her education was slight and she had never had any formal training in theology. Her inspiration was said to come from between three and five hours of daily prayer and the exercise of visionary powers that, according to Father Foley, could unnerve the most hardened and cynical.

Her special ministry to priests and the religious was carried out against the background of a major shift in the Church. Following the upheavals of the Vatican Council in the late 1960s, more than 100,000 priests had abandoned their ministries, leaving an overworked and largely demoralized clergy. A great many priests suffered from sexual difficulties and alcoholism; and there were other, darker problems on the periphery, especially in America, associated with fads in witchcraft, paedophilia, New Ageism, and even Satanism.

Sister Briege had broken through the normal time-consuming process of counseling. She would see each priest alone. Taking him by the hand, she would put an arm around one shoulder and bow her head toward him. After a few brief prayers she would begin to perceive what she called a "word of knowledge" that came unbidden into her head: it was a vivid allegory or emblem. Invariably it illustrated a deep-seated spiritual problem or anxiety; sometimes she would confront a priest with a grave habitual sin. She would begin to speak to him in the words of Christ or the Virgin Mary, using the first person. Often it was a message of comfort and sympathy; sometimes a severe reprimand. The experience was often so stunning that many priests broke down in tears.

For ten years now she had been traveling, always by invitation, ministering daily to scores of priests at special retreats. In the previous year her itinerary had included Brazil, Nigeria, France, Holland, Australia, Taiwan, and the United States. Her time was completely booked for the next two years. These were not lightning calls to capital cities, although she often filled whole stadiums in Brazil and Nigeria; she traveled the length and breadth of each country, visiting remote parishes and mission stations. And she would continue to communicate with her "charges" by telephone and by sending out a daily flood of hand-written "little notes."

The more I heard of Father Foley's glowing report, the more Sister Briege seemed reminiscent of the large energies of the great saints of history, and especially women like Catherine of Sienna, Teresa of Avila, and Catherine of Genoa. I was excited at the prospect of meeting a woman who might one day be looked upon as one of the great spiritual figures of the twentieth century.

But it struck me that by the same token her so-called powers might be no more significant than those of a clairvoyant or a fortune-teller. By any criteria, it seemed to me, she appeared open to accusations of exploiting men who lived unusually stressful and lonely lives and who came to her with high expectations.

A week after my second meeting with Father Foley I flew to Dublin to meet Sister Briege McKenna. The taxi took me from the airport through driving rain toward the city. At length we turned off an avenue lined with suburban homes and entered the gates of a spacious park surrounded by a high wall. There was a sweeping drive through oak trees and ahead lay a long, slate-gray barrack-like building with high curtainless windows; at the far end of the building stood a gloomy neo-Gothic church with flying buttresses. This was All Hallows College, Drumcondra, the largest missionary seminary in the world. The students were now away and it was Sister Briege's headquarters for her retreats when she was in Ireland.

A cheerful lady called Barbara met me at the administrator's desk in the lobby and took me to my room on the first floor. The house was deserted and our shoes echoed on the granite stairway.

"All the fathers are in church," she said crisply. "Lunch is at 1:15."

The room was cell-like. There was a single narrow bed, a small desk and chair, a cupboard, and a washbasin; a piece of gray rug lay on the bare floorboards. A crucifix hung above the bed.

I stood at the window listening to the rain, which fell in a steady curtain smudging the distant mountains in the west. A flock of seagulls wheeled about a flood-pool on the seminary's playing fields. The houses of Drumcondra were hidden by a line of flourishing horse chestnut trees.

I sat on the bed and felt a sense of strange languor associated with memories of religious institutions I had inhabited in my youth; the smell of beeswax polish, the heavy stillness of a large house where time stands still, waiting for the next church service or communal meal. Something about my destined encounter with Sister Briege was nagging me. The atmosphere of the seminary was creating a strange mood in me, evoking shadowy, fearful recollections of guilt in the presence of Irish nuns and priests, figures of strict authority and discipline throughout my childhood.

At length an electric bell rang in the house and there was a knock on the door. Barbara had come to take me to lunch.

Priests by the score were spilling from the church into the cloister. They seemed mostly in their early fifties, many of them with brickred Irish complexions. They walked in twos and threes, hands behind their backs in earnest conversation.

Ill-at-ease at the sight of this clerical conclave, I was on the point of considering withdrawing to the safety of the playing fields, when I was suddenly apprehended and overwhelmed by the presence of the woman herself.

She came upon me in a bustling rush, a profound anticlimax to my image of her as a numinous, wraith-like mystic. Her face was squarish and rather pasty with a hint of freckles around the nose. A widow's peak of dark auburn hair and wide, rawboned features confirmed her Irish origins. Her gray eyes scrutinized me with a daunting frankness. She looked exhausted; there were deep lines about her eyes and mouth. And yet her face had a gentle, youthful appeal of humor and kindness. She grabbed me by the forearms and gave me an affectionate little pat. Her hands were pale, freckly, delicate.

She was physically close, and talking insistently, urgently, although I could not seem to concentrate on anything she was saying. I felt a delightful hint of feminine allure. And yet she exuded an unassailable chasteness as bracing as convent soap and cold water.

As befitting a thoroughly modern nun, she was dressed in a comfortable blouse and handknit cardigan. Her two concessions to religious status were a silver crucifix and a short brown veil.

Leading me to the refectory, she explained the gathering of

priests in a rapid, melodic brogue with a hint of Ulster. The participants, she was saying, had traveled from as far away as Papua New Guinea, the United States, Nigeria, and Australia. There were clerics from a variety of religious orders—Jesuits, Franciscans, Dominicans, Carmelites—and several bishops. Many of them, she said, were Irish missionaries.

Suddenly I found myself seated beneath the glowering portraits of nineteenth-century prelates and a man was serving me boiled bacon, giant spuds, and watery cabbage.

She leaned forward, eager to answer my questions, although I felt self-conscious to be talking in a personal way to a complete stranger about miraculous powers over lunch.

She was looking at me very directly. There was something both deeply mature and yet extraordinarily childlike about her, an impression of wisdom, experience, and innocence. I was conscious of a sense of *holiness,* and yet she was very ordinary. Her features were unremarkable, almost plain, but her eyes and mouth had an impressive, mobile beauty.

I managed to ask, "What is it like, having miraculous powers?" I was conscious, even as I said it, that it was a stupid, journalistic question.

But she treated it with seriousness.

"Nobody could have been more reluctant to believe I had special powers," she began. She had slowed down now, and she was choosing her words carefully. "I used to pray, 'Oh, God, please keep your miracles to yourself.' But they're not my powers; I give them back to God every night of my life." She laughed. "And if I get a headache I usually take an aspirin."

It all began, she went on, with a dramatic healing of her own body. When Briege was twelve, her mother had died of a cerebral hemorrhage. In 1962, at age fifteen, Briege had left behind her tenant farmer father and four brothers to enter a strictly enclosed convent in Newry, County Armagh. Her father was heartbroken, but he told her: "If that's what you want, go ahead, and if it's not want you want, you'll know it." Two years later she developed crippling rheumatoid arthritis in her feet and hands. She remembers the sisters had to put plaster boots on her feet to prevent deformity. "I used to faint with the pain."

She was transferred to a community in Tampa, Florida, but the humid climate only made things worse. "By 1968 I was a cripple on high doses of cortisone. My feet were completely twisted and I had sores."

During this period she was suffering problems with her religious vocation and sat for many hours in the chapel close to despair. "One morning I felt a hand on my head. I opened my eyes and no one was there, but I felt a power going through my body. I looked down. My fingers were limber, the sores were gone, and my feet were no longer deformed. I jumped up screaming, 'Jesus! You're right here!' "

The summer after her healing she returned to Ireland for a holiday and cured a woman dying of cancer in the hospital in Newry.

Sister Briege laughed happily again: "The town was in an uproar looking for the healing nun. Every time they saw a nun in the street in a brown habit they would dash after her."

But the "miracles" were a mere prelude to what she saw as her real mission—the renewal of the Catholic priesthood. She received the call while alone in prayer in 1975. She had been kneeling in the convent chapel thinking about the defection of priests throughout the world and she cried out loud: "O God, what is wrong with the priesthood?"

She began to receive a sequence of visions which appeared vividly "as on a television screen" above the tabernacle on the altar and lasted four hours. "I found myself weeping as I watched the unfolding of this powerful revelation of the priesthood."

A voice told her to go out into the world and lead priests back to God.

As she talked I could not help being impressed by her natural gaiety and frankness. She had the unusual ability to talk about religious matters without seeming nunnish or priggish. But this naturalness and gaiety seemed to mask a core of obsessive determination and seriousness. Everything she said was to the point; there was no small talk. And in rare moments, when her smile failed, she seemed exhausted by the effort. Sitting in the midst of the noisy refectory her attention was devoted entirely to me.

As the refectory began to clear, she stood up, her meal barely touched. She said she would find time to talk with me after supper in the evening. "You must stay for two or three days," she said with a final pat on my forearm. "Don't run away from us just yet."

I wandered out into the cloister. The walls were lined with

Ordination Day photographs of students that told their own story. Up to the 1960s there had been thirty or forty priests ordained every year; in more recent photographs there were no more than four or five.

When I came out into the grounds the rain had stopped and I could see the clergymen strolling slowly together in twos along the cinder paths. I decided to take a walk in the direction of the deserted outer reaches of the football pitches.

"How curious," I thought. "I'm on retreat!" Then I realized that in the past two weeks or so I had also been on a pilgrimage, and during all this time I had given very little thought to the world of journalism and business. And yet, I had not prayed. As I walked around the cinder track at the far end of the grounds, I began to wonder whether I should pray or not. In Medjugorje I had been too busy studying those about me to think of myself. It had not occurred to me for one moment that I should want to pray, nor had I examined my feelings even about the existence of God.

But somehow, in the wake of my meeting with Briege McKenna, the idea had taken a strange grip on me. "Why not do it just to see what happens," I thought. But almost as quickly I said to myself, *"No!"* Prayer meant submission, a loss of independence and self-reliance. I turned toward the college buildings.

Back in my room I fell asleep on the bed and began to dream about putting sheets of paper into a typewriter; every time I took a fresh white sheet and rolled it through, it came out stained with black ink.

Perhaps an hour into my sleep I began to have a recurring dream. I sensed that Sister Briege was "working on my soul": I had no clear idea what this meant, but it was a phrase that kept recurring in the dream. Was she talking to me? Praying for me? Then I became conscious of a cynical voice that kept saying: "There can be no life or experience that is in any way imaginable, or knowable, beyond this body. This is an *absolute* truth."

When I awoke I looked out of the window and saw that it was raining again and that the priests had disappeared.

I wandered down to the ground floor and walked along a corridor looking into the public rooms. At length I opened the door of an oratory. A spacious room full of light, it was furnished with stripped pine chairs and white carpeting. Six or seven priests were praying in various postures; some of them were lying face down on the floor, their heads pointing in the direction of an inner room where I could see a red sanctuary lamp and a tabernacle.

I entered the oratory and found myself a seat. Out of sight of the priests I sat for a while contemplating the silence and the stillness.

The traffic, the streets, the city, seemed infinitely distant; I felt a sense of admiration for this small band of priestly survivors. They reminded me of the peasants in black in the church at Medjugorje. They were irrelevant, impotent really, in terms of the daylight realities of the world, and yet their faith in the presence of God in that little box on the wall gave them a kind of majesty.

I tried to imagine what it must be like to believe that Christ was actually present, a living, thinking being, hidden within the tabernacle; but I found it difficult even to simulate the frame of mind of someone who accepted such a proposition.

Sitting in the silence of the chapel I was suddenly gripped with terror. I was not ready for this, I thought. I was not ready for Sister Briege McKenna. I rose and left the chapel and went straight to my room to pack. I wanted to be out of All Hallows College as fast as my legs could carry me.

Five minutes later, as I stood by the desk in the lobby waiting for the administrator to call a taxi, Sister Briege appeared, smiling.

"Off already?" she said. "Never mind, we'll meet again soon."

With this she took both my hands in hers and kissed me on the cheek.

PART THREE

REAL
PRESENCES

11

The Road to Garabandal

Back in England I spent several days reviewing my notes and pondering the next move. Although I was keen to travel by instinct, I needed an overall plan of the terrain. I was beginning to see a rough shape to the categories of supernatural evidence available in the Christian tradition, and I hoped to seek out contemporary examples of them all, although not necessarily in strict order. This was my first list:

1. Apparitions, visions, voices of supernatural figures including Christ, the Virgin Mary, saints, Satan, angels, and demons.
2. Prophetic utterances as a result of intuition or dreams, and gifts of discernment such as seeing into a person's past life.
3. Miracles of healing.
4. Synchronicities: coincidences with a spiritual or moral significance.
5. Physical prodigies, such as stigmata, odor of sanctity, levitation, bilocation, and speaking in unlearned languages.
6. Material prodigies such as the Holy Shroud of Turin and the liquefaction of blood of Saint Januarius in Naples.
7. Physical prodigies such as weeping and bleeding statues.
8. Psychic experiences with moral and spiritual significance, such as a sense of having returned from the dead or feelings of being possessed by evil spirits or demons.

I was mainly concerned with investigating phenomena that were above suspicion as far as fraud was concerned. And while I wanted to observe and probe and question, and find rational answers, I was not at this stage principally interested in formulating strict rational or scientific answers, and yet the question of "authenticity" was important. If I were not going to consign all mystical experience to "subjectivism" I would have to run the risk of getting personally caught up, as I had learned from my experience in Ireland.

One needed to approach the religious paranormal with all one's antennae engaged in order to grasp the "world," the "milieu," the "culture" of these phenomena, on their own terms. I had no answer to the problem of getting personally involved, except to acknowledge that I must follow my obsession and feelings, wherever they led.

But where next?

I was talking one evening in London with a neurologist friend about the synchronized behavior of the "children" of Medjugorje, and the "spinning suns." He dismissed the latter as a simple case of "saturation of the retinal pigments," commenting that people can "actually get better at doing it"; but he was more intrigued by the synchronized mannerisms and silent speech gestures of the visionaries.

"This sort of synchronized behavior is almost certainly accounted for by cues," he said. "And the fact that you couldn't see the cues doesn't mean that they were not happening. They might be cueing each other by a faint auditory sign, such as a slight intake of breath. Have you never heard of the case of Clever Hans?"

"Clever Hans," he went on, "was a German horse that could supposedly do arithmetic. This involved stamping with its hoof a simple signal for *yes* or *no* in response to suggested answers to arithmetical problems on a board in front of it. Hans was exposed by Osker Pfungst in 1911 when it was demonstrated that the horse failed to perform when its trainer was not in view. The animal had apparently been sensing signals imperceptible even to the trainer, who had been unwittingly relaxing when the correct answer was given.

"The curious synchronized behavior of the children at Medjugorje may well have been managed, perhaps unwittingly, by cues that were imperceptible to the onlooker," said my friend.

The phenomenon of cueing seemed to provide a partial answer to the problem; and yet I was not altogether satisfied with this as a complete "solution," for it seemed to me that there was something that we were missing in the significance of the synchronization in itself. I felt that I was far from understanding the symbolic nature of Marian apparitions, and I wanted to look at the phenomena from that perspective.

Shortly after this conversation I came across another case of highly synchronized behavior in a recent series of Marian apparitions. Through the good services of Father Foley, once more, I had received a curious videotape with some accompanying literature depicting the behavior of four little girls who had reputedly received visions of Michael the Archangel, and later the Virgin Mary, in a remote village called Garabandal in northern Spain in the early 1960s. The Bishop of Mostar and Father Keogh had both mentioned Garabandal, and their reports of the phenomena there had stimulated my curiosity.

The videotape was composed of a variety of contemporaneous still photographs and homemade movies showing the girls in a variety of extraordinary postures and elaborate synchronized gestures and dances. They had received the apparitions mostly at night while on ecstatic or trance-like "marches."

To see the Virgin they leaned backward until their heads almost touched their waists. Yet they rushed about the village in these astonishing postures, and up the hill behind the village, moving so fast—even over rocky terrain and ditches—that they appeared to be flying. If the videotape was to be believed, the antics of these children amounted to an awe-inspiring demonstration of seemingly impossible physical feats; but what made their strange choreography all the more extraordinary was their swift, perfectly synchronized formation. They all seemed to be possessed by a power that played them like a musical instrument.

Were they possessed by good—or evil—spirits? Were they merely cueing each other cleverly? Whatever the case, I was more intrigued by the meaning of the formation activity itself, than by how it was done.

But Garabandal offered other paranormal feats. According to the written evidence, grown men had been outrun by the girls on their ecstatic marches, even when the girls were moving backward. They had also astonished onlookers with acts of levitation, by alterations in body weight, and by the way in which they would fall back to the ground with such force that their skulls were heard to crack.

Another curious feature was the story of a priest, Father Luis Andreu, who became closely involved with the children and eventually began to experience the visions himself. Immediately after witnessing an apparition of the Virgin Mary in conjunction with the girls, he had dropped dead without any apparent physical explanation. He was thirty-six years of age and had been in perfect health. It was claimed that following his death he continued to speak in "foreign languages" through the mouths of the girls.

At the center of the Garabandal phenomena was the leading seer, Conchita Gonzalez, a girl of striking classic Hispanic beauty. The camera lens had focused unrelentingly on her face. She, in turn, knew how to play to the camera and took to her role as budding mystic with considerable skill and verve.

The Garabandal phenomena promised a fascinating mixed-bag of prodigies, including levitation, a Eucharistic Miracle, apocalyptic prophecy, and a promised "Great Sign." There was mention of an unusual miracle of healing involving an Italian-American millionaire called Joey Lomangino, who had dedicated his life to the promotion of the cult from New York.

Characteristically, the Italian mystic Padre Pio was reported to be somehow at the hub of the phenomena, having enjoyed a parallel vision and having guaranteed the apparitions' authenticity. He had talked with Conchita and had specified that she should receive the gift of the lace veil that would cover his face as he lay in state after his death.

My instinct was telling me to attempt to understand what had happened in Garabandal a quarter of a century ago and to discover what had happened to the surviving participants in the meantime.

The four visionaries were still alive and presumably accessible, and I was particularly eager to interview Conchita. But first I wanted to visit Garabandal itself to explore the village and to interview surviving eyewitnesses.

On my way to Garabandal I stayed overnight in Burgos, where I had flown the previous day, and went into the cathedral the next morning. Twenty years after the Second Vatican Council, the principal Mass of the day was still being said in Latin.

Sitting beneath the great Gothic lantern in the nave, I remembered that this had been Franco's capital during the Spanish Civil War. It was in this cathedral that the archdeacon had preached the virtues of Fascism and uttered a chilling curse on the heads of the Republicans:

"You who listen to me, you who call yourselves Christians, show no mercy on the destroyers of churches and priests; may their seed be trampled under foot, for it is the evil seed, the devil's seed."

These celebrants of the late 1980s wore rose silk fiddleback vestments edged with lace. They had grim mask-like faces with pursed lips through which they gabbled their prayers as they hurried about the altar amid clouds of incense. Meanwhile a bevy of pot-bellied canons minced in and out of the choir stalls, flourishing their velvet cloaks and wagging the scarlet pom-poms of their birettas. The spectacle lent insight to Spain's long history of anticlericalism and the deeply buried resentment of women against the male-dominant clergy.

I was glad to be gone and on my way in a rented car. San Sebastian de Garabandal was a half day's drive to the north, beyond the Sierra de Peña Sagra on the edge of the vast wilderness that contains the rugged mountains of Los Picos Europeos.

I arrived in the late afternoon in driving rain and wind. The road climbed a long valley through hairpin bends, and beyond each steeply wooded spur was a hint of wild high country to the west. A river boiled below, cascading through boulders and sudden ravines.

The village remained hidden until the final bend in the road, which had only recently been laid. It nestled at the foot of a dark mountain, a huddle of stone houses with tiled red roofs. On a lower hill immediately above the village stood a grove of pine trees. A Romanesque church-tower loomed above the houses on a platform of rock.

The air of Garabandal was wonderfully sweet, razor sharp. I walked through the deserted lanes until I came to a pension called Meson Serafin; it was on the far edge of the village from the road and immediately below the hill of the pines.

As I entered the pension the huge oak door was caught in a gust of wind and slammed with a mighty bang. I found myself in a simple stone flagged hall with long refectory tables and benches and an open fireplace. There were various holy pictures on the walls of the Sacred Heart, the Virgin Mary, and Michael the Archangel.

A dumpy woman with mild dark eyes and wispy gray hair appeared and asked if I wanted a room and supper. Her name was Pacita Gonzalez, and she was the sister-in-law of the seer, Conchita Gonzalez. She told me that they would eat at seven o'clock after rosary in the church.

My room was an attic under the eaves where the wind drummed on the shuttered, mullioned windows. I slept until I was awakened by the sound of a hand-bell ringing in the street.

Descending the oak staircase, I found the señora laying the table. I asked her about the sound. She explained that a woman walked slowly through the village every evening at sunset ringing a small bell, and that it was customary for someone to approach, kiss the bell, and recite the Lord's prayer for a departed relative or friend.

As Pacita served a Spanish omelette from a pan, several more guests appeared from the attic above. There was a German, a monk-like young man with cropped hair, attended by a blond uniformed chauffeur. The German nodded but refused to speak; he sat with his shoulders hunched and hands joined as if in prayer. The chauffeur informed me in poor English that they were driving to Lourdes and then to Medjugorje.

A Frenchman with pure white hair and a large, fiery-red nose dispensed affable smiles to all present, but he appeared to have only one word in common with the assembled pilgrims, which was "Fatima," whence, I gathered, he was hoping to make his way on foot. He refused the omelette, and when Pacita served him a bowl of watery soup he gave her a grubby holy picture in recompense. She stuffed it in her apron pocket without looking at it.

Opposite me sat a dapper man wearing a navy blue blazer whose tie-pin displayed a number of holy medals. When I commented on them, he said: "Some people wear a pig's tooth or something like that, whereas I wear these sacred objects." Then he drew my attention to a red cross on his lapel.

"See that?" he said. "I am a member of the Order of the Holy Sepulchre, and I am a great supporter of pilgrimages there. I give money for the upkeep of the Holy Places."

He now shook my hand and introduced himself as the Filipino

consul in Barcelona. His hair was an amazing pad of frizz, jet black and with the consistency of candy floss.

Tucking into the substantial potato omelette, the consul told me his story:

"This is my second time here," he began. "I came in 1972, but I stayed only for one minute. I had quarreled with my wife all the way up the valleys from Reinosa. She was frightened of the road and the failing light. We went straight up to the pines. We didn't know you could stay. Anyway, we got up there and my wife was terrified. I begged her to stay; you know, we'd driven across the whole of Spain to get here. But she fled. We sat for forty minutes in the car without speaking. Then I said to her: 'Are you conscious of the smell?' We had both experienced a wonderful scent at the pines and we had somehow carried it with us into the car. I asked her to check that it wasn't in her purse; but it wasn't."

He reflected in silence for a while, then said: "This time I came on my own."

The consul searched in his wallet and brought out a picture of Padre Pio. "See this? This is the great saint of our age. He's at the center of it all. Here, take it, keep it. Padre Pio confirmed that the apparitions here at Garabandal are authentic."

I studied the picture of the peasant monk. "Did you ever meet him?" I asked.

"Meet him? I was given special introductions because of my status. I served Padre Pio's Mass in San Giovanni Rotondo in Italy and went to him in confession. We spoke in Italian, but when we got into conversation I couldn't understand him; it was as if he was speaking a dialect. I said to him, 'Sorry, Father, I don't understand.' With this Padre Pio started to shout and yell at me: 'Oh you don't understand, you don't understand! Get out of here. Come on, out of here . . .' "

"Well that doesn't sound very holy, does it?" I said.

"You don't get it, do you?" said the consul pointing his fork at me. "You see, I was very upset because I'm a proud man, and certainly I wasn't used to being shouted at. I think it was good for my pride; and I think in any case that he was angry because I was wasting his time. His confession was mostly for conversions and reconciliation. I had gone to him out of curiosity."

With this the consul stood up and said an elaborate grace. As he shook my hand he said: "I have a heart valve and a pacemaker and I've got a big journey tomorrow."

Pacita and her husband, Serafin, came to sit next to me. Serafin, a lean, pale man, prematurely bald, was Conchita's eldest brother. We sat talking in Castillian for a while over a carafe of coarse local wine. I asked them about the apparitions.

Serafin began.

"When the visions started I'd been away working up at Leon. On the journey back I heard about nothing else but the visions. As we came up the valley—there wasn't a proper road in those days —there were great crowds of people walking up here. The day after we arrived the children had an ecstasy. From that moment I was absolutely convinced it was from God. I knew my little sister; I know what sort of people we are in this village. We're shy of outsiders, and modest. And here was my sister behaving as if the world did not exist for her. In fact, that's how she used to describe the experience—as if she were *outside the world.*

"There were all sorts of opinions being expressed by so-called experts," Serafino continued. "Eventually Conchita was taken up to Santander by members of the bishop's commission. They interrogated her. They told her that it was all a fairy tale. They said it was a collective hallucination. But where on earth did all that behavior and the messages come from? My sister is intelligent but she was poorly educated and naive. She would never have dreamed all that up. She disowned her visions for a time. But then she confirmed them. Life became impossible for her so she went to America, where she lived incognito for a long time.

"I lost count of the ecstasies I've witnessed. I've even seen them on my own with nobody else present. There were times in the depths of winter when I had to accompany Conchita around the village at two or three in the morning while there was deep snow everywhere. She would climb up to the pines and back again in appalling weather while I followed her.

"I've seen her in her ecstasy running backward on her knees over razor sharp rocks, and there would not be a scratch or a mark on her afterward. Nobody will ever convince me that the phenomena are natural. They *must* be from God."

Here Pacita interrupted, and began to speak excitedly:

"I saw one of the first ecstasies when I was sixteen; I was rigid with excitement and I was completely obsessed with the idea that I was going to see the vision myself. A lot of people felt they would see the vision, but they never did. The children's faces were transfigured, like angels. They were beautifully healthy and normal. But there were times when they frightened us, including the men. They would scream and howl with terror at their vision: 'Who are you? What are you?' All of them screaming in unison together.

"I saw the Eucharistic Miracle. The children said that the angel often gave them Holy Communion, and we would see them kneeling with their tongues out although there was no other sign. Then Conchita announced a little miracle: *El Milagrucu.* The angel was going to make the host visible on her tongue. There were great crowds of people all pressing around her, shining torches on her because it was dark. I grabbed hold of the Guardia Civil's belt and he pulled me through to the front. And I saw it on her tongue, brilliant and dazzling as snow; it was thicker than the normal host and looked spongy. It just formed there on her outstretched tongue as if by magic.

"I've seen strong men unable to lift any of the visionaries off the ground. And one day, Mari Cruz went into an ecstasy while she was holding another girl, Tere, by one finger. Tere was a big strong girl and she was dragged all over the village unable to extricate herself.

"Father Valentin, the parish priest, decided to isolate the girls from each other immediately after the visions to see whether their accounts of what the Virgin had said tallied. They always coincided exactly.

"But the most extraordinary thing I witnessed occurred one night when Conchita was racing backward down from the pines, alone in the pitch black in the middle of the night. It was an absolutely supernatural feat. Nobody could have done that normally.

"The most frightening thing was when they used to go to the cemetery and poke crucifixes through the barred gate for the dead souls to kiss. This kissing of crucifixes and medals and rings was remarkable. They would hold the object up for the Virgin to kiss, and then they would cross themselves, then they would pass it to a bystander also to kiss. All this was done with extremely reverential gestures. One day I was standing in the middle of a vast crowd and I found myself thinking that if one of them brought a crucifix for me to kiss my doubts would disappear for good. Within moments

Conchita came straight over to me and applied the crucifix to my lips even though I was lost in this huge crowd and had only thought my wish in silence. I swear to you that this happened."

"Señora," I asked, "where is Conchita now? Can you give me her address?"

Pacita looked at her husband and shook her head vigorously. She began to clear the table, and refused to speak further. In the meantime her husband brought me a cup of coffee and a book.

"You should read this," he said. "It's a copy of Conchita's diary. It's remarkable. Read it tonight . . . We don't give Conchita's whereabouts. She went to America to get away from the publicity. But there's a man called Joey Lomangino who lives in New York; he talks to people. You'd have to do it through him."

I sat up in bed reading Conchita's diary into the small hours. Outside the winds were so violent that the church bells were ringing of their own accord.

The diary, which was a combination of memoir and journal, was edited by a Father Joseph Pelletier from sixty-five hand-written pages in Spanish. Simple, economic, it clearly constituted the most authoritative subjective record of the Garabandal phenomena.

I was particularly interested in the starting point of the apparitions.

According to Conchita the four girls were playing in the village square on June 18, 1961, when she and Mari Cruz went to steal some apples from a tree belonging to the schoolmistress. With their pockets full of fruit they ran off to eat them in a lane known as the *calleja* (which I gathered was immediately outside the Meson Serafin). It was half-past eight in the evening and she remembers that they heard a violent noise like thunder.

Conchita says that she regretted taking the apples and told the others: "The devil will be happy, and our poor guardian angel will be sad." So they began to pick up stones to throw on their left sides, where the devil was thought to be (their guardian angels, they believed, were on their right). When they tired of throwing stones they played marbles. At this point the vision began.

"Suddenly," writes Conchita, "there appeared to me a very beautiful figure that shone brilliantly but did not hurt my eyes at all. When the other three girls, Jacinta, Loli, and Mari Cruz, saw me in this state of ecstasy, they thought I was having a fit, because I kept crying out with my hands clasped. They were about to call my mother when they found themselves in the same state as I, and also started crying out together."

Conchita went on to describe the almost daily apparitions of this celestial figure, which she identified with the Archangel Michael, from that Sunday June 18, to the next, June 25, the first day of the Virgin's appearance. Only on Saturday July 1 did the angel speak.

"We went to the *calleja* as usual to pray the rosary and the people accompanied us. That day the apparitions occurred very early, at seven-thirty, and it was still almost full daylight and the people were able to see very well.

"At the end of the holy rosary, the angel appeared smiling and said to us: 'Do you know why I have come? It is to announce to you that tomorrow, Sunday, the Virgin Mary will appear to you as Our Lady of Mount Carmel.' "

Conchita records in this same entry, for the first time, a detailed description of the angel's dress. She had already described him as looking about nine years of age, but of immense strength. Now she adds that he was "dressed in a long, flowing and beltless blue garment. His wings were pale rose, rather long and very lovely. His little face was neither long nor round. His nose was very pretty, his eyes black and his complexion dark. His hands were very delicate and his fingernails short. We did not see his feet."

In the entry for the next day, she records: "It was six in the evening and we left for the *calleja* to say the rosary. We had not yet arrived at the scene of the apparitions when the Blessed Virgin appeared with an angel on each side ... They looked like twins. Beside the angel, who stood at the Blessed Virgin's right and at the same height as she, was a large eye which seemed to be the eye of God ... The Blessed Virgin appears with a white dress, a blue mantle and a crown of small golden stars. Her feet are not visible. Her hands are wide open with the scapular [the cloth emblem of protection reputedly given to Saint Simon Stock in England in 1247] on the right wrist. The scapular is brown. Her hair is long, dark brown and wavy, and parted in the middle. She has an oval-shaped face and her nose is long and delicate. Her mouth is very pretty with rather full lips. The color of her face is dark but lighter than that of the angel: it is different. Her voice is very lovely, a very unusual voice that I can't describe. There is no woman that resembles the Blessed Virgin in her voice or in anything else."

Reading Conchita's diary late into the night in that remote and wild spot, it struck me that while some aspects of the iconography of the visions referred to universal traditions going back to the origins of Christianity, there was also something even more primitive, perhaps pagan, and special to this secluded pastoral community.

In the morning the wind had dropped and the sky was crystal bright and cloudless with a cold, damp edge. While Pacita's coffee was brewing I walked out of Meson Serafin into the stone-walled lane that led up to the pines two hundred feet above. A plaque on a post depicted Michael the Archangel, and the legend: "18 Junio de 1961 (Domingo) acqui se aparecio por primera vez a las ninas el Arcangel San Miguel." This was the famous *calleja*. The rest of the way was marked with Stations of the Cross in colored ceramics cemented into cairns. The deep green fields on either side had been cropped by sheep to a carpet smoothness.

The nine pine trees stood on a bluff looking out over the village and beyond to a circle of hills forming an amphitheater reminiscent of the dramatic scene above Medjugorje. The branches of the trees were tied with scarves and handkerchiefs, like the crosses on Mount Krizevac. It was here, "above the pines," according to Conchita, that a great natural sign would occur at some date in the future known only to her.

To the left of the pine grove I noticed an enclosure with a shrine made of aluminum. The gate was locked and I peered in to see a statue of the Archangel Michael striking the serpentine Satan with a lance. Penants depicting the flags of various nations were stuck into the ground.

Standing at the gate of the shrine, I was suddenly conscious of an astonishing scent: a keen, pure, fresh smell of roses in bloom. There was a heavy dew, but there were no flowers, nor herbs, to be seen. Remembering what the Filipino consul had told me the evening before, I felt suddenly haunted and turned away to walk back down the hill toward the pension and breakfast.

When I arrived in the house I found an elderly gentleman ensconced at the refectory table in the company of two ladies bundled in moth-eaten fur coats.

Pacita bustled in with coffee and hot milk.

"This is the *Guardia Civil,* he's come to pay us a visit," she announced.

Brigadier Seco was a tall, upright man in steel spectacles, well groomed with a trim mustache and white hair. He was wearing a starchy blue striped shirt, a black silk tie, and a well-cut dove-gray jacket and vest. But as he stood up to shake my hand I noticed that he was wearing blue waterproof trousers that made a sort of rustling noise.

He told me in sepulchral tones that his full name was Juan Alvarez Seco, and that he had once been the chief of the Civil Guard, Puentenansa sector.

He fixed me with a steely eye. "What do you think of this government?" he asked gravely.

"What did *you* think of Franco?" I asked him guardedly in return.

He stuck out his chest and boomed: "Generalissimo Franco was a man of destiny, without a doubt the greatest figure in the history of this century. What is more, he was a true Spaniard and a devout Catholic."

The women in the fur coats, whose role, it seemed, was to act as silent witnesses to such utterances, nodded their assent.

"The Brigadier will tell you about the ecstasies," said Pacita as she poured the coffee. "Ask him. He remembers all the details."

The ex-policeman put six sugar lumps into his coffee and began to stir the cup slowly.

"I first paid a visit to the village on the twenty-second of June, 1961," he began, "so as to investigate personally the events taking place here, and to compose a report for my superior relative to the alleged happenings."

Brigadier Seco spoke in constabulary parlance with pride and ease. It was if he were addressing a court in session.

"In consequence of my initial investigations," he went on, "I ordered two guards to be placed to watch over Garabandal. The news about the apparitions of the angel was going from village to village and throughout the surrounding countryside, and each day more and more people came, which necessitated increased vigilance. Some three thousand people were witnessing the ecstasies at this time.

"Now. The people going up to see the apparitions were wondering if the children were being hypnotized or being given drugs.

This I investigated fully and satisfied myself that it was not the case. Other people were saying that Conchita was in control of her companions and that if they went at the same hour to the place of the apparitions, it was because she was influencing them. They kept saying she was sick and upon the suggestions of Mari Loli's father, they requested the presence of Dr. José Luis, who, as I have already said, was the incumbent physician for the region. This doctor said the girls were epileptic and sick and everything was happening because of that. But I could see this was nonsense. Why should four epileptics seek each other out as friends? And what were the chances of all four falling into fits simultaneously? Anyway, it was quite obvious that the girls were extremely healthy, mentally and physically. It is important to note that other expert doctors conclusively discounted the thesis of Dr. José Luis at a later date.

"Anyway, the parish priest then demanded that the children be separated, to verify if they would all come at the same time to the place of the apparitions when they felt the special urge that accompanied the onset of a vision. And in fact I can confirm that they did come from different places in the villages under these test conditions at precisely the same time.

"Then all sorts of doctors and priests turned up. During the ecstasies they inflicted pinches and scratches and stuck needles into them. I had to have this stopped. But it was remarkable that none of the children ever reacted to these painful tests; but the marks were all clearly visible after the ecstasies had finished.

"I witnessed many apparitions and I saw hundreds of ecstatic walks and rapid marches, some of them backward, through the streets of the village, while in that state. And when the girls were running to meet one another, some in ecstasy and others in their natural state, no one could keep up with those who were in the ecstasy, not even the other visionaries in their normal state.

"I witnessed many times the way in which, while in full rapture, and after having had objects kissed by the Virgin, the young girls would give each object back to its proper owner, without ever making a mistake."

The Brigadier pulled himself up stiffly and eyed me severely. "I was a policeman, trained to observe accurately and truthfully. The phenomena took place over a long period of time and with great frequency and I was charged with reporting all these things to my superiors. At the beginning of these events I was a Catholic only in name and failed to practice or properly believe in my religion. As a result of the inexplicable nature of the phenomena I returned to full faith and practice."

He turned to the women as if for confirmation, and they both nodded their agreement, vigorously and in silence. "Was there any single event," I asked, "that impressed you more than any other as to its supernatural nature?"

The Brigadier immediately began to nod and to shake his head all at once in a sort of paroxysm of enthusiasm; at the same time he was winking at the women, whose faces were suffused with complacency.

"Now we are talking," he said at last with emotion. "On July 28 I was in the kitchen of Conchita's house. There were others there with me: namely, Dr. Ortiz, a Father José Ramon Vasquez, a seminarian from Reinosa, and a few other people. Conchita was in an ecstasy and she was calling out for help to reach Our Lady, begging us to help her up because she could not reach Our Lady's lips. We said to her, 'Jump. Jump up!' But she said that she couldn't. So three of us, the doctor, the seminarist, and I, attempted to lift her, but we could not raise her one millimeter from the floor; she was like a ton of rock. Jacinta Gonzalez, one of the other visionaries with her, came forward after we had become exhausted with our efforts. Little Jacinta, who was just a slight child, lifted Conchita upward with the tips of her fingers. She lifted her right up to the ceiling."

The Brigadier made another dramatic pause and put his hand on his breast. "What I am telling you, sir, is God's honest truth. After Conchita had made the gesture of kissing her vision all of us saw her float back slowly, right back, until she was absolutely horizontal. Jacinta brought her down holding only her legs. Then she let go and Conchita remained floating about a hand's height above the kitchen floor for several moments. We all stood absolutely amazed. I could have run my hand between the floor and her body, but I was rooted to the spot. I would also add that while Conchita defied the laws of gravity, her dress was never in immodest disarray!"

The women nodded gravely at this.

"Anyway, it was at this point," boomed the Brigadier, "that I was absolutely convinced within myself as a Christian and became a convinced believer in the supernatural events at Garabandal."

* * *

That afternoon I went for a long walk in the lonely foothills of the mountains above Garabandal. Beyond the village the characteristics of the harsh farm economy of the region were clearly evident: the hay fields and arable plots were still worked by hand, mostly by women, and the annual cycle of winter and summer pastures could be clearly seen. It continued to prey on my mind that the ecstatic marches and trances of those prepubescent girls had as much to do with the ancient local folk resonances of this mountain community as their official religion. It struck me, too, that in less liberal times the associations of "night-flying," trances, communication with dead spirits, the Eucharistic mime, and the magical ability to identify talismans might well have been deemed the work of Satan. On just such evidence had girls of even younger ages been condemned by the Inquisition. In which case it made it all the more easy for me to entertain the notion that the phenomena had less to do with the Christian powers of good or evil, and more to do with an aptitude for an ancient and primitive ritual.

My day and night in Garabandal had left me in a state of bemusement. I was deeply impressed by all that I had heard from the locals, and convinced that the children were not fakes. I had found the phenomena of Garabandal more dramatic than those of Medjugorje and yet lacking in any obvious sense of spirituality. All the same, there was an undeniable atmosphere of a "sacred" presence in the vicinity of the pines: but was it the sacredness of Christianity?

Later, when I attended the Mass of the day in the church I noticed that only women were present and the devotion of the small congregation had none of the fervor of the Medjugorjean villagers. As I passed the bar on my way back to the pension I saw the men skulking around the "Space Invaders" machine or playing cards in a great fug of smoke.

As I prepared to leave Garabandal later that day, Serafin Gonzalez came to me with some assorted literature, including a magazine put out by Joey Lomangino, which contained his address and a telephone contact number in America. I knew that I would have to do everything possible to meet Conchita Gonzalez, however reluctant she might be to be interviewed.

On my return to England I came across a report of a case that had curious parallels with the Garabandal girls, and especially their synchronized behavior, although the manifestations were patently evil and violent, as opposed to sacred and benign.

In a document written by a distinguished Zurich psychiatrist, Hans Naegeli-Osjord (published by the New Frontiers Center in Oregon, Wisconsin, in 1988), was the story of two German boys known as the "Lads of Illfurt." The case, I gathered, was well attested by eyewitnesses and supported with plentiful evidence, including tape recordings.

What seized my attention from the outset was the assertion that the experiences had begun, as at Garabandal, with the stealing of an apple from a woman, in this case a stranger who was passing through the village.

The phenomena started on September 25, 1985, when the boys, aged eight and ten, were observed to spin "with incredible speed," like tops, while lying on their backs. Anybody who has seen children doing a "break-dance" will hardly be over-impressed by this. But afterward they proceeded to destroy all the furniture in the house in an exercise of strength that would have been extraordinary even in an adult. At the end of this demonstration, say witnesses, the boys showed no sign of fatigue.

From this point onward the phenomena increased in strangeness and variety. Their legs often gained in plasticity so that they could intertwine them "like supple rods." In this state it was quite impossible for adult observers to untangle them; they were only extricated when the boys decided to exert, as if at will, their power to change the shape of their limbs again. (Naegeli-Osjord was at pains to point out that the flexibility of the boys' bones bore no resemblance to *flexibilitas cerea,* a condition known in catatonic states of schizophrenia where the notion of suppleness of bone is metaphorical rather than real.)

More dramatic yet, the brothers were reported to have levitated, frequently floating "in the air either on chairs or without chairs." These episodes usually culminated in their being buffeted "by what seemed like invisible fists" until they were thrown to the ground. Sometimes, when seated, the boys were thrown with incredible force to one side of the room, while their chairs hurtled in the opposite direction.

They were also subject to strange alterations in weight; they could sit, for example, on the slightest branches of trees without breaking them, as if their bodies had acquired an extraordinary lightness.

While these phenomena were in progress the boys spoke with the deep voices of men, although their mouths were apparently shut. The "voices" spoke in French, Spanish, and English, including various dialects, as well the boys' native German.

Because this behavior defied the skill of psychiatrists and physicians, a Catholic priest exorcist was called. In his presence, it is claimed, the boys began to speak in Latin. The "voices" then threatened to "plague" the Father Superior of a local religious community, whereupon the priest in question, although several miles distant and unaware of the events in the brother's household, was lifted into the air by invisible forces; all the pictures fell off his walls and his furniture tumbled about. The phenomena only stopped when the room was sprinkled with holy water.

On another occasion the boys were offered figs which had been blessed in secret by the exorcist. The brothers apparently cried out in unison: "Away with the rat heads, the blackcoat has grimaced over them." As the psychiatrist remarked: "Such expressions are hardly common in the vocabulary of small boys."

According to the report, house hauntings spread throughout the vicinity of the boys' home to other Illfurt families: the Kleimers, the Brobecks, the Burbachs, and the Dresches. Evidence was collated from all these sources.

The boys were immune to a variety of medical and psychiatric approaches; exorcism similarly failed, both in the boys' home and in the local monastery. Finally the bishop intervened and brought in two exorcists of outstanding reputation from outside the diocese: this at last yielded results and the boys returned to normal.

Hans Naegeli-Osjord, who has served as president of Switzerland's parapsychology society, was not inclined to accept an explanation based on psychosis, hysteria, or hypnosis. He was convinced that he had encountered an exceedingly rare and outstanding case of contemporary possession by evil spirits.

A characteristic of the case that I found particularly intriguing was the apparent flexibility of the bones, as I had come across a similar feature in an article by Herbert Thurston about Christina of Saint Trond, a thirteenth-century saint, known as Christina the Wonderful. "The most remarkable feature," says Thurston, "and the least likely to have suggested itself to the hagiographer spontaneously ... is the flexibility of limbs which seem to belong more to the character of an acrobat or a contortionist. . . . She melted, so to speak, like wax and rolled herself up into a ball . . . she would suddenly and unexpectedly be rapt by the spirit and her body would rotate, whirling like a child's hoop, revolving so rapidly that it was impossible to distinguish the outline of her separate limbs."

It is curious, then, that the same allegedly paranormal symptoms of sainthood in one age are to be found in the demon-possessed of another.

Naegeli-Osjord was principally swayed by the phenomenon of foreign tongues (also an ambivalent symptom, hovering between sainthood and possession); although, personally, I found this less impressive than the reports of levitation, which, if the witnesses were not suffering from delusion, would be evidence of one of the most elusive, albeit frequently claimed, paranormal events one could hope to observe.

My caution on the score of "tongues" was largely due to the writings of Samuel Taylor Coleridge. Coleridge, more than almost any thinker in the English language, had attempted throughout his life to reconcile the possibility of metaphysics and mysticism with rational and empirical methods of investigation; and the more I read him alongside Aldous Huxley, Arthur Koestler, Alistair Hardy, Colin Wilson, and others, the more creative, and sound, I found his approach to the realms of the supernatural.

Browsing through his *Biographia Literaria* (1817), I had come across a case which had occurred in what he describes as a "Catholic town" in Germany a year or two before his visit to Göttingen in 1799.

A young illiterate serving-woman, brought to the local hospital suffering from a "nervous fever," was judged by local priests and monks to be possessed. The principal indication of diabolical influence involved her ability to speak Latin, Greek, and Hebrew, which she did incessantly and "in very pompous tones and with most distinct enunciation." The clergy were all the more convinced that she was possessed since she was suspected of "heresy."

The case had attracted the attention of many eminent physiologists and psychologists throughout Germany, some of whom came to the town and cross-examined the woman on the spot. Her ravings were taken down and found on careful scrutiny to consist of disconnected snatches of texts. Only a small portion of her Hebrew sentences could be traced to the Bible; the rest seemed to be in the rabbinicial dialect. Fraud was soon discounted, and the doctors acknowledged that they were facing a genuine mystery.

A young physician, who was not prepared to accept a paranormal explanation, delved further. Eventually he discovered where her parents had lived and made the journey there. Both parents were dead, but he found a surviving uncle who related how the patient had been charitably taken in by an old Protestant pastor when she was nine years old and had stayed with him some years until his death. The physician next discovered a niece of the pastor's who lived with him as his housekeeper and had inherited his effects. On questioning the niece about the pastor's habits he discovered the solution of the enigma.

It had been the old man's custom for years "to walk up and down a passage of his house onto which the kitchen door opened, and to read to himself with a loud voice out of his favorite books." The niece still had many of these books in her possession. Among them was found a collection of rabbinicial writings together with several of the Greek and Latin Fathers.

"The physician succeeded in identifying so many passages with those taken down at the young woman's bedside," writes Coleridge, "that no doubt could remain in any rational mind concerning the true origin of the impressions made on her nervous system."

The case illustrated to Coleridge, at the end of the eighteenth century, a profound psychological truth evidently overlooked by trained psychiatrists toward the end of the twentieth century: "that reliques of sensation may exist for an indefinite time in latent state, in the very same order in which they were originally impressed."

The "Lads of Illfurt" may well have picked up snatches of different languages from foreign radio broadcasts, and given the evident high concentration of Catholic clergy in the neighborhood it is likely that they had heard Latin in one of the local churches.

But the importance of the parallel with Garabandal, it seemed to me, was the curious association of the apple stolen from the outsider. In Garabandal the "outsider" had been the schoolteacher. The link between both stories and the Snow White motif from Grimm (and, of course, the Eve motif), with its implications of bewitchment, seemed to me irresistible.

The apple incident had in both cases apparently triggered a series of parallel symptoms: synchronized physical actions, dance, abnormal strength, apparent levitation, clairvoyant insight about physical objects; at the same time, the phenomena were performed with the close involvement of clerical witnesses.

Considering both incidents anthropologically, it would surely be unwise to discount the influence of traditional Catholic attitudes toward witchcraft and magic in rural Germany on the one hand, and the long tradition of Marian apparitions in Spain on the other. Moreover, it is surely intriguing that the *Rituale Romanum,* the clergy's handbook on exorcism, lists "bewitchment" as a cause of possession along with some familiar characteristics, including: the comprehension and speaking of foreign languages that are unknown to the subjects; knowledge of secret matters; physical strength that exceeds comprehension; and aversion to holy objects.

To what extent, then, was there unwitting collusion between the children and the clergy, the villagers, and perhaps even the psychiatrists, in the two cases? Reflecting on the synchronized activities of the Illfurt Lads, the girls of Garabandal, and the visionaries of Medjugorje, it struck me that the significance of such patterned behavior was to give onlookers a dramatic impression of *control* from an outside power; the control might be evil, or it might be good, but the importance of the pattern was the impression of possession, and manipulation, by a higher power.

This is to say nothing about "how" such things were achieved; but it seemed to me important at this stage to acknowledge that phenomena involving onlookers, audiences, should be *read,* interpreted, in the light of their mimetic and theatrical meaning, as much as their supposed paranormal potential. It also seemed important to accept that although the paranormal component might fade in the light of rational explanation, the metaphorical and symbolic values would remain.

12

The Virgin of the Ukraine

As I was contemplating a visit to New York to attempt to find Conchita of Garabandal, an opportunity arose for me to cross the Atlantic to do a television interview with a man who claimed to have experienced a number of visions with the Virgin in the Ukraine.

An independent producer of my acquaintance was making a film that would be shown as part of the 1990 "Soviet Spring" series on Channel Four in Britain; he had been intrigued by the claimed apparitions and the way in which they were contributing to the bid for religious freedom in the Ukraine.

The visionary was Josyp Terelya, the leader of the Ukrainian separatist movement, who had been expelled from the Soviet Union in the summer of 1987; his story seemed to complement the cases of Medjugorje and Garabandal. But this time the political overtones were not merely evident, they were overwhelming.

In the time-honored tradition of rural sightings of the Virgin, the apparitions had begun with a twelve-year-old girl, Maria Kyzyn, who claimed that she had seen a "Madonna and Child" hovering above the dome of the banned former Ukrainian Catholic chapel of the Holy Trinity at Hrushiw, which lies a few miles from Poland's eastern border with Western Ukraine.

The Virgin, dressed in black, had looked down in silence. According to Maria, "She glowed in an unearthly light."

Within several days, large groups of women had gathered outside the chapel. They confirmed that they, too, saw the image and that it was identical in every detail with the icon of Our Lady of Compassion, the famous Madonna and Child of Kiev given to Vladimir the Great by his wife Anna in 988 and dating back to the very origins of Christianity in ancient Russia. Within a week, gatherings in Hrushiw of tens of thousands were reported on Soviet television and in *Pravda.* The apparitions were described in an editorial as a "destabilizing miracle," the work of "extremists attempting to undermine *perestroika* ... a political provocation inspired by foreign clerical-nationalistic centers with the help of fanatics and extremists."

But the first apparitions in April, 1987, were occurring not only in the new atmosphere of *perestroika,* but against the background of the long struggle for freedom among the banned churches of the Soviet Union. Those, moreover, with a taste for apocalyptic signals, were not slow to see links with the anniversary of the catastrophe at the nuclear power plant at Chernobyl just 300 kilometers away. And 1988 was the millennium of the advent of Christianity in ancient Rus', to which the Ukrainians make exclusive claim against the rival "pretensions" of the Russian Orthodox. The Virgin seemed to have arrived to demonstrate that history was on the side of the Ukrainian Catholics.

The historical origins of Ukrainian Catholicism, however, were far from straightforward. The Church is a curious blend of Eastern-rite Christianity with an ancient loyalty to Rome; it acknowledges the primacy of the pope, yet its liturgy and music are Byzantine; its bishops are in direct communion with Rome, but its priests are allowed to marry. Its provenance is the subject of contention not only within the Ukraine but inside the Catholic Church itself. While it claims direct and unbroken descent from the eleventh-century missionaries Saints Cyril and Methodius, its local rivals, which include Russian Orthodox, Ukrainian Orthodox, and even Latin Rite Christians, tell a different story, as do the Communists. The alternative view of Ukrainian Catholic history is that Ukrainian Catholicism is a seventeenth-century creation of Polish Jesuits, founded in order to undermine and annex the region now known as Western Ukraine.

The Communists claim, moreover, that all Ukrainian Catholics voluntarily joined the Ukrainian Orthodox Church at the synod of

Lvov at the end of the Second World War. For this reason the Communists referred to them pejoratively as "Uniates." There are rumors, too, originally put about by Stalin, that the "Uniates" had collaborated with the Nazis against the Jews. The official, Communist, view is that the Church simply does not now exist, since it disbanded itself and surrendered all its churches in 1946.

Despite the Ukrainian Catholics' loyalty to the pope, even the Vatican's attitude toward them is equivocal; while Pope John Paul II professes his support for them, Cardinals Casaroli and Willibrands, who masterminded the Holy See's "Ostpolitik," or "Eastern Policy" are known to be antagonistic. The Vatican diplomats believe that the Ukrainians could disturb the delicate politics of ecumenical dialogue with the Russian Orthodox Church and the desire to win freedoms for Latin Rite Catholicism, especially in the Baltic states.

Whatever the historical and political wrangles, Ukrainian Catholics patently do exist and have probably suffered more than any Christian denomination in the long history of religious persecution in the Soviet Union. In the late 1940s eight bishops and almost a thousand priests were executed; thousands of other priests were sent to the gulags, and their churches were closed or given over to the Ukrainian Orthodox.

But somehow the Church survived. In basements, in forest clearings, in abandoned chapels, the faithful continued to gather, despite fines and imprisonment. There are stories of groups that would regularly recite the words of the Mass up to the consecration before disbanding; on the altar they would place an item of the priest's liturgical vestments symbolizing the absent celebrant.

To such a persecuted minority, news that they had been favored with a series of apparitions would have seemed like a beacon of hope lighting up the Carpathian Mountains. And yet, such was the multiplicity of fierce political antagonisms, that I suspected that things might be rather more complicated and ominous.

I flew to Toronto to meet Terelya in what was described as a "safe house" situated in a leafy suburb of the city. There were extensive, well-patrolled grounds and an atmosphere of conspiratorial tension.

Before we started filming, Terelya came out to talk to me beneath a stand of maple trees. He was square, thickset, with a wide Russian face and almond-shaped Slavonic eyes. His thick shock of hair was iron-gray.

He wore a sad, tense expression and I wondered whether he was unwell.

As soon as he sat down he told me that he was forty-three years of age and had spent twenty-three of those years in prisons and concentration camps. He had been sentenced nine times. His brother had been killed in a terrorist action on behalf of a Ukrainian separatist group.

"I have been released," he said, "but not rehabilitated. Gorbachev has not rehabilitated a single political prisoner."

He was eager at once to launch into a description of his visions and the background.

"She appeared," he said, "in a glow of orange and blue light. It was a band of light that seemed to wave, to ebb and flow. She held up a rosary: the Our Fathers were orange, and the Hail Marys were seeds of blue light. Her dress was made up of fiery rays.

"I had not been long out of prison," he went on, "when I heard that the Virgin was appearing near Lvov. I went there straightaway; there were hundreds of militia all over the place. I was spotted and followed; they tried to stop me, but I gave them the slip and got into the churchyard. It was early evening and there were thousands of people gathered.

"All of us were blessed with the sight of the apparition. She did not move her lips, but each of us heard her speak privately . . ."

"And what did she say, to you specifically?" I asked.

Terelya was holding a rosary in his hand. He held it up in the gesture of a clenched fist.

"She told me not to be afraid. She said I must have courage to do what God had chosen me to do."

"And what is that?"

Terelya leaned forward earnestly, his massive shoulders squared.

"The Virgin told me that, because of their sufferings, the Ukrainian Church of Martyrdom would now come out of the catacombs. Because of our suffering we have been tried and strengthened, and specially chosen. We are the just remnant. She told me that through us the Ukrainian people would gain their freedom. We must be brave and prepared to shed our blood anew. In time we would convert Russia itself, bring Christianity to Russia."

"But Josyp," I said, "there is already a Church in Russia, the Russian Orthodox . . ."

"They are puppets of the KGB," he rasped with a dismissive gesture of his hand.

"Even though I was surrounded by KGB informers," he continued, "I stood up among the people and I preached to them for twelve hours after one vision. This is how it went on, day after day. People were coming in from all over the place, even from distant parts of the Soviet Union. There were license plates from the other side of the Urals, from Georgia. . . . People came on horseback, on bicycles, on foot . . .

"The Queen of Ukraine begs and asks us to be penitent and to forgive sins and to be brothers to all Christians of the world, for only through our Ukrainian people will come the universal freedom from the Prince of Darkness."

In the wake of the visions, said Terelya, there had been a spate of mass gatherings of Ukrainian Catholics. Some of their former churches had been taken back by force and there had been frequent clashes with the police. In the midst of this wave of militancy, he had emerged as nationalist leader. Exile had only added to his authority.

He told me that he had continued to enter the Soviet Union in "Scarlet Pimpernel" fashion, and that he sent regular batches of propaganda material, prayer books, and Bibles, released from air-balloons dispatched across the Austrian border.

As he told me these things it occurred to me that he had also emerged not simply as a political figure, but as a holy man, a man of charisma, who would be followed for more reasons than his political and historical arguments.

"We are now five million strong in the Western Ukraine," said Terelya, "and supported by loyal exiles here in Canada and in the United States."

"But Josyp," I said, "are you really in no doubt about your visions? Is it possible that you witnessed an optical illusion?"

He shook his head vehemently.

"Listen!" he replied. "A colonel in the Soviet militia pointed a gun at the vision . . . I was there, I saw this with my own eyes. As he went to press the trigger he dropped down in a faint. He had to be carried off to the hospital. When he came round forty-eight hours later, he was completely converted to the faith. He remembers nothing of his past life. He spends his time traveling around the villages relating what he saw."

"So why did these things happen at Hrushiw?"

Terelya spread his arms expansively.

"She came in the nineteenth century, and during the First World War when she gave a warning identical to that of Fatima: pray or Russia would be lost to God; pray or there will be a second, more terrible war. Again she is telling us that we must pray for the conversion of Russia, or there will be an even worse chastisement. Chernobyl was just a warning. She tells us that we Ukrainians will shortly obtain our own state, which will become the guardian of all those who have accepted Christ as their spiritual leader."

All this time Terelya had been gazing fiercely into my eyes, his forehead creased with tension.

Suddenly I found his vehemence tedious. I had also remembered that orange and blue, the colors of his Virgin, were the Ukrainian national colors. I suspected that he was a man without a trace of humor or irony.

I said to him: "Josyp, you look very unhappy."

It was, perhaps, an undiplomatic remark.

His response was explosive. "Tell me something amusing," he barked, "and then I'll laugh."

It was time to go back into the house to meet with the film crew.

When we had finished filming, I asked to be taken immediately to the airport to catch a plane to New York. I did not want to linger a moment longer with the visionary of Hrushiw.

By the end of the day I had found myself both suspicious of and disturbed by Josyp Terelya's brand of charisma. Quite apart from the question of the authenticity of the phenomena, his claimed visions seemed to me a highly combustible blend of dubious mysticism and fanaticism. I saw nothing wrong with the aspirations of the Ukrainians for independence, nor even with the Ukrainian Catholics making a bid for being the focus of that separatist goal, although there were other powerful claims from other religious and non-religious groups. The ominous element was the attempt to legitimize and bolster such a claim with a series of private revelations that were being spread, evangelistic style, as authentic revelation direct from the supernatural realms.

Against the background of burgeoning ethnic and religious rivalries in Eastern Europe, Josyp Terelya seemed to me to be playing an extremely dangerous game, with all the violent potential of Beirut.

Pondering the peculiar nature of the visions (it was unusual for such large numbers of people to claim to have witnessed a Marian apparition), I recalled that there had been a parallel in Cairo in 1968.

During that Egyptian phenomenon, the Virgin, it was claimed, had appeared in the form of a light above the dome of a Coptic Orthodox church in the suburb of Zeitoun. The series of apparitions had started when some Muslim workmen said they saw a "White Lady" kneeling beside the cross at the top of the dome.

The phenomenon began to occur nightly, attracting, according to some newspapers, as many as 250,000 people at a time. On one occasion twelve people were crushed to death in the pressing crowds, which included both Muslims and Christians. There were reports of mysterious lights, canopies of shooting stars, luminous globes, and blinding explosions of light. Witnesses said that the image shone with an overpowering splendor like the sun in human form, that the vision would glide across domes, bowing and greeting the throngs of people.

Police in Cairo had insisted that the phenomenon was a result of a freak illusion created by the streetlighting. This had been vociferously denied by a large number of witnesses who had written testimonies of what they thought they had seen.

The parallels between Zeitoun and Hrushiw seemed to me too numerous to be coincidental: the proximity of the light phenomenon to the dome, the nightly appearances, the involvement of an ambivalent Christian denomination with Roman affiliations but Eastern cultural leanings. And there had been nothing quite like these two cases in the long history of Marian apparitions spanning almost sixteen centuries. Even at Fatima in 1916 the vast crowd, one hundred thousand strong, had witnessed only a solar phenomenon, and a handful of parishioners at Knock in Ireland in 1879 had seen static and silent visions of Mary and other biblical figures suspiciously reminiscent of a lantern-slide show.

So what was one to make of the Egyptian and the Ukrainian parallels? Was the Hrushiw phenomenon a copycat imitation of the Zeitoun visions? Was there some sort of stage-managed hoax involved, in which clever crowd psychology had been employed? Communist officials had been quick to suggest a contrived "destabilizing miracle," yet nothing definite had been proved. And now that both sets of phenomena had ended, it would be difficult to root out the truth.

One was left, for the time being, with the spectacle of powerful charisma in the making, a charisma emerging from the highly contagious attraction of a leader who is in receipt of divine messages and favors, and who exploits this situation without entertaining the possibility that he and his followers might be deluded or in error. In Josyp Terelya I had encountered, I felt, the dark face of popular mystical experience.

In New York I made contact with Joey Lomangino, the blind millionaire who has dedicated his life to the promotion of the visions at Garabandal.

Joey runs a garbage disposal company called Allied Sanitation. The offices are in Queens and I found him in a cabin out in the yard from which he also runs his Charity House movement for the handicapped homeless.

He was in conference with a group of hulking Italian-Americans; men in business suits were coming and going, shaking ringed hands, being introduced. . . . "Hey! this is my nephew . . . kid brother . . . my attorney. . . ." Meanwhile Joey was taking calls . . . "Hi babe! . . . Hi honey! . . ."

Joey has the mighty frame of a wrestler. His great head with a mop of white hair juts forward aggressively; his full lips seem to be formed in a permanent silent whistle. He peers forward intently when he speaks, as if screwing up his eyelids with intense concentration. But his eyes and brows and the upper area of his nose are entirely destroyed, as if he has been in a high-speed collision with an automobile.

Eventually the men drifted from the room and Joey called me over.

"Never mind that, Johnny," he said, "these are just political people and stuff come to meet my family. You know, Johnny, we're the premier company in New York City when it comes to recycling the garbage. We're so far advanced, we're ten years ahead of the State. . . . Now we talk religion! I'm at your service, Johnny."

He spoke in a marked Brooklyn accent, rapid quick-fire, impatient to get the words out. "Let me share with you my testimony, Johnny, just as the Holy Spirit guides me," he said.

Suddenly he delved into his pocket and brought out an ornate string of rosary beads made of rock crystal and silver; next to the crucifix hung a huge silver Miraculous Medal. Joey made the sign of the cross with the medal and kissed it.

Now he was ready:

"In the name of the Father, and of the Son, and of the Holy Spirit, Amen. We offer this conference, to the greater glory of God, and the destruction of sin, and the salvation of souls. Blessed Mother, help us. Our Lady of Mount Carmel, pray for us. Okay, Johnny. Here we go . . .

"I was born in Brooklyn on October 5, 1930. My mother was immigrant Italian, my father, an Italian-American, born in New York. And when my father was a very young man he contracted spinal meningitis, and as a result my dad could look at you, know that your name is John, and that you're a writer, but couldn't put anything else together. See? So at the age of eight I used to help my father on the ice truck and the coal truck, because that's what Italian immigrants did. They worked labor. And at the age of eleven I was already driving the ice truck to various houses to keep the food from going bad. My father had about three hundred ice customers. My family was poor, but we always made things meet.

"On June 27, 1947, when I was sixteen, I came home on the last day of my third year at high school. I came round the back of the house and went up on the porch and looked through the screen door. And my mother was about ten feet in front of me washing the floor on her knees with a scrub brush. And I said: 'Mom open the door!' And she looked up at me and said: 'Joey, where'd you get that terrible mark across your face?' But there was no mark there. But I thought that maybe there was a shadow over my face that would give her this impression. Then she opened the door and she saw my face was normal. And she said: 'Joey, don't go out there again because I know you're going to get hurt.' Intuition, see? And I said: 'Mom, give me a break. I've got to help dad with the ice truck.' So what happened? I went downstairs, sixteen years of age, stubborn, a box of wrenches under my arm, and I went out. And I could hear my mother's voice crying: 'Joey, you're going to break your mother's heart. I saw the mark on your face, you're going to get hurt . . .'

"I went down to where my father parked the truck and I saw that the back tire was deflated. So I jacked up the truck, and I took the tire off and I rolled it to a gas station. I was putting air in it and my mind was telling me that it was going to explode. So I turned it round so that if it did explode it would hit the ground. But the valve was too long because it was an inside tire, so when I went to put the air hose on it I couldn't fit it under the tire, so I turned it around the other way again face up. As I put the air hose on to it, BAM! it blew, burying steel and rubber two inches into my eyes and forehead. I was in a coma until July 16, the Feast of Our Lady of Mount Carmel. When I come out of the coma I had a whole new life. I was blind, I had no sense of smell; the olfactory nerves were completely destroyed. And I've wrecked my father's living because I can't work for him anymore.

"I was back at home some weeks later, and I'd gone to bed, and I woke with a start in the middle of the night. And I heard this voice of a woman, saying: 'Joey, do you want your eyesight back? . . . Then you pray,' she says, 'every day of your life.' And I said: 'When will you be back?' And she said: 'Soon.' After that I fell asleep again. Next day I told my Mom what had happened, and she said: 'What do I know? Maybe it was an angel.' Anyway after that I prayed those prayers every day of my life.

"In 1949, the priest from the parish took me to blind school. And the first thing they do is leave you in the infirmary for a week to check you out. I was very lonely there, and it was the first time I'd been away from home. And the idea of being blind broke my heart. I laid down on the bed, I took out my rosary, and I prayed. And I cried myself to sleep. And during the night I had a dream and what I saw was something that was equivalent to a golf course. Lush green rolling fields, and in the middle a clump of trees, and I was standing with my back to the trees. When I woke the next morning I had something that took over me, and the only way I could explain it was that it was like a power coming into me; like a strength . . . When I got up the next day I knew that I was going to be all right, but I knew that it was going to be a long haul.

"After I graduated from St. John's a Jewish finance man, a philanthropist, lent me the money to buy my own carting business. My three brothers came with me and my father, and we started to work. And we started to come up. That was 1954.

"By 1961 we were making a lot of money and I took a trip to Europe with my sister. We went down to the Italian Riviera, down toward Rome, and south to Bari. I met my mother's people and stayed on. My Uncle Frank is a teacher of languages at the university, and one day he says to me: 'Joey we've got to go see Padre Pio.' He tells me this priest has got the stigmata. I said 'Get away! Don't give me the story about priests and religion, I don't want to hear it. Every time I go near one they talk about miracles. Hey, look! It's got to be this way! Accept it.'

"But Uncle Frank played it quiet, and kept on at me. The night before I left, Uncle Frank comes to me at three o'clock in the morning. He says, 'Come on, Joey, we've got to see Padre Pio, it's on your way up in the car. Let's go.'

"We got to Padre Pio's church at five o'clock and it was packed. I was at the back and the Mass began, and I knew in my heart that there was something in his voice. At the end of the Mass we were all permitted to go upstairs. I was the last one up, standing in a corner. He comes in from a door and all of a sudden I hear the scuffling of knees, and everybody's whispering, and all of a sudden these arms are around my shoulders and he's kissing me on the forehead, hugging me, bringing me to his heart. 'Joey, I'm so happy to see you.' But I was in sin, Johnny, and I didn't know what to say.

"In 1963 I returned to Italy again, and when I was in Bari I decided I wanted to go to confession to Padre Pio. I made arrangements and at the appointed time I was taken into the church by the arm. I knelt down in front of him, close, face to face. And when I went face to face with Padre Pio I nearly *died*. I thought of all the crazy sins I'd committed in my whole life and I was speechless. So he touches me on the arm and he says, 'Why don't you confess, Joey?' And I said: 'Father, I can't speak.' So he gets me by the arm and in perfect English, he says: 'Joey, do you remember when you were in a bar with a girl named Barbara? Do you remember the sin you committed?' And he goes right down, Johnny, naming the people I was with, the places I was at, the sins I committed. *Right down the line.*

"I was crying. I was sweating and nearly fainting. But I knew that if this was what I had to go through to come back to being happy it's worth it. At the end he put his hand to my lips so that I could kiss the stigmata, and he gives me a little slap round the cheek and says: 'A bit of courage, and you'll be all right, Joey!'

"When I came away from that confessional I felt like a child again. I had a firm purpose of amendment, and I was sorry for every sin I'd committed in my life. I felt so good and so clean I didn't want to talk. And ever since then, February 18, 1963, the cross came off my shoulders. Ever since then I might be a little bit inconvenienced because I can't always do what I want to do, but I don't carry a cross. I don't suffer and I've been free.

"Two days later as I was kneeling down before Padre Pio in the corridor after Mass I got the fragrance of roses that comes from his hands. Now because I had lost my sense of smell, it came as such a shock I was thrown back against the wall as if I'd been hit by a bus. And Padre Pio touched me and said: 'Don't be afraid, Joey!' And from that point on my sense of smell was restored after sixteen years, even though the doctors say that it's impossible, they says it's like getting electric light in a room without wires.

"The next day Padre Pio comes to me again, and he says: 'Joey, I cannot give you physical sight to see with, but I will give you spiritual sight for your soul. I will make you see things that your brothers will never see.'

"Now, from there I was to go to Garabandal for the first time. I had this friend who said that the Blessed Virgin was appearing there. But because of these incredible gifts I received through Padre Pio I didn't want to go. So I asked Padre Pio personally whether it was true that the Blessed Mother was appearing there in Spain, to four little girls. And he said: 'Yes.' And when I asked him if I should go there he said: 'Yes, why not?'

"So I went to Garabandal and I met Conchita, everyone. They described to me the whole village, the fields, the hill with the pines, and told me all the messages from the Blessed Mother about the warning and the day of the great miracle. See this Miraculous Medal? Conchita gave it to me. It was kissed by Our Lady at Garabandal.

"Now in 1964 I was back home in my mother's house and I was lying on the couch saying my prayers and I started to fall asleep, and my mind started to go like this: 'Joey, in the blind school, you had a dream . . . you saw something that looked like a golf course with trees at the back . . . you were looking at something up in the sky . . . Garabandal, Joey . . . Garabandal . . .' Maybe I was uptight; maybe I projected a voice. How how do *I* know! But I'm looking for the truth anyway, and I realize for the first time that the scene of my dream all those years ago is one and the same as the descriptions that have been given me of Garabandal, and I realize that I've been given in a dream a vision of the day of the great miracle.

"I believed in Conchita because Padre Pio told me it was all right. So I wrote to her. And Conchita told me that the Virgin Mary told her to tell me that the voice I heard was hers and that the Virgin Mary would give me the new eyes she has promised on the day of the great miracle.

"Conchita came out here more than twenty years ago. She's married with four children, a holy woman who suffers a great deal. I myself married a wonderful woman I met at Fatima ten years ago and we have two children.

"Conchita and I live in wait for the day of the great miracle, the day on which I shall receive back my own sight. On that day people all over the world will then have a permanent sign of the Blessed Mother's presence in the world. People will be converted the world over, so will Russia.

"A year before the great miracle there will be a warning, when everybody, irrespective of race, color, or creed, will see into their own hearts how they have offended God. Eight days before the great miracle, which will be a permanent sign over the pines at Garabandal, Conchita will announce the date. Then all of those who are convinced of the truth of Garabandal will make their way there. There will be hundreds of thousands, Johnny, because I've been busy all these years setting up Garabandal centers across the world. We'll be there in readiness. Now you have it all, Johnny. God bless you. In the name of the Father and of the Son and of the Holy Spirit. Amen."

All this time Joey had been leaning forward, touching me on the arm with a huge hand; in the other hand he held his rosary. As he came to an end he stood up and pressed the medal on my forehead then put it to my lips.

"And do you really have your smell back?" I asked.

"Anything you put under my nose I can smell. It's a living daily miracle."

"You smell cooking in the kitchen without seeing it?"

"Sure. My sense of smell is normal. In fact it's better than I ever remember it before the accident."

As I shook Joey's hand, he gave me Conchita's telephone number and address.

"It's the best I can do, Johnny. I can't arrange anything for you because Conchita does her own thing nowadays . . ."

As I rode in a cab back to Manhattan I wondered whether Joey's rebirth, the lifting of his suffering, had been a result of his firm trust in an eventual miracle cure, or whether it would have happened anyway. It seemed an extraordinary hope that he would one day receive a completely new set of eyes where he now had none. What was he going to do in the event of disappointment? Would it destroy his faith, both in the Garabandal apparitions and in Christianity? And as for the return of his sense of smell, I had heard of people hallucinating smells in the same way as amputees experienced phantom pain.

Joey's story illustrated both the strength and weakness of the literal approach to supernatural expectations which carried specific promises, and dates.

And what of Conchita? What must she now be feeling as she considered the extraordinary trap into which she had placed herself, and Joey, and all the other hundreds of thousands of the devotees of the Garabandal cult who lived in expectation of the great sign? Had her visions not turned to a nightmare, as the anticipated date drew nigh, threatening disillusion, disaster?

I had found Joey's story, and by association the Garabandal phenomenon, deeply affecting. The problem was seeing how such phenomena could be understood within the framework of beneficent religious experience without the threat of eventual despair and destruction of faith.

13

The Reluctant Prophetess

L called Conchita Gonzalez, now Mrs. Conchita Keena, the seer of Garabandal, six times on the phone. Usually she remained silent for several minutes after she had lifted the receiver. When she eventually spoke it was to refuse to see me. In the end, and somewhat against my inclination, I decided to make the journey to her home anyway.

Late on a summer evening I took a cab out to Queens via the 59th Street Bridge. We drove down Queens Boulevard, to 69th Street, then along the flanks of a cemetery, and into the maze of streets in the neighborhoods of Glendale. I was feeling uneasy and a little conscience-stricken, but I told myself that Conchita's story was in the public domain; if she was convinced that she was the vehicle for a message of supernatural warning to all humankind, she could hardly claim a purely private status.

The cabdriver left me on a narrow street lined with young trees. Children were playing out on the sidewalk. Conchita's house was an anonymous-looking brick building with heavy iron grilles on the windows: it looked enclosed, shut up.

As I approached the front door I was suddenly seized with a sense of foreboding. Something about the house and the prospect of meeting this woman filled me with unease. I turned on my heel and walked back down to the corner of the street. I must have passed up and down the street four or five times before I approached the door again.

I rang the bell. The house was in silence. Almost with relief I was considering walking away, when I cupped my hands and peered through the screen door into the darkened hallway and saw a figure standing motionless in the shadows, staring out at me.

"Hello!" I said. "I'm the English writer who called you. I just wanted to see you, shake your hand ...!"

I was beginning to babble.

She did not move.

In desperation I said: "I bring greetings from Garabandal from your brother Serafin and your sister-in-law Pacita." I was speaking in broken Castillian.

With this she approached the first glass door and opened it a little.

At last she said in English: "I don't give interviews." Her voice was deep with a heavy Spanish accent.

"I know," I blurted out. "I just wanted to tell you how much I appreciate you."

It seemed a false and foolish thing to say.

"I'm nothing special," she said.

"Nothing special! You spoke to Our Lady almost every day for four years and you think you're nothing special?"

She opened the door a little further. I could see her fully now. She was a woman of striking good looks, with high cheekbones and large dark eyes. She was elegantly dressed in a maroon silk blouse and a full black and white skirt. Her arms were bare and suntanned.

She gave a fleeting smile.

"Listen," she said. "When you die and go to Heaven, you will see Our Lady, too."

It was as if she had spoken to a child.

"Can I come in?" I asked.

She hesitated a moment.

Then she opened the screen door wide and let me through.

The hallway led into a sitting room with a dining area. The drapes were drawn. Two walls were covered with mirrors. On the other walls were some icons, copies of Eastern originals.

In the center of the room was a low coffee table on a faded

rug, faced by two white sofas covered in see-through plastic; she invited me to sit down and then sat down herself opposite me, resting her hands in her lap.

"How long have you lived in New York?" I asked her.

She told me that she had come to America at age sixteen. She was now thirty-eight. She had left Garabandal to escape an impossible dilemma.

"In Garabandal," she said, "nobody cared about me for my own sake. They worshiped me because of the visions. I realized that nobody would ever love me or marry me who knew about the visions."

"For a time," I said, "you dismissed your visions. Why did you do that?"

"I went to the Bishop of Santander, and after he had questioned me for hours on end I told him that I didn't believe in them anymore. He gave me absolution and forbade me ever to talk of them again. Then when I got back to Garabandal I felt that I had betrayed the Blessed Mother. I believed in the visions, and yet I couldn't understand how they had occurred. I was torn in two."

"So you came to New York?"

"I worked for a Spanish doctor in the city, and for a year I never spoke to anybody. He wanted to marry me; there were other people who wanted me to marry him. In the end I married someone else."

"Conchita," I said, "are you still expecting the warning, the *aviso* and the great miracle?"

"I'm not sure about anything anymore. I haven't even seen Joey for a long time now ..."

"Are you saying you don't believe in your visions?"

"Everything is against Garabandal," she said. "The bishops, the Church, all sorts of people abuse me. They tell me I'm a liar and a fake."

"So now you think that you were mistaken about your visions?"

"What I am telling you," she said firmly, "is that I saw a beautiful lady who told me she was the Blessed Mother. I saw her almost every day for four years. If this turns out to be false, then *nothing* is true. Do you understand what I'm saying? I mean that nothing whatsoever is true."

Her face was sad. She fiddled with her rings.

"What makes you feel like this, Conchita?" I said.

She bit her lip and looked at me with angry eyes.

"How could the Blessed Mother come to me ... give me all these signs and messages, and then abandon me? How can anything be true?"

She was looking at me challengingly, as if *I* could supply the answer. It was as if she were inviting me to offer her some sort of spiritual consolation to bolster her wavering faith.

"Do you ever wonder, Conchita," I said, "whether you might not have been suffering delusions at the time?"

"We were tested by lots of psychiatrists and psychologists. They said we weren't sick or crazy, or anything like that. I've never had any illness since ... Anyway if that was being crazy, I like to be crazy like that." As she said this she managed a bleak smile.

"Conchita, would you mind my asking you a specific question?" I said. "I've spoken to the old Guardia Civil, Brigadier Seco, in Garabandal, and he remembers you levitating in the kitchen of your house. Were you aware of doing that? Can you confirm that?"

"Look," she said, "when the Blessed Mother came she always appeared out of a bright light; I just wasn't aware of anything else, or anybody else outside of the light. And I wasn't aware of the way I was behaving."

"You know the date of the miracle, Conchita; and eight days before it you are going to travel to Garabandal?"

"That's right," she said, with apparent reluctance.

"What will you do if the miracle doesn't happen?"

She sat in silence for a while, wringing her hands.

Then she said: "That's what I'm telling you, mister. If the miracle doesn't come, then *nothing* is true. What more can I say?"

She hung her head miserably for a while.

"Sometimes," she said, "I wish I'd never have to hear the word Garabandal again.... I'm sorry!"

She stood up. "Look, you'll have to go now," she said.

As she went ahead of me to the door, she stopped and turned to me.

"Would you mind doing something for me?"

"Of course, Conchita."

"Would you pray for me, please?"

The phenomenon of Garabandal had struck me as a dramatic religious mystery, rooted in local folk religion, unlike Medjugorje, which had become trivialized by its extensive promotion by the media. Yet in the view of Catholic officialdom the cult of Garabandal had been an eccentric weed in the flower garden of approved mysticism.

Conchita's temporary denial of her visions before the Bishop of Santander, her sudden lapse of memory when it came to divulging the prophetic secrets, and her later decision to marry rather than enter a convent had put her beyond the ecclesiastical pale. In common with similar phenomena through the centuries, and with Marija of Medjugorje, her visions had outflanked the role of the male-dominated clergy in a peasant region where women were traditionally disadvantaged and disenfranchised. A seer, a prophetess, and a priestess, she shaped and controlled her own liturgy and became the focus of strong religious experience unmediated by the clergy. But she had broken the expected pattern of final submission to the clergy by failing to take the veil and disappear into a convent.

Two of the girl seers had now married at Medjugorje, and I found it significant that Father Svet had accordingly criticized them for failing the challenge of their visions. The failure, ironically, had been to submit themselves to the Franciscans and the discipline of the religious life. Now the promoters were evidently pinning all their hopes on Marija entering a convent, as if this were the final hurdle before official acceptance of the cult could take place.

As it was, Conchita had exiled herself both from the protective custody of the Church and from her country. She had traveled to America, where she knew no one except Joey Lomangino, to escape notoriety in the vast anonymity of New York. Yet as long as she lived she would never escape the burden of her visions nor the implications of having involved herself in the promise of a great visible sign.

I found it moving that she had fled Garabandal and rejected the role of idolized *spirituelle* precisely because she wanted to be loved not for her visions but for her own sake. It argued considerable strength of character that she had been determined to define herself according to her human relationships rather than through the shadows of pietistic adulation.

Entering a convent, of course, would have been no guarantee of psychological and spiritual security. One hundred fifty years earlier, the seer Melanie Mathieu of Salette in Alpine France, had taken the veil, but she ended her life as an alcoholic, wandering from convent to convent throughout France and England.

Yet it seemed to me that Conchita was suffering from both rejection and a lack of comprehension of her experiences. Her predicament underlined the absence in the Church of a coherent theory for popular forms of mystical phenomena.

What was the status of Conchita's visions?

I do not believe that Conchita was sick, nor do I believe that she was a liar. Her ecstasies, like those of the leading seers at Medjugorje, struck me as something primitive, sacred, and real. But did the strange physical feats by themselves indicate the involvement of an alternative supra-natural world? In the absence of incontrovertible evidence under proper test conditions, I was not inclined to entertain the idea. In any case, the question seemed to be missing the main point. The visions, the strange physical feats, were a group experience intended to be observed by the local community in much the same way as an audience witnesses a play, or a congregation the liturgy. Hysteria might well have been involved and some form of kinetic force as yet poorly understood, but the phenomena taken as a whole seemed analogous to an art form, displaying special aptitude, inspiration, dance, and choreography, the exercise of imagination and deep emotion.

The physical feats, the strange backward marches, the apparent levitations lent legitimacy to the central contention that the girls were aware of a sacred, immensely powerful, yet benign presence in their midst. The phenomena needed to be *read*. The "magic flights," the pine trees, the promise of the great miracle sign created a sense of unique focus. It told the participants and spectators that Garabandal could become the center of the universe, a place where a higher power had chosen to make its sacred presence felt among humankind.

The imponderable question was the extent to which the folk religion of the region, the prevailing established religion of Spain, brought this "sacred presence" into the scope of official religious belief and iconography. How much collusion had taken place between Conchita and the women of the village before the precise identities of the apparitions had been announced? In the case of Lourdes the apparition was referred to in dialect by Bernadette as *acquerro,* "that thing," until after extensive conversations had taken place with the pious ladies of the locality.

These thoughts of mine after leaving Conchita by no means indicated a skeptical attitude toward the Christian content of the phenomena. I saw no necessary contradiction between a primitive awareness of sacred presence and a Christian's notion of God's, or Mary's, real presence. Might they not converge toward the same point?

The important question for Conchita, however, was this: what happened when these two notions of transcendent presence and power found themselves in conflict as a result of the dogmatic strictures of Church officialdom?

For Conchita it had resulted in a life of inner torment. A naturally devout person, with an outstanding loyalty to her faith, she was now riven with doubt to the point of speculating whether her private revelations should become a test of her wider sense of faith. Her predicament illustrated the insidious potential of paranormal religious experience.

As it is, Conchita still awaits the warning, the miracle, and possible chastisement. And if, as I now believe she suspects will happen, the warning and miracle fail to materialize, she will not only become a laughing stock but risk losing both her faith in her visions as well as her faith in God.

And yet, something continued to nag me. How special, how unique was the Marian visionary experience? And to what extent was it exclusive to a particular culture and religion?

14

White Ladies

Ihad been spending many
hours in the New York Public Library, which was just a short walk
from my hotel. Browsing through a stack of psychology publications,
I found what I had been seeking for days: confirmation that apparitions of "beautiful ladies" bathed in white light were by no means
the preserve of Christian visions, even in the West.

And there it was before me on the page.

In 1954 the popular Swiss fortnightly newspaper, the *Schweiz-
erischer Beobachter,* had conducted a questionnaire among its readers about paranormal experiences. Some 1,500 responses had come
in and the material had been passed to Aniele Jaffe, the Swiss psychologist and associate of Carl Jung.

Encouraged by a New York psychologist, Martin Ebon, she had
written a paper (published in Dallas in 1978) that established the
leading categories of the experiences. One of her categories was
entitled "Apparitions of the 'Woman in White.' "

Without giving precise numbers, Dr. Jaffe reported that a significant number of correspondents had witnessed the apparition of
a beautiful lady in white light who conveyed a warning of danger.
Invariably the visionaries were girls and boys, and there had been
no specifically religious context attached to the experience.

Among the samples she quotes are the following:

A man wrote that in his boyhood he and a brother awoke to

their father's calls. They went out onto the verandah and in the light of a full moon saw leaning against an apple tree "a woman in white with her hair hanging down in plaits." They jumped down into the orchard and ran toward her. When the correspondent was a few feet away from the apparition he asked what she was doing there. She stared back in silence. "Two dark eyes were fixed on me, imploring me, with sadness and reproach, not to disturb her," he wrote.

He tried to grab hold of her, but his hand remained empty.

With a gentle, apologetic smile she glided away. They ran after her. "Then the miracle happened. As if borne by an unseen power, she glided swiftly away from us, and the next moment had vanished."

In another submission a woman wrote that in her childhood she once went to meet her mother who was returning from work. At a lonely spot on the road she saw a "beautiful lady" before her, "not very tall and snow-white." The apparition was wearing a long dress and veil and had floated along a little way behind her, hovering just above the ground. The girl had stopped again and again to look back at the "wonderful figure."

When her mother approached, the apparition disappeared.

Another woman recollected that once, as a child, she awoke during the night plagued with thirst. She called out for a glass of water and waited for her mother to come, raising herself in the bed in anticipation. At that moment a figure of a woman appeared at the bedroom door. "It was a completely strange figure, a woman, tall, beautiful, in a flowing white robe, with long black curls hanging down." The apparition approached the bed and stood for several seconds gazing at her before returning slowly to the door. At that moment her mother appeared with a glass of water. "I saw the two figures quite distinctly side by side—my tall mother looked small beside the apparition—then suddenly it vanished as if dissolved in air."

Another woman wrote that when she was about ten she was walking with her mother on a lonely footpath next to a wood when they had seen a woman "dressed all in white walking slowly along." As they gazed at the figure, it suddenly vanished.

In her analysis Dr. Jaffe attempts to relate these contemporary experiences with a wide range of parallels in what she calls the "old texts," and notably the *femina alba*—Venus, or Aphrodite, the Goddess of Love. Why though, she asks, does the White Lady so often seem a harbinger of misfortune?

Her suggestion is typically Jungian: "If we are to understand such a strange contradiction," she writes, "we must bear in mind that, as long as they are unconscious, all archetypal contents are twofold and ambiguous. In the unconscious the opposites are not yet separated; an unconscious content becomes conscious only through discrimination of its latent opposites. When the two sides stand face to face they can be comprehended and the conscious mind can grasp them."

Aphrodite, Jaffe points out, is not only the goddess of love; she is also the queen of the underworld or of death. In Germanic mythology, moreover, the corresponding goddess is Frigg or Freya, who is both radiant goddess of love and the goddess of the dead known as Hel.

In an alternative pantheon, Jaffe goes on, there is a still more powerful manifestation known as Erda or Hertha encompassing both the great powers of light and darkness. "This goddess of earth, or the archetypal figure of the 'Great Mother,' " she says, "has to be understood as a personification of the unconscious. The unconscious is the maternal, instinctive foundation of man as a living creature, it is the 'mother' of his mind and consciousness as well."

While her interpretation struck me as rather woolly, the ambivalence of the archetypal figure suggested a great many echoes, from Isis through to Keats's "La Belle Dame Sans Merci," the loving harbinger of his own fatal disease.

And the less clinical, more poetic approach, it struck me, found echoes in the rich materials gathered by Robert Graves in his *White Goddess*.

Graves points out that in medieval Irish literature the Virgin Mary is identified with Brigit the goddess of poetry and Brigit the patron of healing. Brigit is also known as the White Swan, as the bride of the White Hills, and as Bride of the Golden Hair. Brigit, or Mary, has a variety of mythic prototypes, he claims: in the Aegean she is Brizo of Delos, a moon goddess, and she was associated in Britain and Gaul in Roman times with healing incantations at sacred wells.

Jaffe remarks in conclusion that the White Lady appears invariably to girls at the point when they are becoming conscious of their femininity. The female principle, says Jaffe, is their future fate, and the divine or mysterious phantom is like an intimation of what they have yet to become. This does not imply, however, that the child has grasped its meaning. "Nature is lavish and reveals herself to the blind as well as to the seeing eye ... Nature, or the unconscious, presents itself, and leaves it to consciousness, to ask questions or seek for a meaning."

Like dreams? Like poetry and mythology? Like theater?

Jaffe comments that visions of the White Lady are frequently encountered more than once by the seer. And she suggests that questions raised by such impressive dreams or childhood experiences are only asked later, in adult life.

Throughout the discussion she is not in the least concerned with the *reality* of the phenomenon: that is, with *accounting* for the apparition in terms of imagination, dream, or hallucination. She is more interested in the timeless, "archetypal" constants.

But what was one to make of this evidence in relation to the seers of Medjugorje and Garabandal, or any of the other 230 recorded series of major sightings of the Virgin Mary throughout the twentieth century?

Jaffe's material, it occurred to me, complemented the fascinating work done by the social scientist Michael Carrol at the University of London, Ontario, published by Princeton University at the time of my visit to New York. Carrol had put the details of many hundreds of apparitions of the Virgin into his computer in order to discover an empirical pattern. Among the most constant features were these:

- The Virgin appears to girls at about puberty.
- The favored seer usually colludes with the local community before announcing the Virgin's identity.
- The seers are normally working children, who are out looking for lost cattle or sheep at the time of the first phenomenon, which usually occurs as a light.
- The seer has lost a mother, or a mother figure (with Bernadette of Lourdes it was her elder sister), in the previous *eight* weeks. As exact as that!
- The Virgin imparts secrets and warnings of doom if certain religious formulas are not adhered to.

There was clearly an interesting overlap between Jaffe's and Carrol's work; yet did this indicate a conclusion altogether inimical to religious faith?

It seemed to me that the White Lady phenomenon might even add depth to the significance of Marian apparitions provided one was not looking for specific and literal quantities and values. At the heart of the experience was the impression of encounter with a supernatural presence that was not so much the procuring of a state of feeling, or the apprehension of an object (such as might be acquired by drugs, or techniques of meditation), as a meeting of two presences, the supernatural personality having *chosen* to manifest itself, or herself, to the mortal.

The paradigm of gift and response in the suggested relationship between a human being and an awareness of a sacred presence seemed to me far more potent than a highly specific and literalist approach, which asks questions such as How was she dressed? Was she three-dimensional? What specific instructions did she give? What is the precise date of the chastisement? And so forth. How much are *these* sorts of questions, in any case, the result of collusion with those eager for precise eschatological answers?

The mysterious, poetical context, suggested in particular by Garabandal (and, by inference, Medjugorje) did not preclude a spiritual, a Christian interpetation.

On the other hand, I was finding it increasingly difficult to fit Conchita into a clinical or pathological pattern. A recent psychiatric study has attempted to link the incidence of hallucinatory experiences in non-psychotic children with specific mood problems and family circumstances. In the study, published by the Academy of Child and Adolescent Psychiatry in 1987, psychiatrists at the Royal Ottawa Hospital assessed eleven children who had experienced spontaneous hallucinations without any evident signs of mental illness. In ten of the cases the content of the hallucinations was frightening or threatening and involved male or "monstrous" figments of presences. In only one case was there a female presence, described as a "white woman," who urged the child to do "good things." According to the authors, "most children presented mood disturbance, mainly anxiety . . . the children were socially inept or withdrawn."

The picture of typical "mood disturbance" and social ineptness observed in the Ottawa study clearly has no bearing, as far as I could ascertain, on Conchita's personality and circumstances, and from this point of view a psychiatric, a clinical diagnosis or "solution" seems unhelpful.

If, however the miracle does not come to pass (on the date only she knows), I suspect that this will weaken Conchita's sense of the *literal* nature of her vision's messages without undermining her conviction about its reality. It seems a pity, though, that her Church cannot offer pastoral and psychological advice in advance and eliminate a further possibility: that she may come to identify her visions with the "powers of darkness."

Reflecting once more on my conversation with Conchita, her diary, and the village testimonies, I realized that her story conveyed, above all, a conviction that she had encountered the real presence of a beautiful lady. The reality of her experience, the reality of the relationship, was impervious to any sort of rationalization or contradiction.

Conchita had been able to identify her vision with the Blessed Virgin Mary without doing violence to the reality of the encounter. She was not, however, prepared to sacrifice her vision in the interests of Church doctrine and discipline when it attempted to contradict the reality of her experience.

Even if the Church, even if the pope himself, were to tell her that the Virgin Mary had not appeared to her, even if she were to be betrayed by the non-fulfillment of the secrets, she would continue to believe in the reality of her beautiful lady. This suggested to me an impression of presence more profound and striking than anything encountered in neurotic states, or, indeed, in normal religious conviction. Perhaps this gave new meaning to the Jungian term "archetype" and the significance of a primitive religious experience. Perhaps it was a clue to the powers of religious imagination, little acknowledged and seldom understood.

PART FOUR

WOUNDS AND HEALING

15

Briege's Gift

Toward the end of my stay in New York I came in from the library one evening to find a phone message to call Sister Briege McKenna at a Long Island number.

When I got through to her I was reassured to learn that she had not been indulging in ESP. Father Foley, with whom I had been in contact, had told her of my whereabouts when he had discovered that she was coming through New York.

"I wanted to ask how your work is getting on," she said cheerily. "You've been in my thoughts and prayers. . . . Come and have lunch tomorrow."

She gave directions and hung up.

So I found myself the next day riding the Long Island Railroad to Manhasset. Passing through the pleasant wooded suburbs, I thought of Thomas Merton, the Trappist monk and writer, who had described this journey in his autobiography *The Seven Storied Mountain*. He had been riding this very train on the afternoon war was declared in Europe and had come up with the extraordinary thought that one mortal sin might have been responsible for the outbreak of World War Two.

At the station a man was waiting for me. He held up a card with my name on it.

We drove in silence along Shelter Rock Road and eventually

141

turned off and through a gateway where two men scrutinized me and waved at the driver. There was a track through thick woods of beech and maple, then another gate with more guards. At length a vast and rambling country mansion came into view with half-a-dozen Labrador dogs lounging around on the terrace.

I gasped. What sort of convent was this?

The driver heard me. "This," he said with evident pride, "is the home of Mr. and Mrs. Peter Grace."

I knew only one thing about Mr. Peter Grace: he was one of the richest men in America.

At the front door I was greeted by a secretary, who ushered me into an elegant drawing room. Sister Briege would be down directly, she said.

Suddenly a figure swept through a doorway, a youngish-looking woman in a silk turquoise dress and white high-heeled shoes. Her hair was well coiffed and she was wearing a string of pearls. She was laughing pleasantly as she came toward me.

It was Sister Briege McKenna.

"Don't worry about this," she said, patting her hair, "I'm on my holidays. How are you, John?" With this she gave me a hug and a kiss on the cheek. With her freckles and friendly grin, she looked like a mischievous urchin who had been playing dress-up.

She led me through to another drawing room full of Victorian furniture and family portraits and sat me down on a sofa. There she explained that her work had been sponsored by the Grace Foundation so as to relieve the burden on Third World missions that were keen for her ministry.

"I come here for a few days every year to unwind," she said. "Now, John, I just wanted to check up on you, to see how you are. We've a few minutes before we go in to lunch. Is there anything you'd like to talk to me about? How is the miracle hunt?"

I was speechless.

She touched me on the arm and laughed teasingly, and I realized at that moment that I felt attracted to her more than was good for me, and despite my better judgment.

I noticed that she had been holding her right hand clenched all this time, and slightly extended toward me. She now opened it to reveal a small black Celtic cross with a thin leather string to go around the neck.

"I want to give this to you," she said. "It's made of compressed

Irish peat." Next she stood up and came around behind me. Before I could protest she had placed the cross on my chest and put the loop over my head.

"There. Put it inside your shirt."

As I did so the cross felt uncomfortably cold next to my skin. I felt embarrassed, imposed upon, and it must have shown in my face.

Briege looked at me for a moment, then laughed happily and tapped me on the cheek with two fingers. The blow was strong enough to hurt a little. She was looking directly at me, and her eyes were filled with tenderness. I felt as if I had known and loved her all my life.

She sat down again and took my hands in hers. She had guessed that I was upset.

"Take it off later," she said, "it's not important to wear it ... but keep it. You might want it one day."

Then she said with feeling: "I *love* you, John. I *really* love you ..." She was looking into my eyes with an amused and quizzical expression.

With this she took me in her arms and kissed me on the forehead and on the cheek.

As we went in to lunch I was conscious that my face was burning.

Before I left for the station to return to New York, Sister Briege gave me a picture of the alleged face of Christ on the Turin Shroud; there was an address on the back.

"Here's another little present for you," she said. "There's a convent in the Bronx where some Carmelite nuns claim some extraordinary occurrences. I wonder what you'll make of it. Tell them I told you to call."

As I got into the car, she told me: "I've a feeling we'll see each other again before too long."

She stood at the doorway waving. As soon as she was out of sight, I took the crucifix from around my neck and put it in my pocket. And I looked at the "face" of Christ. It conveyed an impression of deep sadness and resignation. I put it in my wallet, amid my plastic credit cards.

When I called the Convent of St. Joseph on the telephone, a woman's voice said: "Praised be to Christ!"

Sister Mari sounded dubious about receiving me, but she relented when I mentioned Sister Briege's name.

I was driven from midtown Manhattan by a Bengali cabdriver who got hopelessly lost for one and a half hours. When we finally arrived at our destination in one of the poorest parts of the Bronx, I wondered whether I had made a mistake about the address. I had been expecting a Gothic building with a chapel. The driver left me outside a dingy apartment building.

A young man opened the door and directed me up a stairway smelling of cabbage to the apartment above. At the top was a statue of Saint Michael the Archangel, trusty champion against the snares of the devil. I was surveyed through a grille by a pair of eyes, then a door opened and a nun greeted me. She was small and rounded with a bright red face and was dressed in the full habit of the Carmelite order: brown robe with a scapular back and front, a white wimple, and black veil. This was Sister Mari; another nun, tall, stooped, and pale, stood beyond her: she was introduced as Sister Gertrude.

The nuns' habits were so voluminous that they could hardly move in the narrow confines of the apartment. The floors were covered in linoleum and the walls painted an institutional green. The place was spotlessly clean but smelled of damp.

Sister Mari invited me to sit down in a sort of kitchen area comprising a sink and a gas cooker, but it was merely part of a corridor. She pointed to a glass door beyond which I imagined there might once have been a proper kitchen or bathroom.

"That's our chapel," she whispered. "We have perpetual adoration of the real presence. We maintain silence within the convent, it's our rule; but I can talk in special circumstances."

The rest of our conversation was continued in a stage whisper as if this somehow mitigated the breaking of the vow of silence.

Sister Mari told me that she was the superior of this convent, which numbered just three nuns. For ten years they had been running an experiment in conventual living in inner-city areas.

"We were part of a regular convent in upstate New York, but we're bringing the contemplative life into the heart of the city," she said.

They had no money or back-up resources. Neither did they beg. They waited for gifts of food and donations. Whenever they had an excess beyond their needs for a day or two, they gave it away. They fasted regularly and they were vegetarians. They believed in the power of prayer and encouraged local people to come and join them in silent contemplation and adoration.

"We make ourselves free to pray for those who cannot pray for themselves," she said.

All this was said with a directness and simplicity that belied any sense of spiritual pride or sanctimoniousness.

Their lives were not without anxiety. Several times they had been turned out of their rented apartments. "This usually happens," she said, "after we have cleaned and renovated the place. The landlord then sees that we have made it more commercially valuable and puts up the rent."

Then she told me how the miracles began.

On the previous Christmas the nuns had entered the chapel for the third Mass of Christmas day and had noticed that something strange had happened to the child Jesus in the crib. On both sides of the hand of the twelve-inch-high wax statue had appeared the likeness of a wound. Then, on the feast of the Holy Innocents the statue had shed tears on two different occasions. Still during the Christmas period, on the eighth day of the feast, the left foot had began to swell. Gradually, another wound had shown itself and a red substance looking like blood had flowed from it.

"It took some time before we realized that this was the sign of the stigmata," said Sister Mari. "We had to mop up the substance with a napkin."

"What was your first reaction?" I asked.

"We were cautious," she replied. "But it's difficult to know how it might have happened naturally. Nobody has access to the chapel except us. We know each other well, and it's inconceivable that any of us would have engaged in a deceit. And what would be our motive? We don't look for miracles. We're not mystics; our spiritual life is based on faith and prayer."

"What happened next?"

"Six months later, on the feast of Corpus Christi and the Precious Blood, the two feasts are now combined, we noticed that the host which was being used for the exposition was oozing red drops; in a matter of hours it had darkened in just the way that blood is affected by contact with the air."

The nun now took me through into the chapel where there was barely enough room for more than eight people standing. It was simple, austere.

She opened the tabernacle behind the altar, genuflected and opened the door with a tasseled key. There, on a gold mount, was the subject of the claimed miracle, a circular wafer of unleavened bread, about an inch in diameter. Most of the surface of the wafer was a dark brown color, exactly that of a bandage which had been stained with blood for a day or so before.

I asked Sister Mari if I could take a photograph, but she signaled that this was not allowed.

Next she took me into a small room, no more than a cubicle, which served as a vestry or sacristy. There, on a chest of drawers, was the effigy of the child Jesus in its crib. The brown stains were still clearly visible on one palm and one foot.

"Has the substance been analyzed, both from the host and the effigy?" I asked.

"A bishop came, and several scientists; everything has been taken to Rome. They say the liquid isn't blood, but a mystery substance they cannot identify. It could be years before anything is decided."

We fell silent for a moment. I was wondering whether the nun would offer me a cup of tea or coffee.

Then she said: "Excuse me, sir, but if that is all—we have a life of prayer to get on with."

I felt suitably rebuked. I had somehow assumed that these nuns, with their prayer life, were nevertheless ladies of endless leisure.

"One more question, Sister," I asked. "Why do *you* think that this miracle happened here in this little community in the Bronx?"

"I've no doubt whatsoever why it happened," she answered promptly. She fixed me with a look of complete frankness.

"A few days before the phenomenon somebody had placed a human fetus in our garbage and we found it. We saw in that dead little creature the image of the crucified Christ. Somehow the effigy with its stigmata was pleading for that link to be made more firmly, perhaps, and for prayers of reparation to be said . . ."

"So. It's a sort of political statement," I said.

"I don't know about politics, Mr. Cornwell," she stated. "I see only the facts. There are five million unborn children aborted every year in the United States. That's the equivalent of the Jewish holocaust once a year in this society."

"Nevertheless," I went on. "The occurrence of a miracle here lends support to the antiabortion lobby."

The nun smiled wanly. "I don't know ... We've made no attempts to publicize it. We simply observed it and reported it to the bishop. You are the first writer to come here and observe the phenomenon. We didn't ask you to come."

The nun's coolness impressed me. I wondered, though, whether she was aware of the precedents of Eucharistic Miracles and whipped and bleeding statues which had been prolific during the Middle Ages and which had widely supported the grotesque blood libels against the Jews—reports that Jews routinely desecrated the sacred host and crucifixes and shed the blood of Christian babies for sacrifices.

As she was walking me to the door of the apartment I asked her whether she had studied in a university.

"I was at Fordham in New York and was a postgraduate student at Freiburg University in Germany. I took a doctorate in mystical theology."

As I descended the staircase with its atmosphere of boiled cabbage I decided that Sister Mari was probably better aware of the precedents than I.

I took the subway back to Manhattan, all the way mulling over the strange experience of the afternoon. I could not discount the notion that the stains on the wafer had been caused by a species of mold. And yet, that would not have accounted for the prior phenomenon of the stigmata on the effigy.

The simplest explanation, then, was fraud. And yet, why should they do this, and keep quiet about it? Surely, the only motive for perpetrating a hoax would have been to create publicity for themselves. I was thinking of a case in the town of Entrevaux in France in the 1950s, when blood appeared on a broken finger of the statue of the Virgin in the church; it was tested and found to be human blood. After two million pilgrims flocked there, and many miracles had been reported, a local man confessed that he had devised the "miracle" in order to put the church "on the map."

In another case in my files, a man in Stockport, England, had recently confessed to having pulled off a holy hoax forty years earlier involving flowers. In 1947 the roses before the statue of the Madonna failed to fade or shed their petals during a period of three years. The man admitted that the miracle of the "eternal roses," which drew hundreds of thousands of pilgrims from all over England, had been a trick devised by the parish priest and a local florist.

It seemed to me that the Eucharistic Miracle of the Bronx had the unmistakable characteristics of a hoax, and yet I found it difficult to believe that the nuns themselves would have perpetrated it.

There was an element of mystery, then, closer to Agatha Christie than to genuine mysticism. But what did it matter? The prayer lives of these heroic women, who had chosen to accept all the drawbacks of the religious life with none of its consolations, would impress me for a lot longer than their "miracle."

Back in midtown Manhattan I went into a shop that sold religious publications and found on the shelves a book containing some thirty accounts of Eucharistic Miracles spanning the eighth to the twentieth centuries. It had been published in Rockford, Illinois, in 1987, with the imprimatur of the Archbishop of New Orleans, Philip M. Hannan.

I bought it and took it off to read over dinner.

The majority of the accounts occurred in Italy, Spain, and France. Most involved priests who had suffered doubt and whose faith had been restored by the miracle of a bleeding or fleshly host. There were other sorts of accounts, such as those of Saracens, French revolutionaries, and Republicans in the Spanish Civil War whose attempted depredations of tabernacles had been foiled by dramatic prodigies of flying and disappearing hosts. And there were instances in which a miracle had occurred to expose the use of the consecrated host in acts of sorcery. Like the woman of Altari in Italy, who had removed the Eucharist from her tongue, and then later returned it to her mouth again in order to captivate a young man in a kiss. Or the housewife of Santarem in Portugal who stole and ground down a host to make a love potion to win back her philandering husband.

Sacrilege had been revealed by the appearance of a telltale sign: the host would "bleed," or go dark brown. But how often, I wondered, did the discovery of a molding host lead to the search for a fantastic cause?

Then, to my dismay, I came across a type of eucharistic tale that I had hoped had been long expunged in modern hagiographical collections. But here it was, written up in this recently published paperback: a repetition of the Jewish blood libel.

The story was entitled "The Miracle of Brussels," and I recount it here in outline, as it reveals that dark face of the "miraculous" that once raged through Christian Europe and clearly still smolders in contemporary pietistic literature.

A Jewish resident of Enghien named "Jonathan," the tale goes, purchased from a Christian some sixteen consecrated hosts for sixty-two gold coins. The hosts eventually ended up in the synagogue in Brussels, on April 4, 1370. "After laying the sacred hosts out on a table," the author continues, "they inflicted upon them both verbal and physical abuse. At some point during the sacrilege, knives were drawn and the hosts were stabbed."

Then the miracle happened. Before the "stunned" eyes of the Jews, blood gushed from the stab wounds. Terror-stricken, the perpetrators fell to the ground.

According to the legend, an accomplice of the thief reported the crime to the curate of the local bishop and the Jews were rounded up and imprisoned. The modern author tells us that there are alternative endings to this story: in one version, they are banished from Belgium by the Jewish community; in the other, they confess their crime and are all burned at the stake.

Commenting on the guide book to St. Michael's Cathedral, where the remnants of the hosts are kept to this day, and where the story is depicted in stained glass, the author refers, with complacent naiveté, to "a very surprising notice" that reads:

"On December 30, 1968, the diocesan authorities of Maline-Brussels Archdiocese declared the charges of theft and sacrilege of the Blessed Sacrament in 1369–1370 which were brought against the Jewish community of Brussels were unfounded."

The author is clearly irritated by the disclaimer and assures the reader that "tourists and the faithful of Brussels still honor the miracle by visiting the chapel where the miraculous Hosts were kept."

Pondering this story, and the scholarly explication of the Jewish blood libel myth by historians such as Po-chia Hsia and Norman Cohn, it struck me that there was a deep irony in the survival of this powerful relic of suffering. At a deeper, more primitive level, it was a commemoration of the prejudice against the Jews as Christ killers not only as they are remembered in Christian scripture and passion plays such as Oberammergau, but in those vicious eras when they were tortured and murdered in the name of Eucharistic Miracles. The Eucharistic Miracle of Brussels is surely a relic of astounding irony for it perpetuates unwittingly the agony of innocent medieval Jews who might otherwise have been forgotten.

The Eucharistic Miracle of the Bronx reminded me that supernatural phenomena in the Western Christian tradition tend to alternate between Marian "presences," on the one hand, and the stark images of Christ's blood and wounds on the other. Marian apparitions were recently depicted by Pope John Paul II (in his encyclical *Mater Redemptoris,* 1987) as signifying the Virgin's journey through time and space on a pilgrimage toward the Second Coming and the final victory over Satan. Her appearances in different locations, moreover, can be explained in the light of popular folk religion in a tradition that goes back to pre-Christian times in Mediterranean communities, but the Church amplifies these specific occurrences so as to fit them into a pattern that coincides with universal doctrine: Mary is the Second Eve, the woman who cooperated in our redemption by becoming the Mother of God. She is the Immaculate Conception, the Mediatrix of all graces, and she has a major apocalyptic role yet to come: to foil Satan in the last days of the world.

Like the rosary itself, which exemplifies the story of Mary's joyful, and sorrowful, journey on earth as well as her glorious status as Queen of Heaven, there are periodic pauses in which the devotee dwells on Christ and particularly his passion and death. Physically this is illustrated by the dominant image of the crucifix which hangs from every set of rosary beads. The emphasis on Mary as a regular heavenly visitor, rather than Christ, is possibly explained by the dominance of the divine, male "real" presence in the Eucharist. Mary thus provides the female, motherly presence, not only available in apparitions but in countless effigies which are often endowed with supernatural attributes.

Paranormal manifestations of Christ, as opposed to Mary, invariably emphasize suffering, pain, sacrifice, wounds, blood, the cross and the instruments of Christ's passion, the veil of Veronica, and the holy shroud.

If Mary exemplifies a preoccupation with birth, gentleness, motherhood, mediation, and bereavement; then Christ-centered iconography emphasizes death, violence, sacrifice, blood, and instruments of torture. The contrasting figures of Mary and Christ are perhaps best strikingly illustrated by the depiction of the Virgin suckling Saint Bernard at her breast while Christ inflicts the stigmata on Saint Francis of Assisi.

In the varied storehouse of Catholic tradition there are countless instances of the physical manifestations of Christ's passion on favored persons. One sixteenth-century example involves the Blessed Clare of the Cross. After her death the sisters opened her heart with a razor and found, fashioned out of muscle and tissue, not only the image of the Cross, but representations of "the Whip, or Scourge with which Christ was beaten ... the Pillar, the Crown of Thorns, the Nails, the Spear and the Pole with the Sponge ..."

But the most dramatic and consistent physical manifestation of the passion of Christ since early medieval times is clearly the phenomenon of the stigmata, in which Christ's wounds appear in vivid form on the appropriate part of the hands, feet, and side of a "servant of God."

The very first recorded "authentic" instance of stigmatization is believed to be that of Saint Francis of Assisi in September 1224. Thurston, however, cites the curious story of an Englishman who in 1222 allowed himself to be crucified and thus bore the wounds of Christ by "artificial" means. The unfortunate fellow was either imprisoned at Banbury or burned to death, possibly both, his self-crucifixion being judged a blasphemy. (In a more recent case, in which two laborers crucified a man on Hampstead Heath in London, it was the crucifiers who were charged, and fined, even though their victim admitted that he had requested the treatment.)

Imbert-Goubert, author of *La Stigmatisation* (1894), reckoned that of the 300 and more stigmatics (deemed authentic or otherwise), 280 were female and only 41 were male.

Italy has been most favored with stigmatics, but the phenomenon has also occurred in France, Spain, the Netherlands, and the United States. At the time of writing current cases involve an Australian (a nurse who believed that she was in need of expiation) and an Anglican Englishwoman in Derbyshire, the wife of a bus driver.

A typical stigmatic, according to clinical descriptions, is a single woman, invariably a Catholic and a member of a religious order, who shows an excess of religious fervor in youth, including self-denial and penance. Before the onset of symptoms she will have suffered prolonged physical and psychological illness necessitating invalid status and long periods of confinement to bed. In nearly all cases the stigmatic will have experienced trances, visions, raptures, and intense contemplation of the crucified Christ. The stigmatization invariably involves great pain at the site of the wounds.

I was very keen indeed to meet a "genuine" case.

16

The Stigmatic of Montreal

I had asked my guide, Father Foley, if he knew of a current stigmatic and he readily recommended a seventy-four-year-old woman in Montreal called Georgette Fanielle, who, he said, was probably the most authentic living example in the world today. On the way back to Europe I took a side trip to Canada to meet her.

It was arranged that I should go straight from the airport to the headquarters of the Society of the Holy Apostles near the Olympic stadium where I was to meet my contact.

It was an imposing, brick house next to a concrete church. As I rang the bell the door opened immediately to reveal the astonishing spectacle of identical middle-aged twins; the fact that they were both priests made the phenomenon all the more strange. The brothers were Father Guy and Father Armand Girard, one Georgette's spiritual director, the other her spiritual adviser. They were dressed in pale blue clerical shirts with Roman collars and identical gray pants, moccasin shoes, and eyeglasses. They had open, grinning, childlike faces and wore their hair in straight fringes monk-style.

Father Guy was deputed to take me in his car to Georgette's home. On the way he filled me in on her story.

Georgette was the daughter of a modest painter of religious murals. At the age of six she began to experience inner locutions,

153

voices that "resounded in the depths of her heart." She believed that Christ and Mary spoke to her. Often she heard the voice of Satan, too, telling her that she was deluded and damned. Eventually her most constant voice was to be that of the "Eternal Father," the first person of the Holy Trinity.

Trained to be a pianist as a girl, she practiced at home on a cardboard keyboard, because her family did not possess a piano. Nevertheless, she took the gold medal in her final year at the Montreal conservatory. But at the age of twenty she fell ill with inexplicable paralysis and pain. She became a chronic invalid. Her suspected illnesses were legion, from cancer to rare forms of bone disease; the doctors never reached a definitive diagnosis. For the next half century she was to be virtually bedridden, spending her life in constant pain and prayer. She never left the apartment in downtown Montreal.

She says that she suffers the pains of Christ's wounds, and that she bears the vestigial signs of stigmata. She sleeps no more than an hour or two each night, as this is the time, she says, when she travels spiritually throughout the world tending the needy through prayer and her suffering.

She started at an early stage to commit her inner locutions to paper; her writings now fill many volumes in manuscript.

In her late twenties she met a Jesuit, Father Joseph Gamache, who believed that she was a genuine mystic; he became her spiritual director, seeing her daily until his death twenty years later. He encouraged her to take vows of poverty, chastity, and obedience.

Another Jesuit called Father Paul Mayer then came on the scene and advised her for the next seventeen years until his retirement. And now the Girard twins had been looking after her spiritual life during the preceding six years.

She lived an intensely private, reclusive existence, although stories of her peculiar life and powers reached the outside world from time to time.

This is how Guy Armand came to hear of her.

"One day a friend told me that a sixty-two-year-old holy woman had become pregnant," said Father Guy. "Naturally I didn't believe it; but I was fascinated and wanted to meet her. It turned out to be Georgette. She had a young, non-Catholic friend who was pregnant and wanted an abortion for fear of the pains of childbirth. Georgette offered to take upon herself all the discomforts of the pregnancy if the woman would have the baby. From that time Georgette developed the symptoms of pregnancy. On the day of the birth Georgette suffered all the pain of the delivery, while the young woman did not have the slightest discomfort in giving birth."

Even though Father Guy related his story in a calm, matter-of-fact manner, the story of the phantom pregnancy did not encourage me to believe that all was well with Georgette.

We eventually drew up in front of a modest clapboard apartment building with staircases on the outside of the building. Father Guy let himself in through a door on the ground floor and we mounted a staircase painted emerald green and pink. At the top we were admitted by an elderly housekeeper called Regine. Behind her, standing still and silent, was a small figure in pale blue pajamas and a dressing gown. It was Georgette.

The moment I set eyes on her I knew that there was something unusual about her. Although she was elderly and pallid with evident pain and illness, she had the pure and youthful eyes of a very young child. She looked straight at me with a curious gaze of affection and innocence. I found her captivating from that very first moment; yet it did not stop me from wondering whether she was a lunatic or a fraud.

She led the way through a door across the lobby. One half of the room was a simple sitting area decorated with a few items of cheap furniture. Two love-birds fidgeted in a cage.

In the second half of the room was a double bed covered in imitation satin. The bedroom area had been constructed as a shrine with the bed as the central piece; there were some plastic Doric pillars, festoons of dried flowers, votive lamps, and holy pictures. The scene made me feel uneasy.

Georgette sat down and talked for a while in French with Father Guy. She was saying that she was not happy about giving an interview as she did not want publicity. But Father Guy continued to persuade her that it was all for the good.

At last she turned her attention to me and smiled apologetically. I felt embarrassed.

She asked me how I would like to begin.

I had been looking at her limbs to see whether she was showing any signs of the stigmata. Her fore-wrists were monstrously swollen with rounded protuberances the size of tennis balls, but there was no sign of a bloody wound. Woolen socks and bedroom slippers covered her feet.

"Jesus has talked with you?" I said.

"Yes."

"How does he address you?"

"He calls me beloved, his little bride, his little victim of love."

I felt as if I were talking to a sick child.

"Was anybody cruel to you when you were young?" I asked.

She thought for a moment. "There was a nun ..." she said. "I was looking up adoringly at the host during Mass when I was six years of age. She slapped me around the face and told me that I would be seized by the devil to show such lack of respect in the presence of God."

I gasped as she said this, but she continued to smile in a self-deprecating manner.

"Father Guy was telling me that you had a spiritual director from a young age ..."

"Father Gamache."

"Can you tell me something about him?"

"He was sometimes strict."

"For example?"

"When I first met him I was very young and a pianist. I told him that I had a license in music. He said to me 'So what! Even dogs have licenses.' "

Georgette's eyes lighted up and she laughed gently.

"When did you begin your prayer life?"

"From the age of four. Throughout my childhood I prayed at least one hour each day. I thought it quite normal to hear the voice of Jesus. I thought this happened to everybody."

"When did Jesus begin to tell you that you were his bride?"

"On February 22, 1953. He told me that he was everything and I was nothing. He asked me to wear a ring and have it blessed by my spiritual director."

"Was your life filled with happiness after this?"

"No. I got tired and disgusted with the demands his love put on me. I threw away the ring. I went through a period of dryness. There were struggles and attacks from Satan, who wanted me dead. The sacraments were disgusting to me and I couldn't even stand the presence of my spiritual director. I did not believe him anymore, or the purification he was demanding of me. One day Father Gamache told me that his direction of me was costing him much in prayer, self-denial, and fasting. He said that he was trying to liberate my soul."

"How did you come out of this?"

"My spiritual director persuaded me to write the story of my spiritual life."

"Anything else?"

"I committed myself to greater denial. I severed myself from my family, friends, inclinations, and possessions."

"And the stigmata? When did that begin?"

"That began earlier, in 1950."

"You have the wounds?"

"Yes. In my wrists and on my feet. Also in my heart. And I received the crown of thorns on April 25, 1953. I was not worthy, but it was God's will. I also have a sixth wound, which is the pain that Christ bore from carrying his cross. This wound was revealed to Saint Bernard of Clairvaux. Christ told him that while carrying his cross he had a wound three fingers deep and three bones were laid bare on his shoulder."

"Do these wounds give you a great deal of pain?"

"It's always worse on Friday and during Mass," she said, "especially at the consecration. But the inner sufferings of Jesus were much greater than his physical sufferings. He died of too much love."

"Are your wounds visible?" I asked.

"For many years there was no sign," she said, "even though the pains were real and intense. But in more recent years there have been clear signs, although they do not bleed. And in 1982 on the Feast of the Precious Blood, God manifested himself with a terrible pain and by leaving a sign in my flesh in the shape of the figure two."

This item of information surprised me; it was certainly an unfamiliar emblem in the long history of physical phenomena of mysticism. "Did the number have a special significance?" I asked.

"The sign indicates that God and I are two in one same flesh."

"Have you had these marks checked by a doctor?"

"Oh, yes," she continued. "The doctor examined it with a magnifying glass and said that it was unbelievable . . ." She smiled and seemed to be pleased with herself. "It looks like luminous neon and the blood can be seen circulating. He also said that the number was made up of seven dots, which Jesus has told me indicate the seven gifts of the Holy Spirit. Jesus also said that the name of this sign should be known as the Alliance, indicating the intimacy of God with the soul and a greater indentification with the suffering of the crucified Christ."

"As you get older, Georgette, do your pains decrease?"

"No. They are worse. Much worse. I frequently have a pain like a burning arrow in my heart." Her face clouded as if with memory of the pain. "The pain is even more intense when the arrow is withdrawn. At that moment I experience great joy in my soul. I offer up this suffering to God for the whole Church."

"Do you take pain-killers?"

"No," she said promptly.

"As we were coming along," I said, "Father Guy told me that you had heard the voice of Satan. What sort of thing did he say to you?"

She sighed a little. Again she seemed like a little child.

"Satan told me even when I was a child that I was going to Hell because I had made bad confessions and committed sacrileges. Now he comes to me and tells me that my whole life has been wasted in spiritual pride and that I am his, and damned. He plays tricks on me."

"How is that?"

"He distorts the way I say my prayers. He makes me say: 'Thank you Jesus for allowing Satan to wander throughout the world for the good of souls,' or 'I hail myself Mary, Satan is with me.' "

"Anything else?"

"Sometimes he attacks me physically. He has tried to strangle me. Father Guy will confirm that the bruises of his fingers have been left on my neck."

Father Guy now suddenly intervened to say that he was going to prepare to say Mass and that Georgette would attend the service in the bed because her pains would become so severe.

I remained sitting in an armchair while the priest vested and prepared the mass receptacles on a table at the foot of the bed.

In the meantime Georgette went into the bedroom area, took off her dressing gown, and got beneath the sheets.

Before he began the Mass the priest said: "Mister John, you will notice that at the consecration the birds will begin to sing."

It was a short service, and I remained sitting.

Just as Father Guy had said, at the words of the consecration the birds began to sing in extraordinary cadences. At the same time I could hear Georgette gasping and moaning as if wracked with pain.

When the Mass was ended she came out slowly into the sitting area again, holding onto the furniture as she moved. Deathly pale and seemingly exhausted, she was breathing with difficulty and making little sighing noises. She sat down and whispered to Father Guy and then turned to smile at me.

The priest said: "Oh! Georgette says that she had a inner locution about you from the Eternal Father during the Mass."

Georgette smiled. "The Eternal Father hovered over you," she said. "I saw him as I sometimes do in the form of protective hands. He gave me a message for you. I feel so happy, because I have had no messages for these three months. The Eternal Father said this: Mary and I were overjoyed to see our son bowing before the real presence of Jesus. And I have put my hand on him to bless him in a special manner, giving to him all graces that he needs in his work and upon those whom he has in his heart and in his prayer. All those things he asks for will be given to him in accordance with his faith and trust. He will live happy days."

It was nicely put, I thought, and it would have been lovely to believe. It made me feel cozy, despite my natural skepticism. But a little voice inside my head was saying: "Give me a break!"

In the mood of new contentment that now seemed to fill the room I took advantage of the situation to ask if I could examine Georgette's wounds.

She smiled warmly, saying that there was not much to see that day. However, she would show me her feet. With this she beckoned me over to the sofa where she was sitting and began taking off her slippers and socks.

She allowed me to hold both of her feet one by one and to examine them closely.

Her feet and ankles were very badly swollen and in the center of each foot was a distinct deep, purplish mark, slightly discolored and flushed at the edges. The skin of the whole foot looked extremely tender and inflamed, but it was neither broken nor showing any signs of blood. It was as if the sign of the wounds had been painted on. As I scrutinized the marks very closely, the images seemed to me to be composed of broken or distended capillaries as a result of some trauma below the skin's surface.

Both feet looked extremely painful.

Next I looked at her wrists. There were no similar vivid signs except for monstrous swellings which had the appearance of an unusual kind of arthritis. The skin was drawn taut almost to breaking point and although I touched the pressure area very gently she shut her eyes and gasped as if agonized with pain.

"And what of the sign that you call the 'Alliance'?" I asked.

"Georgette will only show you that mark in her little chapel," said Father Guy.

After a short whispered conversation between the priest and Georgette it was agreed that I would be shown this final sign.

The chapel was a tiny adjacent room with just enough space for the three of us to stand side by side. There was an altar and a statue of the Sacred Heart and the Virgin. Georgette and Father Guy faced the altar and began to sing a hymn.

When they had finished Father Guy asked me to go down on my knees and face Georgette.

Then she raised her dressing gown and pulled down her pajamas a little so that I could see her bare hip. The sign of the number two was quite distinctly visible; it was apparently composed of seven bright scarlet spots. It was strangely impressive, and yet I could hardly restrain myself from laughing.

What on earth was I doing here in Montreal, in the middle of a working day, kneeling before an old lady who was pulling down her pajama bottoms to show me her spots!

After the exhibition of Georgette's Alliance it was time to go. At the door she asked if she could kiss me. She touched the back of the nape of my neck and kissed me gently on the cheek.

As I was about to go out of the door I paused and came back.

"Georgette," I asked, "why do you have all this physical suffering? What is it for?"

She smiled. It was as if I had at last asked the one question that really mattered.

"My wounds," she said, "are a great grace. It is by Christ's wounds that we are healed. I share my wounds of the heart with the souls God entrusts to me, especially those of priests. There is a prayer of Saint John of the Cross: 'Lord wound me with a wound of love which may be healed only by being wounded again.'"

*   *   *

Georgette's life seemed morbid, unhealthy, and self-absorbed. But how much of this was her fault? I was wondering about her first spiritual director, Father Gamache. Was it possible that he had been a manipulative fanatic, dominating and shaping the young Georgette until she was entirely his prisoner like the girl in John Fowles's novel *The Collector?* What hidden layers of self-interest and vicarious satisfaction may not have lurked beneath the story of that first "spiritual" relationship?

Then, looked at in a clinical light, the characteristics of Georgette's symptoms were distinctive, and obvious even to a layperson. Episodes of depressive guilt; periods of elation; the hearing of often conflicting voices; the experience of multifarious and excessive pain with no very clear diagnosis; susceptibility to suggestion; phantom pregnancy and dramatic dermatological signs; years of self-absorbed chronic ailments requiring invalid status: Was she not a classic hysteric?

But what did that mean?

Hysteria, as far as I knew, was an extraordinarily vague and outmoded term. Originally deriving from the Greek word for "womb," the condition focused on the idea of unbridled, neurotic female emotion, manifesting itself in imaginary illnesses. Then there was Freud's more specific *conversion hysteria,* the notion that repressed sexual conflicts were manifested in physical symptoms precisely symbolizing stifled wishes and desires. Having met Georgette, I was eager to study the link between hysteria and stigmatism more closely.

Yet even at this first acquaintance with the phenomenon of stigmata I was reluctant to accept that Georgette could be dismissed entirely by psychological or neurological explanations. She was clearly a gifted and exquisitely sensitive woman, imaginative and affectionate. Her personality did not strike me as altogether neurotic, even though she was clearly highly strung and had suffered traumas in her childhood and youth.

Above all, it seemed to me that the dedication of her life to prayer and contemplation was genuine. And what if one accepted for a moment the idea of the efficacy of prayer and sacrifice? Was she not pursuing an unusual interior vocation of great courage and nobility?

I was far from satisfied that I had completely grasped the character of Georgette Fanielle, and my perplexity had much to do with the mystery of suffering, so central to the Christian idea of the passion and crucifixion. A positive vocation to suffering and solitude seemed an alien and a neurotic thing from the perspective of a busy and healthy twentieth-century life.

17

The Shroud Mystery

In Montreal I had decided to fly on to Italy to take a closer look at the life of the most famous stigmatic of the century, Padre Pio. But before heading for San Giovanni Rotondo in the Gargano Peninsula, I planned to linger in Rome for a while. Among other things I wanted at this point to explore the significance of one of the most mysterious, and yet contentious, "paranormal" manifestations of Christ's wounds in history, the Shroud of Turin, believed by many to be Christ's winding sheet,

Ever since my visit to Briege I had taken out the picture of the "face" on the Turin Shroud and pondered its haunting expression, finding it difficult not to believe that this was the face of an actual person. As a student I had spent several summers working as a hospital porter on geriatric wards; I had consequently seen a great many faces in death. Whatever else it might be, the face on the shroud seemed to me unquestionably to be a highly accurate representation of a *dead* person.

The shroud is a fourteen-foot piece of linen showing a full-size back and front image of a crucified man. Pathologists examining the full-length image have identified a large number of "particularities" consistent with the marks of scourging wounds, and the cap of thorns, and the signs of crucifixion.

There had been a variety of tests already, most of them pointing to the conclusion that the shroud might well have dated from the beginning of the Christian era and confirming the mysterious nature of its creation. Some thirty scientists had concluded, as a result of tests conducted on sticky tape-lift samples, that the image had been formed by blood and other bodily secretions. A Shroud of Turin symposium of researchers, had declared in 1982:

"We can conclude for now that the Shroud image is that of a real human form of a scourged, crucified man. It is not the product of an artist. The blood stains are composed of hemoglobin and also give a positive test for serum albumin."

Pollen tests, moreover, seemed to demonstrate that the material had originated in Palestine, and laser technology indicated sophisticated techniques of image-forming quite beyond the scope of pre-1980s science.

It seemed that the shroud had revealed more and more of itself at each stage of the century's technological advances. The negative image, of course, remained hidden until 1898 when the first photograph was taken. Was it possible that the shroud was a fifth gospel? The Sign of Jonas for an unbelieving age? Was it a unique example of God's revelation discovered through science and technology?

Despite the excitement generated by the indications of authenticity, the evidence never did altogether point one way. There were some nagging problems. The surviving first record of its existence, for example, was ominous. We first learn, in history, of the shroud as a fake relic contrived in order to extort money from the unsuspecting faithful. The evidence centers on a memorandum sent to Pope Clement VII in 1389 by Pierre d'Acis, Bishop of Troyes. Referring to the shroud, he writes: "Eventually, after diligent enquiry and examination, he [Bishop Henri of Poitiers] discovered the fraud and how the said cloth had been cunningly painted, the truth being attested by the artist who had painted it, to wit, that it was a work of human skill and not miraculously wrought and bestowed."

Nor had the scientific evidence remained entirely undisputed. Between 1978 and 1979 an American microscopist, W. W. McCrone, was involved for one whole year on a set of spectroscopic tests on sticky tape-lift samples from thirty-two spots of representative image and non-image areas of the shroud. He examined some 40,000 linen fibers and other loose particles and concluded that the marks were made by paint pigment, namely red ochre, an iron oxide of variable degrees of hydration.

McCrone claimed that thin paint-layer paintings were known in Europe only from about 1275 to 1425; taking all the other evidence into account, in 1980 he put the shroud's date at 1356 or very slightly earlier. In subsequent debates with the pro-authenticity lobby, he frequently pointed out that the thirty scientists who disagreed with him on the sticky tape tests were neither analytical chemists nor microscopists.

The dispute, however, had now been conclusively resolved.

Before I arrived in Rome, scientists in Arizona, Zurich, and Oxford had completed carbon dating tests on samples of the shroud and found that the cloth was from the mid-fourteenth century. The implications of the exercise, conducted in the full glare of media publicity and reputedly under meticulous test conditions, had caught the imagination of the world. The question of the shroud's provenance had been settled for once and for all. The image on the cloth was not that of Christ.

But did it matter? What had ultimately been at stake?

It was nonsense to suggest, as did some commentators, that the faith of many millions of relic-loving Catholics had now been entirely undermined. Nevertheless, it was clear that an unfavorable result was a severe blow to those who were hoping that in this instance science would act as a prop to religious belief.

From my own point of view I was particularly intrigued by the reactions of the losers in the argument. The exercise was about to reveal much about the psychology of scientific evidence in support of cherished belief, or unbelief, and therefore the extent to which tangible phenomena really do aid faith or the lack of it.

First indications were that the "believers" had by no means braced themselves for a climb-down. Fierce champions of the shroud's authenticity had already fired their first shots from what looked like a precarious fall-back position. They had claimed in the Catholic press that anything from bucketfuls of water used to douse a fire which nearly destroyed it in 1532, to a hypothetical release of ionizing radiation from Jesus's body, when forming the mysterious imprint, could have affected the carbon dating reading.

Other shroud believers, like Leonard Cheshire, the famous wartime RAF bomber pilot, had commented in the expectation of bad news: "I do not believe you can prove it scientifically or logically, any more than you can give a man faith through a rational argument."

There were others who were capable of sitting comfortably on the fence. Gerald O'Collins, a Jesuit professor of theology at the Gregorian University in Rome, had described the shroud as a "both/and rather than an either/or," meaning that even if the shroud were not of first century origin it might be regarded as a spectacular icon and revered like any other holy and mysterious artifact: a sort of "have-your-cake-and-eat-it-too" solution.

The most ingenious suggestion from the "believers," however, came from those who argued that the image was indeed an authentic "apparition," which had occurred during medieval times on a medieval piece of cloth. The exponents of this view pointed to the sixteenth-century apparition of Our Lady of Guadaloupe on an Indian peasant's *tilda* outside Mexico City, which was to become the focus of the shrine of Our Lady of the Americas, currently visited by some sixteen million pilgrims a year. They could also cite numerous instances of miraculously formed icons in the Eastern Church, and, above all, the reputed appearance of the Virgin on an airborne shroud to save the Greeks of Constantinople from an Arab invasion in 910.

The shroud is kept safely wrapped and secure in a casket in Turin and is only rarely taken out for public view; the last occasion was in 1978 when some three million pilgrims, among them Pope John Paul II, were allowed to witness the object with the naked eye.

Those wishing to see a full display of the shroud in photographic form along with an array of other evidence relating to its significance and authenticity must go to the Centro Romano di Sindonologia in Via Pio XII near the Vatican City.

The center is directed by Monsignor Giulio Ricci, who has spent forty years of his working life studying the shroud in minute detail.

I visited the center shortly after my arrival in Rome and found Monsignor Ricci weary and ailing in the midst of his gruesome exhibits, which included plaster models dripping with blood; reproductions of the crown of thorns, the scourge, and the nails; and hundreds of lighted enlarged color photographs of details of the shroud. The place had the chilly, blood-stained atmosphere of a butcher's shop.

The focal point was a life-size model of the crucifixion, a monstrous spectacle of explicit cruelty quite unlike any painting of the crucifixion I have ever seen. It was minutely based on the evidence of the shroud, and one look at it convinced me once and for all that the Turin burial cloth had not been a work of imagination.

But if the "model," the victim, was not Christ, then who was it?

I asked Monsignor Ricci how he thought the image had been created. Was it blood? Was a miracle involved? What did he think of the popular sci-fi theory going the rounds that Christ's body had emitted a radioactive flash at the Resurrection, thus causing the image?

"No, it's certainly not a miracle!" insisted the monsignor. "Everything about the shroud is natural. The marks are composed of the natural secretions from the Shroud Man's body and the myrrh and aloes which were used for embalming. No miracle. No radiation flash."

I was intrigued by his reference to the "Shroud Man," as if he were prepared to leave room for an area of doubt. Such historical courtesy seemed admirable in a Roman monsignor.

Forty years was a long time, I said, to devote to studying one relic.

"A very *short* time," he replied, ". . . to meditate on the conclusions."

The monsignor drew my attention to an enlarged photograph in which the supposed marks of scourging could be traced.

"We are not simply engaged in cold research," he said in a mournful voice. "One is overcome by deep emotion when one attempts an accurate analysis of the numerous whipstrokes."

"And how accurate is that analysis?"

"The shroud tells us the precise nature of the flagellum," the monsignor went on, "the number of soldiers inflicting the strokes; the number of strokes; the direction of the strokes. Teams of pathologists have confirmed the very precise geometrical implications of the marks on the shroud . . . Is it possible to believe that a forger would have known all this?"

Unless, I was thinking, the forger had used a human "guinea pig."

"After considering all the scientific evidence we are virtually certain that the scourge was composed of three thongs; and at the end of those three thongs were five further strands, each weighted with two pieces of lead or heavy bone.

"The Shroud Man received his whipping while bending over a post; 120 strokes at the very least, from two distinct directions. We can trace every mark in the throbbing flesh."

The priest gazed at me with tears welling into his eyes. He seemed to be carrying a huge burden of sadness.

"How can we imagine such a punishment?" he went on. "His scourged body—from the soles of his feet to the top of his head—must have looked like the body of a leper."

He fell silent for a few moments.

"When they untied him," he continued, "he must have fallen exhausted into a pool of blood. He might have pondered the words of Isaiah: 'I have trodden the wine press alone; and from the peoples no one was with me.'"

The monsignor seemed to groan inwardly and hung his head a little to one side.

At last he said: "Look, I am very tired."

I bade him farewell quietly, and left him pale and exhausted among his terrible exhibits.

As I walked back to my lodging I kept thinking about the arresting face of the Shroud Man. Devout Christians had spoken of its majesty and peace; I had read a remark by a theologian to the effect: "What kind of man can it be who after such torturing, can show serenity in death?"

What kind of man indeed. For if the image on the shroud is *not* Christ, then who was it? And how was it produced? And can the faithful continue to venerate the image with an easy conscience?

And it is here that those impressive "particularities" of the wounds present a chilling prospect in the light of the carbon-dating tests. The remarkably accurate pathological details of the scourging wounds, the crown of thorns, the symptoms of crucifixion, including the accurate effects of the severing of the median nerves, have always suggested the presence of an actual human being, a man who perhaps endured these appalling torments and death, in order to make the image possible. As for the image's special quality of "serenity," it is only in fiction that dead faces are frozen in horror, suffering, or beatific smiles. In reality, facial muscles, be they of saints or sinners, ultimately relax into a semblance of peace whatever the expression at the moment of death.

A true icon is an idealized image produced in circumstances of prayer and devotion as an object of veneration. It would be consoling to think that the shroud was reproduced by an artist of preternatural visionary and mystical powers; but, as we have seen, the first historical mention of the shroud in 1389 is in relation to its status as a bogus relic. The auspices of its provenance, then, do not encourage us to believe that a mystic was on hand in its making. But such is its awful sense of visual "authenticity" that we are forced at least to speculate that a human subject was involved, and that the man was almost certainly a Jew since, according to experts such as Professor Carlton S. Coon, his facial characteristics correspond exactly with the "Sephardic Jew or Noble Arab" type.

While the possibility had existed that the image was first-century, it had seemed to me that Christians were justified in hoping against hope that they were gazing on the body and face of Christ. But now that the carbon test points to a medieval date, we can no longer postpone reflecting on the possibility that the image is an unspeakable anti-Semitic product of barbarism manufactured in the interests of ecclesiastical commerce.

But even as I write, shroud "believers," I understand, have announced that the carbon dating process was not fairly conducted and that its findings are therefore false.

I went to visit the Church of the Santa Croce de Gerusalemme which houses, it is claimed, the true cross of Christ.

There I saw the wooden placard on which was carved in Greek, Aramaic, and Latin the inscription "This is Jesus the Nazarene King of the Jews."

There were dark spiky things behind glass, which purported to be the nails which had pinned Christ to the cross; the finger bone of Doubting Thomas (that, of course, which he had placed in Christ's side); two needles from the crown of thorns; a fragment of the column on which Christ was bound during the scourging; a piece of the tomb in which he had been buried ...

As I looked on these things I felt troubled. There were pilgrims passing to and fro among the relic cases whispering in pious awe, and others kneeling at prayer in an ante-chapel; it was not for me with my phlegmatic English sensibilities to pass judgment; but I wondered whether the archaeology of science was going to stop at the Turin Shroud. How long would it be before the carbon dating experts put these instruments of the Passion to the test, and then on and on through Rome's leading relics?

To the modern mind these tarnished impedimenta, of dubious spiritual resonance, let alone provenance, smack of superstition and simony, the sin of making profit out of holy objects. Perhaps there are some strong arguments to enlist science to sweep it all away. And yet, how would the Christian Church have fared had the cult of relics never existed? There is a theory, eloquently argued by the scholar of Christian Antiquity, Peter Brown, that without them, and the spread of their unique sense of holy presence in the early Church, Christianity might never have become a universal religion.

If the spread of relics had not established a major place in Christian piety, Brown argues, the spiritual landscape of the Christian Mediterranean might have been very different. It might have been more like that of the later Islamic world: the *holy place* might have been permanently restricted to a few privileged areas, such as the Holy Land, and cities where the saints were buried, such as Rome. There might have been a Christian Mecca or a Christian Kerbela, but not the spread of the sense of *presence* of the major saints, such as Peter and Paul, far beyond the ancient frontiers of the Roman world.

But the spread and the cult of relics eventually brought commercial exploitation in its trail; by the Middle Ages it had become a widespread trade, involving lies, fraud, fakery, and theft; and the attendant scandals echo to this day.

The reliquariums jealously guarded in Rome's hundreds of churches are an instrinsic part of the attraction of the Eternal City; but they linger in an uneasy limbo of authenticity, from which they could soon be expelled into oblivion by the scientists. The extremes of picturesque fakery satirized by Boccaccio and Chaucer have long gone, among them the feather of the wings of the Angel Gabriel, and the receptacle preserving the breath of the ox in the stable at Bethlehem. But with three rival heads of John the Baptist, seventeen arms of Saint Andrew, and five breasts of Saint Agatha, there are still a great many fakes around, and the scientists could make short work of proving them so.

With these thoughts revolving in my mind, I called in later that afternoon at the medieval convent of Santa Lucia, the only place in the world where Catholics may acquire relics that carry a stamp of authenticity. The religious house and church, which is the official repository of relics in Rome, is situated in Via in Selci, a quiet street near the Colosseum. You enter the principal door by a steep flight of steps; to the right is a grille and an electric bell. Above is a piece of card with the legend *"Ho Sete"* ("I thirst"): Christ's cry from the cross.

A diminutive nun with a shiny, dark rounded face peered through the iron bars. When she had ascertained that I was in the business of acquiring relics she disappeared, then reappeared as quickly at a side door to admit me into the convent.

I entered a vast and lofty whitewashed parlor with another huge iron grille set in the wall. She seated me at a plastic table, then popped through another door to reappear on the other side of this second gate.

She announced herself as Sister Cathy and asked me which saint's relic I required.

"Would it be possible," I asked her, "to acquire a relic of the true cross?"

She looked at me askance.

"For you personally? Or for a church? Are you a priest? No, you are not a priest!"

Sister Cathy told me that a splinter of the Holy Cross was a very major relic available only for churches or religious institutions and required an application from a bishop.

But seeing me crestfallen, she asked me whether I would like another sort of relic.

I told her that I had as a boy possessed a relic of Thérèse of Liseux, which I had lost. Would it be possible to have another?

"Of course," she said with a smile. "But I'm sorry to hear that you were so careless as to lose the first."

We talked for a little.

The monastery of Saint Lucia, she told me, had a special re-lationship with the "Vicariate" in Rome, the office which dispenses the licenses for relics. There were forty nuns in the community, and the majority of them—like Sister Cathy—were Filipinos.

"We have deposits of 2,000 relics," she said. "These are of three different classes. First-class relics are actual pieces of the bone of the saint; second class are items of clothing; and third class is a piece of the saint's tomb."

"Are some relics more popular than others?" I asked

"Oh yes ... Saint Rita of Cassia, Saint Benedict, Saint Lucy ... and, of course, Sainte Thérèse."

"So what happens," I asked, "if you run out of a popular relic?"

"We tell the Vicariate, and they find us some more," she said simply.

"And what about the Virgin Mary, could I have a relic of hers? I believe you have a bit of her veil?" I said, teasing her.

Sister Cathy suddenly burst out laughing.

"Who told you that? That isn't true," she cried.

"There *are* relics of Our Blessed Lady," she went on, "but they are third class, because Our Lady was assumed into Heaven without corruption. It's possible to have a relic of the rock of the assumption, or an item of her tomb, or a piece of the Holy House at Loreto."

She was referring to the extraordinary proposition, widely credited by Italian Catholics, that angels had transported the house of the Virgin from Nazareth, via Yugoslavia, to the Italian Marches, where it arrived in 1294, to become one of the great shrines of Europe. Our Lady of Loreto, not surprisingly, was to become, in the twentieth century, the patroness of air pilots.

Sister Cathy, whose order was permanently enclosed and took vows of silence, seemed to have enjoyed our little colloquy, but she now urged me to the business in hand.

What kind of reliquarium would I like to purchase?

With this she produced a display case with some twenty or thirty different glass and metal receptacles ranging from objects the size of a coffee cup to tiny lockets to be hung around the neck. The prices, which were written on labels next to each sample, ranged from 10,000 up to 70,000 lira.

I chose one at 13,000 lira.

"There is an extra charge for post," said Sister Cathy. "Five thousand lira to send your relic to England when it is ready; and then there is five thousand for administration that goes to the Vicariate."

As we said farewell, I passed a small donation through the grille to the smiling little nun.

"Allow eight weeks for delivery," she said.

As I walked back to my lodgings near the Campo de Fiori in

the old city it gave me a warm feeling to think that I would once again possess a relic of Sainte Thérèse.

I could understand, and feel, how vulnerable were the Holy Shroud's devotees to the sophisticated machines and charts of the carbon dating experts.

18

Dinner with Briege

I'd heard it said that people who are getting close to religious experience begin to encounter peculiar coincidences fast and thick. Jung and Koestler were so astonished by the incontrovertible proliferation of such "synchronicities" in some peoples lives that they speculated that there might be some sort of quantum theory explanation.

Whatever the case, walking across Piazza Farnese the next day I ran into a coincidence that seemed too extraordinary for comfort. Bustling toward me came Sister Briege McKenna with a broad smile, and a look that said: "Here we are again!"

She was back in her religious habit and wearing a short veil.

"I was just thinking about you!" she shouted.

"I think you're following me, Sister," I said. "How come you nuns manage to gad about the world like this?"

"This is nothing," she said, giving me a resounding kiss. "The day after tomorrow I'll be in Papua New Guinea ... but I've got to dash now, I've got a meeting with some people. Have dinner with me tonight?"

I felt suspiciously privileged. People traveled halfway across the world to spend a few minutes in private with this woman, and I couldn't get away from her.

We agreed to meet that evening in a trattoria near the Gregorian University.

174

*   *   *

Throughout the rest of the day I could not get the coincidence out of my mind: I had heard from so many people that Briege McKenna's life buzzed with nonstop paranormal happenings all of which she accepted as perfectly normal; added to which, I had been sensing the beginnings of a serious infatuation with her, not so much overtly sexual, perhaps, as an obsessive inclination to think about her.

As I set off to walk from the Via di Monserrato to the restaurant that evening I had a feeling that our assignation was "meant" in some way.

It was a modest restaurant, and empty. Sister Briege was sitting in a back room and jumped up to embrace me.

She looked tired. Grumbling about keeping her weight down, she ordered some fish and accepted a glass of white wine.

During the meal we talked about our families, the troubles in Northern Ireland, her frequent journeys to South America and Africa. As we talked, I had to keep reminding myself that this was a woman who spent, so I had been reliably informed, up to three hours in silent prayer each day.

Did it show?

She was warm, affectionate, humorous, deeply human; all common qualities of natural goodness. But there *was* a difference in her sort of goodness that was hard to define; it had something to do with an impression that in everything she said, in every gesture and nuance of her physical presence, there was a quality I can only describe as intense purity of heart. And she had the capacity to speak, constantly and directly, from her heart.

While she spoke I kept wondering what it would be like to be married to such a person, thinking about the waste of a life dedicated to chastity.

When the dishes were cleared and the waiter had left us to ourselves, I said: "Do you mind if I ask you some straight questions about yourself? And do you mind if I take a record of it?"

"That's okay," she said. Then she punched me playfully on the arm. "But don't expect too much at this time of the evening."

"I want to understand your healing gift. You talked about it briefly in Dublin, and I wanted to ask you more . . . but I got itchy feet . . ."

She was silent for a while, as if putting her thoughts together.

She fiddled with the gold ring which she wore on the third finger of her right hand.

"I was born on Pentecost," she began, "and Pentecost has always been a special time for me.

"In 1971 on the eve of Pentecost Sunday, when I was twenty-four years of age, I was praying in our oratory in the convent in Tampa. I was just sitting there, saying: 'Jesus, here I am.'

"After about five minutes I sensed an extraordinary stillness in the chapel; it was like a cloud descending. I heard a voice say: 'Briege.' I turned round to look toward the door, thinking that somebody had come in. But there was no one there; yet I was conscious of a presence. As I looked toward the tabernacle again, I heard the voice saying: 'You have my gift of healing. Go and use it.'

"I felt a burning sensation going through my body. It was as if my hands had touched a live electrical current. The burning sensation went through and out of me. Then the sense of stillness seemed to lift.

"On Pentecost morning I woke up to a voice roaring in my head: 'You have the gift of healing: go and use it.'

"That day I was invited to pray with a sick child. I only learnt years later that the child had been healed after that prayer.

"I told no one about my voices, but in the next week or two several people came to me to say that they were convinced that I had a gift.

"People would come up to me sometimes and say that they knew that I had powers of healing, but I rejected it, because I didn't trust it, and I didn't want people to think I was some kind of religious maniac.

"Then things came to a head in my life. It was the early seventies; everybody seemed to be looking for a mystical key to everything. I heard that a group of women were going to see a guru who claimed to be a sort of prophet. I got the idea in my head that he could help me.

"This so-called prophet turned out to be dangerous. He fixed me with his eyes and asked all sorts of questions. Then he said: 'Have you had a man?' I thought that was a strange question to ask a nun. He said all sorts of things, but nothing that I didn't already know.

"A couple of weeks later a nun I knew came to stay and I told her about my visit to the prophet. 'I want to see him, too,' she said. I thought that maybe it would do her some good so I went again.

"As soon as he saw me, he said: 'Have you been with a man?' I said he was not much of a prophet if he didn't know that I hadn't. Then he said to me, 'You need your head cut off,' and he traced his finger along the back of my neck and around to the front. He kept saying that I shouldn't be a nun, that I was wasting my young life."

As she said this Briege seemed to be looking at me intently. It was as if she had read into my thoughts a few minutes previously. I was quite thunderstruck by this, but I pretended as if she had said nothing unusual.

"Anyway," she went on, "I was arguing with him, and he was gazing into my eyes. After half an hour I felt as if I was in pieces. Nobody was any good or worth anything, and I was wasting my time thinking I could be of any good either. I had never questioned the existence of God in my entire life, and now I was riven with doubt. I came away weeping and distraught.

"That night in bed I felt as if I was being choked where the man had touched my neck. I couldn't even cry out for help. It was like a dark power over me, tempting me to deny Christ and stop serving him. I tried to pray and I couldn't. Somehow, though, I managed to utter the name Jesus, and the choking stopped.

"For days I was in a state of misery, convinced that I was going to get out of the religious life. I went on a trip to a convent in San Francisco, and all the way I kept saying, 'God, please help me.' When I got there I just stayed in my room. I took the Bible and said, 'Jesus, I know this is your living word. Please tell me what I am to do, and where I should be.'

"I opened my Bible and the words leapt out of the page at me. It was the passage in the first letter of Saint Paul to the Corinthians, about committing yourself to the single life for the Lord. I was filled with peace and joy. I also knew that God had work for me to do.

"After that the opportunities kept arising in which I prayed over people and they were healed. It even happened over the telephone. People came to me and said that I had appeared by their bedsides when I was two hundred miles distant. For the first six months I was very skeptical. People were healed; I saw it again and again with my own eyes, but I still wouldn't believe Jesus would work through me. It didn't seem possible that I could be of any use until I was changed and perfect.

"But I knew very little in those days about *real* sickness. One day at a prayer meeting a woman stood up and asked me to pray for a friend who was blind and paralyzed. I was convinced that this was far too big an order for me, but I went to see her anyway.

"I found that she was very bitter and angry and had given up on God. I put my hand on her paralyzed arm and prayed with her, and as I did so I felt the sensation of needles, just as I had in the chapel when I had been given the gift of healing. But I wasn't confident that I could do anything for her.

"A few days later she asked to see me. She had received her sight, and the power had come back in her arm. But as we talked later I realized the woman's spiritual attitude had totally changed. The woman's inner, spiritual healing, was more important. It also enabled me to see that psychological and physical healing often follow in a natural way from spiritual healing.

"If you believe, as I do, that our bodies, our minds, our souls are one entity, it stands to reason that the healing of the body might follow from spiritual healing."

For the space of an hour, Sister Briege related stories of healings, of prophecies, of amazing coincidences, of miracles major and minor. She talked of voices and visions, and divine interventions, as if they were normal daily occurrences. And the more she talked the more exasperated I became, not so much with the woman herself, but because she seemed to inhabit a world in which God behaved like a fixer, favoring some more than others with no very good reason. It wasn't Briege McKenna that annoyed me so much as her God.

"Briege," I said eventually. "I need to ask you something . . . I've no doubt that all these things happened just as you've described them," I began. "But what puzzles me is why God should favor one person with healing rather than another? What sort of God is this that goes around allowing one person to suffer in agony, and another to escape? And why does he answer your prayers rather than mine?"

Sister Briege leaned forward; her face was kind and gentle, without a trace of sanctimonious zeal.

"During the first few months of the healing ministry," she said,

"I had those thoughts myself. I asked that question all the time. I got all sorts of books on healing written by recognized experts, on why certain people don't get healed. On the first day I read a chapter in one of these books, and the next morning I couldn't remember a thing I'd read. I was on retreat at the time in a Franciscan convent in Birmingham, Alabama, where Mother Angelica runs a Catholic satellite television network. Finally Mother Angelica took me into the chapel. She pointed up at the altar to the Real Presence of Jesus, and she said, 'Let Jesus teach you.'

"That day I made a commitment to spend up to three hours a day in personal prayer. And the Lord started to teach me that I didn't have to answer all these questions. Not everybody is going to be healed physically, and that isn't my problem. Nor do I need to defend God, or apologize for the way in which he works; our job is to proclaim him, not defend him."

I felt myself smiling inwardly at this "cop-out," and yet it seemed an ingenuous answer true to her character. I was glad that she had not given me some complicated theological rationalization, and yet I understood that all debate, argument, and probing would be useless.

She was observing me, as if wondering how I had taken her answer. Then she said: "Jesus has a *way* of healing that is tied in with his teaching. Every healing in scripture is an opportunity to teach. Through prayer I began to learn about his healing in the same way. And so he enabled me to be more effective in letting him work through me."

She fell silent for a moment, as if waiting for this to sink in.

"I am not the healer," she went on. "Jesus is the healer. And we shouldn't be surprised when he answers prayer by suffering, and even by taking someone we love back to himself."

She stopped, as if uncomfortable with the didactic way in which she was talking.

"Some years ago," she went on, "the father of a little girl came to see me. She was dying of leukemia. He had heard that I had been instrumental in the healing of many children sick with the disease.

"I went to the hospital with him. The child was in terrible suffering and obviously dying. As I knelt down and took her hand, I felt as if she were saying to me: 'I don't need healing, but my father does. I'm happy to go.'

"Outside the ward I spoke with the father and mother. I took their hands and said: 'I'd like to be able to tell you that Mary is going to be healed the way you want, but I have no idea how she is to be healed. I just know that Jesus will not disappoint you.' As I spoke to them they couldn't accept what I was saying. They were distraught.

"We often act as if we can manipulate God into doing what we want him to do, by saying the right words, or making promises, or having sufficient faith. But God teaches us through prayer that he doesn't do anything to suit us. In prayer and through prayer we change to fit into God's will.

"About three days after my visit to the hospital, the parents phoned to say that Mary had died. I went to see them at once, thinking that they would be badly in need of comfort. The father came up to me and embraced me and said: 'I realize that healing doesn't mean getting my own way, but getting the strength and the grace to say yes to God's way. Mary wasn't mine. She didn't belong to me. I didn't have the strength to accept this until the moment that she had died.' You see, John, whenever we can say yes to God, we will never be hurt. He is a God of love and you should never put limitations on him. It is only in our resistance and pulling away and saying no to God that we get hurt."

Briege was talking rapidly and earnestly. I could see that we could never have a discussion about any of these matters; she had only two roles, as explicator and mentor. It was clear from what she had told me that there had been doubts in the early days, but her whole world picture was based on an extraordinary act of continuing faith. She was consequently impervious to anything I, or anybody else, might say to challenge her.

And yet, I felt she was both sane and sound and she radiated a sense of love and warmth. There was not the slightest hint of mania, or pride, or eccentricity. Nor did she strike me as sentimental or pietistic. Her mission and her beliefs had a sort of bracing purity, like mountain air. The problem was, how on earth could one live in the real everyday world and cope with such beliefs?

"Have you kept records, Sister, of the various miracles you have performed? Have they been properly recorded and checked by medical experts? Can I see some tangible evidence?"

I was conscious that in attributing the miracles to her and not to God I had invited her to make a pietistic disclaimer.

She ignored the invitation, and said: "I'm not really interested in doing that. You'll get that sort of thing at Lourdes. In any case, people who have faith don't need that sort of proof; and those who are without faith won't be impressed by any kind of evidence ... even priests."

I wanted to ask a final question that contained a bit of a mean performance test. It was the question of the Third Tempter in T. S. Eliot's *Murder in the Cathedral*. Even as I framed it I felt ashamed.

"Are you never worried, Sister," I began, "by the idea of spiritual pride? There are a lot of people who think you are a saint. Are you a saint? And do you behave in the way you do so that you will achieve sainthood?"

"Listen, John," she said, "the most important thing to be in life, the most beautiful thing, is to be human. Never mind being a saint, whatever that means. And if you're asking whether I have normal human weaknesses, of course, I have plenty of them. And self-indulgences ... I like going to the beach, and going out to dinner with friends, which a lot of nuns would think outrageous ..."

With this she looked at her watch, and sighed, "Talking of which," she said, "I must be off." And she stood up at once to go.

On the way back to her convent lodging she put her arm in mine.

"You know," she said, "belief in miracles is an unpredictable business. A priest once came to my retreat with a gangrenous leg; there was talk of him having it amputated. He said to me: 'Briege, just cure this foot and my faith will know no bounds.' I prayed over him that night, and asked God for healing. The next morning he appeared at breakfast all red in the face. His trouser was rolled up as he walked into the refectory. The leg was completely healed. He just sat there staring at it, but he looked unhappy. 'I don't know, Briege,' he said, 'it might have cured itself ...'"

As we embraced at the door of her convent, she said: "I might send you a miracle tomorrow. I wonder what you'll make of it."

I was staying in Rome at the Venerable English College near the Piazza Farnese. In the middle of the morning on the day following my dinner with Briege I was reading in the college library when a message was sent up from the porter's lodge that I had a visitor.

The visitor turned out to be a Sister Margaret Scully from

Sydney, Australia, a very tall nun dressed all in blue, clutching a document file.

"I'm your miracle," she said with a loud laugh. "Got any coffee in this place?"

She was a rangy, raw-boned woman with high coloring and swift movements. In her plain spectacles and uniform she looked rather severe, but she had an open, mobile face, and a ready wit.

We repaired to the college staff kitchen and she explained that she was a friend of Briege's and was studying a course in Rome for the year.

"Briege McKenna healed me of a very nasty, chronic disease in 1986," she explained. "So I've brought along my papers to show you, although Briege says it won't make any difference to a hard-headed chap like you!"

With this she began her story.

She said that she was fifty-six and that she had been a Sister of Charity since the age of eighteen. From early childhood she had suffered a digestive problem which became progressively worse as she got older.

In 1979 she began to experience severe abdominal pain and vomiting. She was admitted to the hospital and a test revealed that she had an "utterly abnormal esophagus." But too little was known about the condition to provide any help other than a diet of soft food and liquids.

At this point in her tale Sister Margaret delved into her file and brought out a sheaf of letters with impressive letterheads from consultant physicians in Australia. They referred to matters such as "esophageal motility," "diffuse spasms," "peristalses": all of which I took on trust. Her doctors described hers as a "serious problem" with a long history of postprandial vomiting and consequent weight loss. She had suffered a "congenital motility" disorder involving "essentially the esophagus."

"Now," she said, "this is where Briege McKenna comes in. In 1986 Briege was doing a tour of Australia and I attended one of her retreats. I was sitting in the kitchen of the convent one day and Briege came through and saw me consuming my usual diet, which was a soupy mess from the blender. She said to me: 'Sister, why are you eating that muck?' When I told her about my trouble, she said: 'We'll have to do something about you.' At the next healing session in the convent chapel Briege laid her hands on me and

DINNER WITH BRIEGE   183

prayed for healing. After I returned home I was preparing some food in the usual way with the blender when I had the most incredible desire, for the first time in my life, to have a lamb chop. I cooked a couple of chops and boiled potatoes and I ate them and enjoyed it! And I've been eating normal meals ever since. A few weeks later I went to the same specialist and he confirmed the complete cure."

The nun now handed over a second sheaf of letters, dated in the spring of 1986.

According to state-of-the-art tests it seemed that she was now completely normal. The same Dr. Talley could say that according to his examination she now had "normal esophageal motility." Writing to her general practitioner, he also commented, in relation to the possibility that she had responded to "faith healing," that he was "quite prepared to have some faith in this sort of cure in certain circumstances."

Having made her point, Sister Margaret jumped up from her seat and said: "I'm going to get out of your hair now, Mr. Cornwell. But never let it be said that Sister Briege's successes could not produce proper documentation. You can keep all that stuff, they are copies."

As I showed Sister Margaret to the door, she said: "My doctor said an interesting thing to me after my healing. He said he believed that when something like that happened to someone it was not just for that person's sake, but so that it could be shared with others."

As I returned up the stairs I found myself wondering about the implications of her last remark; it smacked too much of "proof" and "legitimacy" for my liking.

Sitting in the library I went through her batch of letters very carefully once more. In the midst of them I found at least one skeptical testimony. It was from one of the second opinions, based at St. George's Hospital in the University of New South Wales, although Sister Margaret appeared to have excised (unwittingly I am sure) part of the letter and the consultant's name and status.

The consultant wrote that in reviewing the tracing from 1979 he was unable to demonstrate a sphincter but that he was not at that time using a "sleeve catheter." He had seen several "synchronous contractions" consistent with an abnormal esophage motility pattern, but the tracing, he believed, was not characteristic of "scleroderma," "diffuse esophageal spasm," or any other specific motility disorder. The current tracing, he was convinced, had none of the abnormalities noted on an earlier tracing, but the changes were not "dramatic." He believed there was some "improvement," but nothing more than that.

At this point the letter had been excised.

Should I have been impressed by the fact that Sister Margaret had included this opinion, and the doubts expressed? Did it matter that her "miracle" was not so dramatic after all?

Reflecting on the nun's visit, I had to admit that her claims, and the manner in which she had presented them, made me uncomfortable. But why? Hadn't I set out to find exactly the sort of "evidence" she was giving me?

I was glad for Sister Margaret's sake that she felt better, and I had no doubt that Briege McKenna's intervention (mediation?) had something to do with the improvement in her health. But Sister Margaret's approach to her miracle exemplified an antagonistic divide that seemed characteristic of most claims for miraculous healing.

There is obviously a widespread hunger among religious believers for evidence that their faith is justified, and in this context the phenomena of sudden, inexplicable cures associated with divine healing can be dramatic and "demonstrable." After all, this is an opportunity to enlist science in favor of the divine! If the doctors say it's true, it *must* be true! On the other hand, such "evidence" can be extremely annoying for those who have set their minds against the possibility of divine intervention of this sort and who associate such "proofs" with crude attempts to force the skeptical into submission.

For my own part, I was not inclined to take up a position on either side of this divide. If there was such a thing as a miracle of healing, it seemed to me that something more gentle and subtle was at work than counters to be used in religious polemic. Was it possible to believe in miracles? What did they mean? And what were they for?

At the outset of my inquiry I had opened a file on miracles of healing with a view to collecting some current case histories supported by evidence and opinions from specialists. After my conversation with Briege McKenna, and Sister Margaret's visit, it seemed a good time to review some of the significant items in my file, including the most recent material from cures at Lourdes.

There is a common skepticism toward miraculous healings which focuses on the fact that, outside of scripture and medieval hagiography, it is difficult to find a *real* miracle: for example, the appearance of a new eye or a new leg. For the most part, miracles of healing tend to involve illnesses that may well have resulted from a psychosomatic cause and are therefore amenable to psychological suggestion. At very best, they appear to involve "inexplicable" *remissions* of diseases as opposed to the growth of new organs or new limbs. Healing therefore involves a dramatic process of nature, a return to wholeness, rather than a display of *magic:* now you see it, now you don't.

The problem for the skeptic is therefore a simple one: do not dramatic remissions occur as often in nonreligious contexts as they do in the milieu of divine healing?

In my file I had two recent cases of startling remissions of terminal cancers reported in *The Times* of London:

> *"Mrs. Kathleen Matthews aged 45, was told she had cancer of the pancreas and would survive another 12 months after an operation last December at Queen Alexandra Hospital in Portsmouth ..." reported the newspaper on August 24, 1988.*
>
> *"Mrs. Matthews made a will and settled all her affairs before leaving on holiday for Australia. ... While in Perth she visited a hospital and showed doctors a letter she carried from Portsmouth explaining what was wrong with her. When doctors in Perth put her through a scanner they told her they could see no sign of cancer."*
>
> *Mrs. Matthews returned to England in perfect health. In the meantime the responsible consultant in Portsmouth declined to comment.*

The second story, published on April 6 in the same year, involved a cinema projectionist who twelve months previously had been given a one percent chance of living longer than six months.

> *"Three separate medical tests all concluded that Mr. Albert Oxley, a widower aged 52, from Stockton, Cleveland, had cancer of the stomach which was spreading to his liver. Doctors told him that the condition was both inoperable and terminal ...*
>
> *"Seven months after the original diagnosis, he returned to*

North Tees General Hospital for a further blood test, which showed that his liver was functioning perfectly ... Last month further tests revealed that there were no longer any traces of cancer. A stomach tumor had also disappeared ..."

Dr. Tanner, Mr. Oxley's consultant gastroenterologist, had commented that "although it's possible for some malignant tumors to disappear it was virtually unheard of when they were located in the stomach."

There was no question of divine healing in either case, nor were the cures referred to as "miraculous" even in a metaphorical sense. So what was the difference between the merely inexplicable and the miraculous? Would the International Medical Committee (CMIL) at Lourdes have declared such incidents miraculous?

I had discovered that few medical bodies are as painstaking and cautious over the term "inexplicable" as the CMIL.

The council, which convenes once a year, is composed of twenty-five members, mostly from major West European countries, the majority of them being French. They represent a wide range of specialities and at least ten of the panel hold chairs in major medical schools.

An exhaustive report is drawn up for the scrutiny of the members. The original diagnosis must be proven correct with all the appropriate evidence of laboratory investigations, X-rays, endoscopies, biopsies, and so forth. The committee must be convinced that the disease was organic rather than psychological, and that the natural history of the disease precluded the possibility of spontaneous remission. Nor will the committee accept cures that might have been effected by medical treatment.

The cure must be "sudden" and "complete." In the case of multiple sclerosis, for example, it would be normal for the committee to wait up to six years before making a final declaration of a "cure." Even so, the CMIL does not announce a miracle as such. The members are posed the following question: "Does the cure of this person constitute a phenomenon which is contrary to the observations and expectations of the medical knowledge and scientifically inexplicable?" The final decision is made on the basis of a simple majority. It is the Catholic Church that declares whether or not the cure was of supernatural origin and therefore a miracle.

In a rare medical presentation by an English member of the

CMIL, Dr. St. John Dowling (MB MRCGP) has described the relevant details of the latest Lourdes cure in the *Journal of the Royal Society of Medicine* (77: August 1984). The cure involves a girl called Delizia Cirollie, who lives in a village on the slopes of Mount Etna in Sicily. [At the time of publication the case is still the most recent to be approved as a miracle by the Catholic Church.]

"In 1976 when she was twelve years old she presented with a painful swollen right knee," writes Dr. Dowling. "An X-ray showed bone change, so she was referred to Professor Mollica at the Orthopedic Clinic of the University of Catania. After further X-rays he did a biopsy which Professor Cordaro reported as showing a bony metastasis of neuroblastoma. The surgeon advised amputation; the family refused. He then advised cobalt irradiation and she was transferred to the Radiotherapy Unit, where she was so unhappy that her parents took her home the next day, before she had had any treatment.

"Her teacher suggested that Delizia be taken to Lourdes, and a collection made locally enabled her to go with her mother in August 1976. There she spent four days attending the ceremonies, praying at the Grotto, and bathing in the water. There was no improvement and X-rays in September showed extension of the growth.

"The child went downhill and her mother began to prepare for her funeral. Nonetheless, the villagers continued to pray to Our Lady of Lourdes for her cure and her mother regularly gave her Lourdes water.

"Shortly before Christmas she suddenly said that she wanted to get up and go out, which she did without pain but she was not able to get very far owing to weakness; at this time she weighed only 22 kg. [less than 50 pounds]. Her knee swelling disappeared, leaving her with a degree of genu valgum, and her general condition returned to normal. X-rays showed repair of the bone. The following July she returned to Lourdes to present herself to the Medical Bureau and did so again in 1978, 1979, and 1980. X-rays of the thorax and abdomen showed no sign of the calcification often seen in neuroblastoma.

"There was no doubt that she had been cured but the exact diagnosis proved more difficult. The histological opinion of Professor Cordaro of Catania was a metastasis from a neuroblastoma. He sent the biopsy slides to the Lourdes Medical Bureau and they were submitted to French histologists eminent in the field of bone tumors. Professor Payan of Marseilles gave his opinion that it was a Ewing's tumor. Professor Nezelof of Paris agreed that the diagnosis of a metastasis from a neuroblastoma could not be absolutely excluded, but concluded that Ewing's tumor was the most likely diagnosis. Dr. Mazabraud and his colleagues at the Curie Institute reached the same conclusion. Spontaneous remission of neuroblastoma has been reported, but very rarely, and never after the age of five years. Spontaneous remission of Ewing's tumor has not been recorded.

"The CMIL studied the case in 1980 and 1981 and at their meeting in 1982 they decided that Ewing's tumor was the correct diagnosis and concluded that the cure was scientifically inexplicable. The fact that the moment of the cure was at home in Sicily and not in Lourdes was irrelevant to the work of the Committee."

The difference between a report of an inexplicable cure at Lourdes and any other claimed cure, then, is clearly the wealth of painstaking detail and the cooperation between a very large number of doctors, albeit Catholic doctors. The Lourdes assessment leaves little area for doubt as to the original diagnosis; in fact, it probably errs on the side of caution and for this reason official Lourdes cures are few and far between. In the absence of such stringent criteria we shall never know whether the case of Mr. Oxley of Stockton and the "virtually unheard of" disappearance of his stomach cancer constitutes a cure just as inexplicable as that of Delizia's tumor.

All the same, it is worth emphasizing the little-known fact that of the estimated two million sick pilgrims who have visited Lourdes since 1858 (nowadays there are an estimated 65,000 seriously ill persons each year out of a total of four million annual visitors), only 65 have been accepted as miraculous cures by the Catholic Church. That is an extraordinarily small number, roughly one person in 130,000 every other year. There are medical statisticians who acknowledge that on the basis of the figures the statistical link between Lourdes and cure is therefore utterly insignificant.

Naturally these figures have little bearing on the enormous number of people who claim to have benefited spiritually and psychologically as a result of making the Lourdes pilgrimage; nor do they reflect those sick people who have experienced an alleviation of their physical symptoms, but without official recognition. That number is estimated to be in the region of 2,000 since 1858, but it is doubtful whether the figure is any better than the number of "cures" at any of Europe's famous secular spas.

The paucity of cures at Lourdes, and indeed at other centers (such as the Anglican healing center at Burswood in Sussex, England), is unlikely to disappoint mainstream Christians who regard divine healing as a means of teaching or reemphasizing religious truths. In this sense modern claims of "miracle" healing can echo the significance of miracles in scripture.

On leaving Medjugorje I had promised myself that I would read the gospels, something I had not done for almost twenty-five years. I had been as good as my word, and I had rediscovered the multilayered, symbolic nature of the miracle narratives as expressions of the story of redemption, indeed that Christ repudiated the notion of performing miracles merely as a display of power: "An evil and adulterous generation seeks for a sign; but no sign shall be given to it except the sign of the prophet Jonah."

Christ's miracles are in no sense "magical"; there is no hint that he is engaging in a formula or ritual technique. His healings and exorcisms are invariably performed in a context in which he challenges the Jewish rules of separation, the divide between the clean and the unclean. He heals on the Sabbath and he cures people who were considered beyond the pale of Jewish piety—lepers, tax collectors, a woman with a menstrual flow. And his healing contains clues and foretastes of salvation.

In the case of the raising of Lazarus from the dead (John, Chapter II), Christ deliberately delays his arrival at Bethany so that he might "waken him out of his sleep." Martha rebukes Christ for coming too late, and Christ replies that he *is* the resurrection and the life, and that those who believe in him, if they die, will live forever.

The story of Lazarus is clearly more than the mere raising of a corpse. The miracle anticipates the promise of eternal life and conveys a clear signal that out of those who respond in faith to Christ will come a new people, "to gather into one the children of God who are scattered abroad." The raising of Lazarus, like other miracles in the gospel of Luke and John, is symbolic of the promise of a new people of God and of eternal life.

I had been intrigued by Briege McKenna's assertion that there was always something to be "learned" through *praying* for miracles, whether the results were "successful" or not, for it carried the implication that the lessons were not always obvious. Before they could be fully understood, miracles of healing, perhaps like apparitions, must be "read," almost as one would ponder the meaning of a poem, a narrative, or play. The more one concentrated merely on the power, the "proof," the manipulation and the magic, the more one scrutinized the purely medical and scientific data, and the less one was capable of understanding the spiritual implications.

And if one were to accept that there is such a thing as *spiritual* healing, in the sense of discovering faith and confidence in a power beyond oneself, is it so very difficult to accept that such a renewal might culminate in psychological and even physical benefits?

Our understanding of the operation of the autonomic and immune systems on the control of pain and spontaneous remissions, is still rudimentary, but the gathering evidence looks incontrovertible. It is certainly clear that what people call faith and hope can elicit both subjective and objective changes in the body involving psychological and physiological effects that are measurable. And why should this be surprising? Whatever a person's philosophy of the relationship between mind, body, and soul, our thoughts are incontestably, if not merely, electrochemical events which can bring about physical events.

Advances in our understanding of the effect of endorphins, opioids and other neuron transmitters on pain and illness may soon threaten the assumptions of the Lourdes criteria for miracles, to the point where the notion of the "inexplicable" may disappear altogether. To invoke the notion of the "inexplicable" is to appeal to a temporary state of affairs, is to put the phenomenon of "divine" healing at the mercy of scientific progress: what is inexplicable today may be very much understood tomorrow.

Is this to veer, once again, toward reductionism? It is common nowadays for historians of medicine to harp on the gap between medical knowledge and superficial symptoms that so easily led to miraculous conclusions in the past. During the Middle Ages, for example, only the very learned had guessed that the pulse might be a sign of life in a body; people relied mostly on skin color, body temperature, and lack of obvious breathing and, as a result, miracles of revival from the dead—as with Lazarus—were not uncommon.

As I scanned contemporary commentaries on miracles, however, I could take little comfort from the idea that *most* "miracles" of the past could be dismissed as inaccurate diagnoses.

In a revealing article in the *British Medical Journal* (287: December 24–31, 1983) Dr. Rex Gardner, a consultant obstetrician and gynecologist, draws parallels between miracles of healing in Anglo-Celtic Northumbria and some contemporary cures associated with religious auspices in the same district.

One example of the seven cases he cites should suffice. In his homily on Luke written in the eighth century, the Venerable Bede tells the story of a woman suffering from hideous ulcers who was healed by prayers and the application of salt and holy oil. As a modern parallel Dr. Gardner cites the case of a young woman in Northumbria who had a "deterioration in a large varicose ulcer of the leg which had been troubling her for many years. . . . She asked for prayer at the monthly charismatic meeting. A general practitioner present examined the leg and judged that even were the ulcer to heal, it would require skin grafting." By the next morning the ulcer had almost healed, and after a second prayer meeting a week later the cure was complete. Dr. Gardner comments: "This story is so bizarre that it would not have been included were I not one of the doctors who examined the patient's leg."

But the crucial point he wishes to make involves the relationship between expectation of miracles and their fulfillment. Bede's stories of miracles and especially those of Saint Cuthbert, says Gardner, have up to now been discarded as mere copies of New Testament incidents written for hagiographical purposes. Indeed, he says, there is evidence that during his own lifetime Bede himself believed (probably encouraged by Pope Gregory the Great) that the age of miracles had passed. Gardner's study is a salutory warning both against seeing miracles *purely* as a metaphorical or hagiographical device, and against assuming that they arose out of our ancestors' ignorance of medical matters.

On reflection, and paradoxically—considering my starting point—what worried me most about miracles, as defined by the churches (and especially the Catholic Church), was their attempt to institutionalize the quality of "inexplicability." The notion smacked too much of magic as opposed to *mystery.*

Isn't it enough that the cure should be unusual, surprising, or mysterious? Surely the crucial factor should be that the cure follows prayer or religious ritual; it is the context, the narrative of the cure that matters. In other words, as with apparitions, or visions, or stigmata, I could not see, from a believer's point of view, why there should be any contradiction involved in grace or spirituality building on natural processes. But this does not satisfy the literalists who condemn such an approach as "subjectivist" and "rationalist."

Pondering the case of Delizia of Catania, I had to admit that there seemed to be more than a purely coincidental link between Lourdes and her cure. But by the same token, I was equally impressed by the alteration in a terminally ill friend of mine whose pilgrimage to Lourdes earlier in the year resulted in the overcoming of bitterness and depression and a sense of renewal and hope, despite the absence of a physical cure.

The more one puts limits and rigorous criteria on the meaning of miracles, or apparitions, or any of the other physical phenomena of mysticism, the more, it seemed to me, the value-laden, nonmaterialistic significance of these events seems to recede and elude us.

The best illustration I can offer is a strange miracle-in-reverse that I had first heard of on my journey through America after my dream. It occurred to my friend Tobias Wolff, the American writer, and I quote it in full, for it illustrates, as can no amount of discussion or ratiocination, the insights, the ironies, the potential for growth and self-understanding that can arise in a place like Lourdes. It says something too, I think, about the role of imagination, irony, and narrative, in the most humble of religious experiences.

> I don't see well. It's a condition I've always resented. As a boy I wouldn't even admit to it until I began to suffer from headaches, and could no longer read the blackboards at school. I hated my glasses and wore them only upon necessity, walking around most of the time in a blur, as if under water. Later I tried contact lenses but my eyes wouldn't tolerate them. Anyway, they made me feel like a fraud. What I really wanted was perfect vision.
>
> I mention this by way of preamble to a story about something that happened to me in the summer of 1972, during a pilgrimage to Lourdes. But first I should explain how I got there.
>
> At my mother's wish I was baptized a Catholic at the age of ten, but faith, conscious faith, played no part in my life until I was in my twenties.
>
> That's not true. It did play a part in my life, an active part,

because I was vigilantly suspicious of it, understanding instinctively that it would subvert the plans I had for myself, mercenary, vainglorious as most of those plans were. And I believed that faith would somehow blind me, keep me from seeing things clearly. Certainly it would change me. I was afraid of it. I went on being afraid of it, go on being afraid of it even now, years after it entered my life irrevocably.

In my twenties, as I said, faith became a possibility for me. Why then? I can think of reasons. But reasons don't, in the end, explain faith any more than they can create it. Something happened, an inward turning, a sense of being both cornered and upheld. But even in this turning I felt a sense of reluctance and doubt.

In the summer of 1972 I went to Lourdes for a week. I lived in a barracks with other men. We weren't there very much—only to eat and sleep. The rest of our time was given over to performing different services for the sick, to whom Lourdes is dedicated. We worked in the dining halls, in the hospitals, in the baths— wherever we were needed. I worked mostly at the baths, volunteering again and again because the experience was strange, and harrowing, and therefore, I thought, good for me.

Good health makes provincials of us; we take the border between ourselves and the unhealthy as ordained, fitting, and eternal, and do not give much thought to what lies on the other side. At the baths I was, at least for a time, shaken out of this provincialism. There were four of us in each bathing pool. Our task was to receive the men and boys who were brought in to us and to separate them from their wheelchairs and braces and walkers, then undress them and carry them into the water, where we prayed over them. I saw the human body under every kind of attack. It was good to recognize that hope and faith and even joy could live on in such ruins. But the experience also appalled me, and I was not displeased to be taken out of the baths one afternoon and driven with some other volunteers to the local airport, where we were to help a group of disabled Italian pilgrims embark for the plane ride home. It was a hot, muggy day. The heat hung over the tarmac in a haze that made the light harsh, almost blinding. At first things went smoothly. We wheeled a number of people out to the plane, where they were taken up a ramp by crews of nurses and medics. Then there was a mix-up. They told us to wait at the bottom of the ramp. We waited for a time, and then, outrageously, someone shut the airplane door.

I was with a little girl about two years old. She was completely paralyzed, and had tubes in her nostrils that drained into bags under the sheet that covered her. She looked up at me calmly, too calmly somehow; I couldn't tell whether she heard me or not when I murmured to her in what I hoped was an encouraging tone. I moved her gurney into the shade of the fuselage and fanned her face with my hand. Still they kept us waiting. Then the flies discovered her. I couldn't keep them off, no matter how hard I tried. They swarmed on her face, over her lips, around her eyes. I kept brushing at them but they came right back, humming, persistent. I became desperate with anger. My anger went beyond the situation. It was fundamental, unreasonable; it had to do with the scheme of things. By the time they opened the airplane door again I was weeping, though only I knew it—by now all our faces were flushed and glistening with sweat.

The little girl was with the last group of passengers. After the plane took off I got on a bus back to Lourdes, and it came to me along the way that something peculiar was happening. I had taken my glasses off earlier in the afternoon because they kept slipping down. They were still in my pocket, but I could see as well as if I had them on, could read license plates and make out the features of people we passed, see sheep grazing in distant fields. I couldn't understand it. I squinted and blinked and rubbed my eyes, thinking it must be a lens formed by sweat and tears, but it didn't go away. I felt giddy and restless, happy but uncomfortable, not myself at all. Then I had the distinct thought that when we got back to Lourdes I should go to the grotto and pray. That was all. Go to the grotto and pray.

But I didn't do that. The bus let me off at the barracks and I went inside for a moment to cool off, and fell into conversation with an Irishman I'd gotten to know. He was sharp and honest and very funny. We sat down on his cot and talked, and all the while I was aware of what I wasn't doing and what I wasn't telling him. I had no reason not to mention what had happened—he would have been keenly interested, not at all derisive—but I didn't say a thing about it. We talked and laughed for a couple of hours, then went to dinner, and I never made it to the grotto that day. Next morning I was wearing my glasses again.

Later I told this story to a priest I knew, Father Michael Hollings, and he said, "O ye of little faith." He said it with a smile, but he meant it.

What happened? Possibly it was, as I first suspected, a film on my eyes. Possibly it was an illusion—I only thought I was seeing clearly. It would seem ungenerous, un-Godly, to make such a gift conditional, and to take it back. Of course there's no way of knowing what really happened, or what would have happened if I'd gone to the grotto that afternoon.

What interests me now is why I didn't go. I felt, to be sure, some incredulity. But this wasn't the reason. I have a weakness for good company, good talk, but that wasn't it either. That was only a convenient distraction. At heart, I must not have wanted this thing to happen. I don't know why, but I have suspicions. I suspect that I considered myself unworthy of such a gift. And if I had secured it, what then? I would have had to give up those doubts by which I defined myself, in the world's terms, as a free man. By giving up doubt, I would have lost that measure of pure self-interest to which I felt myself entitled by doubt. Doubt was my connection to the world, to the faithless self in whom I took refuge when faith got hard. Imagine the responsibility of losing. What then? No wonder I was afraid of this gift, afraid of seeing so well.

PART FIVE

SAINTS, ANGELS, AND PRODIGIES

19

In the Gargano

Throughout my journey I had been constantly reminded of the reputation of the astonishing stigmatic, Padre Pio, and his legendary powers which, by all accounts, he had continued to exert beyond the grave.

The time had come to discover for myself an impression of the life and influence of this great recent "saint" by visiting his shrine, and by talking with the man who was urging his canonization. Would I feel that sense of *potentia* which, according to Catholic tradition, is exerted at the tombs of those of outstanding holiness through the special presence of God from whom all miracles and wonders spring? Would I be enticed toward belief by the example of his holy life?

Or would I, on taking a closer look at the phenomenon of his stigmata, decide that he was a neurotic fraud, a creation of primitive Italian superstition?

I rented a car in Rome and drove across Italy to San Giovanni Rotondo in the Gargano Peninsula, the site of the monastery where Padre Pio lies awaiting the deliberations of his Church on whether or not he is to join the calendar of the saints.

In the early Middle Ages there were three great pilgrimages in Europe, known as the journeys to the Man, to the God, and to the Angel: to Rome and Saint Peter; to Jerusalem and the Son of God;

and to Gargano and the Mount of Saint Michael (the Monte Sant'
Angelo).

The Gargano Massif, the spur on the boot of Italy, is an austere,
high tableland of rock and forest jutting out into the Adriatic Sea.
Isolated, harsh, poverty-stricken, it was for centuries a haunt of
mystics and pilgrims. Monte Sant'Angelo, on a beetling peak dominating the peninsula, is the site of the cave where, according to
legend, Michael the Archangel—the champion of the Powers of
Light against Satan—appeared three times to shepherds in 491. It
is a windswept, melancholy place, of vast skies and arid landscapes.

Pope Gelasio the First and the local bishop of Manfredio were
quick to confirm and authenticate the shepherds' visions, and before
long a trail of kings and princes, bishops and priests, and armies
of the faithful, were making the arduous journey to this mountain
fastness to encounter a unique token of holy presence. It was popular, too, among saints: Saint Bernard, Saint Anselm, Saint Bridget,
and Saint Alphonsus came to fast and pray; Saint Francis of Assisi
received the stigmata shortly after completing his pilgrimage.

From the end of the Middle Ages until recent times the place
fell into neglect; but, it has enjoyed a revival by association with the
man known as Padre Pio of Pietrelcina, who lived for most of his
religious life in a monastery in the small town of San Giovanni
Rotondo just a few miles below the old shrine. For fifty years or
more people trekked to Gargano to catch a glimpse of this man,
who seemed to rival the greatest saints of old both in his evident
heroism and in his extraordinary paranormal powers.

Padre Pio died in 1968, but the faithful have not ceased to
journey there.

I arrived late in the afternoon at the monastery of Our Lady of
Grace after driving across a featureless plain from Foggia, the largest
city of the region some forty miles distant to the west.

There is a square with a modern barn-like church to the side
of the monastery; but Padre Pio's vast hospital, set back a little to
the right of the church, dominates everything. The hospital is one
of the great ironies of the place: for this man who was famed for
his gifts of divine healing, and who lived in retirement under a vow
of poverty, established before his death one of the biggest, most
heavily endowed, best-equipped hospitals in the south of Italy.

From the outside the church looked like a political convention
hall: there were posters of Padre Pio stuck all over the facade.

Middle-aged Italian women were barging their way through the main doors, many of them dressed in black. I joined an entering party.

Inside, the church was light and airy and free of ornament save for a mosaic mural behind the high altar, a crowned Madonna and Child surrounded by pink and pastel green angels.

There were a few pilgrims kneeling in prayer, but the majority of people were coming and going down a flight of steps that led to a crypt. I followed the flow.

The crypt was cold and smelled of damp plaster, like an underground shelter. But the principal and most startling impression was the echoing sound of droning, crooning, humming women, circulating in swarms around a gray slab of marble situated behind a steel grille. This was the tomb of Padre Pio, the goal of their pilgrimage.

There were two prominent signs on placards attached to the grille. One depicted a recommendation of the shrine by Karol Wojtyla in 1974 when he was Cardinal in Cracow; two years after his ordination the future Pope John Paul II had visited Padre Pio, and the living saint had prophesied, according to reasonable evidence, that the young priest would one day be pope.

The second notice warned: "NON GETTARE MONETTE SULLA TOMBA" ("Don't throw money at the tomb").

There were capacious collection strongboxes situated around the walls, announcing: "OFFERTE PER LA CAUSA DI BEATIFICAZIONE DI PADRE PIO" ("Offerings for the cause of the beatification of Padre Pio"). Canonization costs money.

The vast basement reverberated with an alarming hum of primitive belief in the *power,* the efficaciousness of the supposed presence of the "saint" who lay within the tomb. Part of me was repelled by the crude irrationality on display here. But part of me felt glad, in a way that I could only dimly understand, that there were places in the world, like this, where men and women could find solidarity and reassurance by standing in the presence of the spirit of a fellow human who had been transformed in life by a heroic imitation of Christ.

I found the office of the vice postulator behind an electronically operated steel gate surmounted by spikes. No groups of formidable women could penetrate *this* sanctuary. A rascally looking monk with immense girth took me through a modern office complex to my appointed meeting.

It is the job of the vice postulator (he is the key person in the operation, the postulator himself being a bureaucrat in Rome) to act as impresario in the long, expensive, and difficult task of persuading the Church to accept a "servant of God" as a candidate for sainthood. In the case of Padre Pio the vice postulator is a Franciscan called Father Gerardo di Flumine. He greeted me at the door of his room, yet another rotund friar with a polished bald pate and the enigmatic lineless face of a buddha. He seemed to narrow his eyes with suspicion as he shook my hand. In the business of sainthood publicity counts for much.

He glanced down at my shoes, which were black.

Suddenly he was smiling. "Are you a priest?" he asked.

"No," I said. At which the smile came down like a well-oiled trap.

"It's so difficult," he murmured, "to tell the difference nowadays between the clergy and the laity. . . . But never mind."

He invited me to sit, while he placed himself at a vast desk. Behind him, and all around the room, were shelves of box files and weighty-looking theological tomes; in the offices on the way, I had gained a fleeting impression of blinking computer terminals, banks of filing cabinets, documents by the ton.

"It would take me several lifetimes to tell you about Padre Pio," he began. "I will give you some books, and you can do your own homework. There's no other way . . ."

With this he began to take books out of a drawer in his desk and bang them on the table in front of me.

"But how, Father," I asked, "are saints made?"

I had a second question, too: What are they for? But that could wait for the time being.

The priest blew a silent whistle and raised his eyes to the ceiling.

"Many years. Much expense. And much patience," he said, shaking his head. "There are three stages toward canonization," he went on, "Venerable, Beatus, and finally Saint. We only started working toward the venerable status of Padre Pio in 1983.

"You see, although he died in 1968, for a number of years you are not allowed to do anything. We gathered together eighty major

testimonies to present to the tribunal, which has two branches—
the president on the one hand, and the lawyer on the other—known
in popular parlance as the Devil's Advocate.

"The second stage is what we call a historical commission, in
which we collate all the letters, journals, memoranda, books—edited and unedited—documents—official and unofficial . . ."

The priest droned on and on, describing the proliferation of
depositions, the weighing, the sifting, the difficulties, the hurdles,
the obstacles, the sheer time-consuming drudgery, stage after stage.

"Finalmente!" he said. "If all is okay, the responsible cardinal
goes to the pope and presents the evidence to await his verdict . . .
and if he says yes, then he becomes Beatus, and the process starts
all over again as we present his case for sainthood. . . . It could take
another fifty, sixty years . . . And even then that would be fast."

"So what is your biggest headache, Father?"

The priest smiled.

"Every year when I think that I have completed the collection
of Padre Pio's correspondence, something new turns up."

I picked up the pile of books that Father Gerardo had given
me.

"Tell me something, Father," I said. "Do you believe in the
Holy Shroud of Turin?"

He looked at me quizzically.

"Of course I believe in it."

"On the shroud, Christ is pierced in the wrists. So, if Padre Pio
received the genuine marks of the crucifixion from God, why are
his wounds in the palms of his hands?"

The priest narrowed his eyes. "How interesting," he said, "we
had a congress on the stigmata and Padre Pio just last September
and this question came up . . ."

Father Gerardo stroked his well-trimmed beard. "The answer
my friend is very obvious when you think about it.

"Listen," he said, "if God speaks to you, does he speak in Italian,
English, or Chinese? Do you get my meaning? If God did not operate
for the benefit of the receiver he would have to perform *two* miracles; he would have to enable you to speak a language you did
not understand. . . . *Now* are you with me?"

I nodded, eager to move on from these casuistic quibbles,
which were, after all, of my own making.

"In any case," said Father Gerardo with finality, "the important thing is that he lived for more than fifty years as a living crucifix. The wounds, the sufferings, were *intensely* real . . ."

As I rose to go with my stack of books, the priest shook my hand.

"Make up your mind after you've acquainted yourself with his life," he said.

Padre Pio's real name was Francisco Forgione and he was born in 1887, one of five children, at Pietrelcina, near Naples. His father, a migrant worker, twice made the voyage to the United States to earn money to support his family.

As a boy he witnessed a miraculous event that was to have a profound effect on the course of his life. In August 1895 he accompanied his father to the shrine of San Pellegrino. The statue of the saint stood on the high altar before a great crush of pilgrims who had come to attend the ceremonies associated with miraculous healings.

In the midst of the ritual, a "raging, disheveled" woman started to scream. She pushed her way to the front until she stood before the statue. In her arms she held a child with a huge, hydrocephalic head and shrunken, paralyzed limbs; unable to talk, the child made a horrifying squawk "like a crow."

The woman cried out ceaselessly for a miracle, and threw herself on the ground before the statue. Next she began to abuse the saint, screaming and cursing up at the statue. At this point Pio's father decided that it was time to leave, but Pio refused to budge. He stayed on, earnestly praying for a miracle.

Suddenly the woman let out a final scream and hurled the child at the statue. "Why don't you cure him?" she yelled. "Well, keep him! He's all yours!" The child bounced off the statue and fell to the floor of the sanctuary, hitting its head with a loud thud on the marble. The people surged forward to restrain her, but the child stood on its feet, completely healed, and ran toward her, calling out, "Mother, mother!"

It is clear that Pio associated the healing with his *own* prayer, rather than the efficacy of the saint, and he saw his defiance of his father's wishes as an important element in the story: he was already about his *real* father's business.

The incident, whatever its retrospective accretions and exaggerations, anticipates the central significance of his life: more than any holy man in Christendom this century he was to provide proof, according to his countless devotees, that God intervenes in direct and observable ways in human affairs.

Pio grew up in a region which outstrips even the rest of Italy in its manifestations of popular folk religion. Toward the end of the nineteenth century there were estimated to be as many as 10,000 churches, chapels, and shrines in the region of Naples. The proliferating legends of its saints featured heroic self-denials and extravagant paranormal behavior, including levitation, flying, and bilocation. Its local Virgins, its relics, and ubiquitous "incorrupt" bodies of saints provided a complete and alternative world of the sacred. Ritualized miracles were a familiar part of people's lives.

As a child Pio was deeply religious; even allowing for the hagiographical excesses that surround his memory, it is clear that he believed he enjoyed visionary experiences of angels and conversations with Mary and Christ. He heard celestial choirs, and bells, and was aware of holy odors, and he believed he was harassed by "assaults of the devil."

It comes as no surprise to learn that his hobby was making statues, his favorite figure being Michael the Archangel.

Pio grew up with the single-minded ambition to be a Franciscan priest, and after a haphazard education he entered the seminary at the age of fifteen. He was ordained eight years later.

From the very start his superiors found him a problem. He went in for excessive self-denials, fasting, long hours in private prayer. He was frequently ill, running phenomenally high temperatures and prone to migraines, constipation, and vomiting. He often slipped into ecstasies, and he took nearly two hours over a Mass service that should have taken thirty minutes.

The solitude and inactivity occasioned by his frequent illnesses created further opportunities to pursue his intense interior life. In the early years of his priesthood he spent months on end living alone in a tower at Pietrelcina. We next hear of demonic and poltergeist activity; neighbors talked of crashes, bangs, and shouts, like "drunken brawls." Pio was to confirm later that he had been locked in dire struggles with demons. "They hurled themselves upon me," he wrote, "threw me on the floor, struck me violently, and threw pillows, books, and chairs through the air and cursed me with exceedingly filthy words."

He was called up for army duties in the First World War but simply went absent without leave and never returned to duty. In desperation his spiritual director had him removed to the remote monastery of Our Lady of Grace at San Giovanni Rotondo.

There his mystical life deepened. And its focus was a powerful dedication of himself as "victim," to suffer with Christ on behalf of others: "Deep down in my soul," he wrote, "it seems to me, God has poured out many graces of compassion for the sufferings of others ... When I know that a person is afflicted in soul or body, what would I not do to have the Lord relieve him of his sufferings! Willingly would I take upon myself all his sufferings to see him saved."

At times this vocation for self-immolation seemed to go beyond the norms of even the most radical expressions of spirituality: "Punish me and not others ... Even send me to Hell, provided that I can still love You and everyone else is saved."

His "visions," his "locutions," his insights in prayer seemed to be of two kinds: on the one hand, they fall within a rigorous, peasant folk tradition; on the other, they approach the classic high mysticism of Teresa of Avila and John of the Cross.

He has left accounts of jocular, scolding, Browningesque conversations with his "guardian angel," whom he referred to as "my boy": "Angel of God, my angel—aren't you my guardian? God gave you to me ... Are you a creature or are you a creator? ... You're a creator? No! Then you are a creature and you have a law and you have to obey. You must stay close to me whether you want to or not ... You're laughing! ... What is there to laugh about? ..."

At the same time, he was engaged in that long and arduous climb through the "dark night of the soul" to the pure, airy summits of unitive prayer: "My ordinary way of praying is this: hardly do I begin to pray than at once I feel my soul begin to recollect itself in a peace and tranquility that I cannot express in words. ... The senses remain suspended ..."

He writes of being "forever lost in that immense ocean of good ... and enjoying that by which He Himself is blessed."

Again, he describes a vision of Christ in which "The Lord immersed my soul in such peace and contentment, that all the sweetest delights of this world, even if they were doubled, pale in comparison to even a drop of this blessedness."

In Padre Pio, the peasant piety of southern Italy seems to meet and blend with the higher reaches of spirituality and prayer, suggesting that the rituals and images of Mediterranean folk religion, commonly regarded as uncouth, superstitious, even pagan, have immense potential for powerful spiritual insights.

Pio's mystical states were by no means a succession of sweet and ineffable experiences. It seems that for the most part he was subject to a long chain of afflictions, both physical and psychological. His spiritual director was convinced that Pio had been specially chosen as a "co-redemptor and victim" by God, and an indication of his special status was an experience referred to by mystics as "The Assault of the Seraphim," in which he was struck in a vision by a fiery weapon that delivered a "mortal wound in the depths of my soul, a wound that is always open and which causes me continual agony."

Nothing could have illustrated better the marriage of vivid, traditional iconography, and the deeper implications of Pio's self-surrender, than the phenomenon of the stigmata. He had gradual warnings of its arrival, with incipient pains and visible symptoms over several years. Then, at the age of thirty-one, things came to a crisis. On September 20, 1918, after eight years of intermittent pain in his hands, feet, and side, he received the stigmata proper. The five wounds opened up fully, and poured with blood. He was the first male stigmata on record since Saint Francis in the thirteenth century.

He wrote to his spiritual director:

"After I had celebrated Mass I was suddenly filled with great peace and abandonment which effaced everything else and caused a lull in the turmoil ... While this was taking place I saw before me a mysterious person ... his hands and feet and side were dripping blood ... The vision disappeared and I became aware that my hands, feet, and side were dripping blood. Imagine the agony I experienced and continue to experience almost every day. The heart wound bleeds continually, especially from Thursday evening until Saturday ... I am dying of pain because of the wounds and the resulting embarrassment ..."

The phenomenon of the stigmata in Padre Pio was to last for more than fifty years; in addition to the pain he would suffer both unwelcome adulation and aggressive skepticism.

A succession of psychiatrists and physicians trooped down from Rome to San Giovanni Rotondo over the years. They marveled at the fact that they could make their fingers meet through the wounds in his hands and that the blood, which remained constantly fresh, seemed "perfumed." Many declared themselves to be baffled and proclaimed that here was a genuine mystery to science. But others accused him of fraud, hysteria, self-hypnosis, and even of being in league with the devil. An archbishop set spies on him and asserted that the phenomenon was perpetrated with aid of eau de cologne and carbolic acid, which he claimed had been found under the monk's bed. The archbishop was in time discredited, but the rumors and accusations persisted until Pio's death.

His life was fraught with paradox and controversy. Many hours of his day were spent in contemplative prayer, and yet he conducted an outward-going energetic ministry right up to the day he died, spending as long as twelve hours a day in the confessional and performing a host of good works.

His spirituality seemed "private," elevated, unattainable, and yet his attachment to familiar pieties kept him in touch with the people. All spoke of his evident saintliness, yet he could be irreverent, brusque, sharp-tongued, and comic. He lived a sheltered life enclosed in his monastery, and yet he had an impressive grasp of what was happening in the local community, in Italy, and around the world. Italian Communists scoffed, calling him "the richest monk in the world." His hospital was free to the poor, but he was criticized for his insistence that it should be built with the finest materials; there was too much marble in it, they said. There were wrangles over the building contracts, rumors of financial scandals. Rome was suspicious of all this, and of his popularity; people flocked to him by the hundreds of thousands.

The attraction was undoubtedly the curiosity of his stigmata, and there was an abundance of miraculous and "paranormal" occurrences associated with the cult of his personality. The number of miracles of healing claimed in his name would run into many thousands. It was believed that he regularly bilocated; in the books that Father Gerardo di Flumine lent me there were scores of testimonies from people who claimed that on meeting Padre Pio they realized that they had encountered him before, on a sickbed, on a battlefield, in a church confessional, in a dream. There were even accounts of airmen who had seen his bearded figure over the skies of Italy. Invariably these experiences were accompanied by an arresting perfume. When he was challenged as to his awareness of these episodes he would invariably wink and quip cryptically: "Oh, these little visions and voices!"

A brother monk claimed that Padre Pio had come to him while in the hospital and healed him of a fatal illness, although it was known that Pio had not been outside the monastery. When his superior asked him whether he had bilocated, Pio said: "Is there any doubt about it? . . . Yes, I went, but do not say anything to anyone."

His long struggles with demon presences had given him, it was believed, unparalleled efficacy as an exorcist, and in confession he was credited with a discernment tantamount to clairvoyance. People would say that he "saw the whole of one's life at a glance." It was in confession that he was most often angry, especially if he detected pride or mere curiosity in a penitent; or worse still if a person came to him who was living "in sin" with no evident purpose of amendment. He could send people away with an earful of abuse and without absolution, and he was known to slap faces and box ears. Many people quaked at the idea of confronting him in the confessional; many backed out at the last moment.

But the high point of the day at San Giovanni was Padre Pio's Mass. He would rise at 2:30 in the morning to prepare himself in prayer and meditation. The people would be let in at five, and there would be a race for the best places. A bevy of local women would always be at the front, and there were stories of uninitiated pilgrims being trampled, bitten, and knocked to the ground in the rush to the altar rails.

Once started, though, the silence and concentration during every moment of the Mass became an unforgettable experience for the congregation. As a fellow monk wrote: "His Mass produced such an impression that time and space between the altar and Calvary disappeared. The Divine Host, raised by those pierced hands, made the faithful more aware of the mystical union between the offering priest and the eternal priest."

He seemed to struggle with waves of emotion, trembling and weeping as he passed through fear, joy, sadness, anguish, and pain. From the expression on his face the people could follow his interior meditations. Often his whole body would be shaken by sobs.

Padre Pio wrote: "When I celebrate holy Mass I am not standing, but hanging on the cross together with Jesus, and I suffer inadequately all that Jesus suffered on the cross, as much as is possible for a human creature. The Lord has deigned to associate me with the great work of human redemption, and this despite my every demerit, and only because of his supreme goodness."

As he grew older his physical suffering increased. He was confined to a wheelchair and seemed prematurely aged. The monks prepared a tomb fit for a saint in the crypt of the new modern church. In the final year of his life the stigmata began to disappear. When he died on September 23, 1968, there was no sign of the wounds. Hundreds of thousands flocked to his requiem mass, which was celebrated in the presence of cardinals and bishops. The famous "perfume" filled the church where he had lain in state.

20

Physical Phenomena of Mysticism

I had a disturbed night. Whenever I slept I dreamed vividly about Padre Pio; he seemed to be hovering in the room, a powerful, ambivalent, haunting presence, demanding to be understood. I had acquainted myself with his personality merely through spoken and written testimonies and photographs, but here in San Giovanni Rotondo I could sense something of the immense charisma as if I had known him intimately all my life.

What did I believe about Padre Pio? Was I convinced that his stigmata offered irrefutable evidence of supernatural intervention?

In preparation for this trip to Italy I had studied, among other things, the relevant chapters on his case in Herbert Thurston's *Physical Phenomena of Mysticism,* to discover that the Church had seriously wavered on the question of the significance of his stigmata.

In 1923 the Holy Office in Rome had declared, after "due investigation," that his stigmata were definitely not of supernatural origin, and that pilgrims should not visit him or correspond with him. Although the official attitude softened in later years, the early investigations are of great interest, especially the medical reports that Thurston managed to secure for inclusion in his study, for these were thorough and impartial in the days before Padre Pio's widespread adulation began.

One of these investigations, conducted in 1919 by a Professor

A. Bignami, an agnostic pathologist of Rome University, confirmed the existence of "superficial scars" on the hands and the feet and the form of a cross on the left breast. He commented that the "wounds" were marked by extreme sensitiveness (hyperesthesia) and he was quite convinced that they had not been artificially produced. Professor Bignami's verdict was, nevertheless, that they were of "neurotic origin," and that their symmetrical arrangement indicated "unconscious suggestion."

Another distinguished physician, a Dr. George Festa of Rome, who was a Catholic, examined Padre Pio four months after Bignami. He saw drops of blood trickling from the scar on the breast, although he commented that the "wound" was not "open" in the sense that there was a rift in the flesh with "open lips." He also found drops of blood oozing from the scab on one of the hands.

Both doctors remarked on the exacerbating effect of iodine and carbolic acid that Pio used to cleanse the wounds and prevent infection.

There nevertheless seems to have been serious disagreement as to whether the "lesions" really were superficial or not. Padre Pio's local physician, a Dr. Andrea Cordone, and a Dr. Luigi Romanelli of Barletta, insisted that the wounds were deep; Cordone reckoned that he could "see light" through them, as did members of the monastic community who cared for Pio every day of his life.

The disagreement is important as superficial bleeding, even in the apparent form of stigmata, has come to be related in recent times with a condition called psychogenic purpura, in which spontaneous hemorrhages can occur with no current physical trauma. In my researches after meeting Georgette Fanielle I had unearthed a description of this phenomenon in a paper published in *Archives of Internal Medicine* (109:1969) by Drs. D. P. Agle and O. D. Ratnoff. According to the study, the phenomenon of painful spontaneous bleeding can follow trauma such as an automobile accident, but may not occur until months or even years later, during times of emotional stress. It occurs in people of "hysterical predisposition" and may be reproduced with a hypnotic procedure. Their work was remembered in 1972 in Oakland, California, when a ten-year-old Baptist girl, Cloretta Robinson, experienced the stigmata during the Easter season, apparently influenced by the book *Crossroads* by John Webster. During subsequent examinations the girl's "wounds" were scrutinized with five- and ten-power magnifying lenses and showed no skin abnormality or lesions. During the fourth examination investigators "observed the blood to increase in volume fourfold, welling up in the center of the palm and spreading over the palmar creases. After wiping the wet blood away, no lesions were present with the exception of a pea-size bluish discoloration remaining in the palm of her left hand for approximately three minutes." The phenomenon was considered to be in all respects similar to psychogenic purpura.

Yet even if Padre Pio's wounds had indeed presented more than purely superficial lesions, there is still evidence available that his stigmata were psychological rather than supernatural.

Father Herbert Thurston's book, published in 1952, contained a reference to a remarkable, although little-known, pamphlet by a Dr. Alfred Lechler, published in 1933 in Germany. The pamphlet is still to be found in the library of the Jesuit house at Farm Street, London, where Thurston lived for most of his life.

In 1928 Dr. Lechler, a German psychiatrist, took on a Lutheran Austrian patient he calls Elisabeth K. She was highly neurotic and hypochondriacal and had been in and out of a number of psychiatric clinics without avail. One of her principal problems was that she manifested the symptoms of any illness she heard about. Her sufferings seemed real enough to her, at least, and she had attempted suicide on several occasions. Lechler was interested in her case and decided to take her into his house as a domestic so that he could study her at close quarters.

On Good Friday, 1932, Elisabeth K. went to a cinema to see a slide show of the Passion realistically depicted. When she returned home Lechler saw that she was upset and complaining of pains in her hands and feet. The idea then occurred to him of hypnotizing the girl and suggesting that she, like Christ, had been pierced with nails in her hands and feet. He renewed the suggestion several times and the appropriate wounds accordingly appeared. With subsequent suggestions he induced tears of blood to flow freely from her eyes and bleeding punctures to appear on her forehead representing the crowning of thorns. Photographs of the wounds are reproduced in the pamphlet.

According to the text the wounds are described as "open," and the flesh "torn." In subsequent sessions Lechner succeeded not only in healing the wounds by the same hypnotic process but in bringing them back once more by non-hypnotic suggestion.

While some doubt must remain, then, as to whether an auto-hypnotic process could bring about wounds through which the "light" appeared, there is sufficient disagreement about the actual depth of Padre Pio's stigmata to suggest that the phenomenon owes more to the psychological than the supernatural, both in the case of the monk himself and those who observed the phenomenon. It is surely significant that only those who knew him well and came from the locality spoke of such drastic fissures.

And yet, even though the evidence tended toward an explanation based on hypnosis and hysteria, I was not inclined to minimize an element of essential mystery in his stigmata, although that sense of mystery had less to do with miracles than a rare combination of poetic and spiritual aptitudes.

The more I pondered Padre Pio's stigmata against the background of his life and character, the more I was reminded of that powerful eighth-century Anglo-Saxon poem known as "The Dream of the Rood."

The dreamer has a vision of the Rood, the tree of the cross that bore Christ. The Rood addresses the Dreamer, telling of its humiliation at the hands of those who made it an instrument of torture for criminals, its sense of unworthiness when the hero Christ mounts it, and its joy as it is restored thereby to glory. Throughout the poem the tree's meditation is related to the sadness and loneliness of the sin-stained Dreamer. What is most striking, however, is the powerful sense of empathy and identity with the wounds of Christ, which reveals the spiritual and poetic potential of the state of stigmata:

The young hero stripped himself—he who was God almighty—strong and stouthearted. He climbed upon the high gallows, valiant, in the sight of many, for he would redeem mankind. I shook when the warrior embraced me, yet I dared not bow to earth, fall to the ground's surface: I must stand fast. A cross was I raised; I lifted up the Mighty King, Lord of the Heavens; I dared not bend. They pierced me with dark nails—on me are the wounds seen, open hateful gashes. Nor did I dare do harm to any of them. They mocked us both together. I was all wet with blood shed from the sides of that man by the time that he had sent forth his spirit. Many bitter things I had endured on the hill. I saw the God of Hosts cruelly racked. Darkness had covered with its mists the Ruler's body, the bright splendor. Shadow came forth, dark under the clouds. All creation wept, bewailed the King's fall: Christ was on Cross.

Padre Pio was apparently not neurotic, self-absorbed, or in any sense egotistical. His holiness was of a selfless, humble kind that proclaimed the invitation to imitate Christ in a radical and heroic manner. His way of life was essentially simple: he said the Mass with deep and sincere feeling; he spent his entire day in prayer and ministering to souls, he meditated ceaselessly on Christ's passion. More than this he was a down-to-earth, loving member of his community, and he built before he died, in the face of immense obstacles, one of the largest hospitals in the south of Italy.

Wordsworth in the "Preface" to the *Lyrical Ballads* describes good poetry as "the spontaneous overflow of powerful feelings" and a poet as one "who being possessed of more than usual organic sensibility, had also thought long and deeply." It seems to me that Padre Pio was a holy man who combined the sensibilities and powerful feelings of a poet with an unusually sensitive psychosomatic disposition (clearly capable of non-pathological hysteria and self-hypnosis) that enabled him to make a poem of his own body. Was this a miracle? In the sense in which most of us understand that word, the answer must be "no."

If there was a miracle in his story, it surely consisted in the fact that he lived the life of Christ without compromise, and yet managed to keep both feet more or less firmly on the ground.

In the morning I went up to the monastery to return the books. An American priest called Father Bill came to greet me as Father di Flumine was saying Mass. Father Bill had been very close to Padre Pio and had cared for him physically in his declining years.

He took me through the building to see Padre Pio's room, which is preserved exactly as it was at the time of his death. It was a simple cell, about ten feet by seven with an iron bedstead, a *prie dieu* and a washbasin. There were some nasty-looking exhibitions of blood-stained bandages behind glass.

"It was all in his eyes," recalled Father Bill. "Right up to the day he died he had the eyes of a young child. The whites were astoundingly clear, and they gave the impression of the most extraordinary innocence and love ... you just could not resist those eyes."

As he said this I remembered the strange childlike gaze of Georgette Fanielle in Montreal.

As Father Bill led me back to the door of the monastery, I said "You lived with him here for many years in this monastery; what was he like as a fellow monk? Were you in awe of him, or was he genuinely a friend?"

Father Bill stopped in his tracks.

"I'll tell you what he was like. Toward the end of his life, when he could only move with difficulty and great pain, I got up on the morning of my saint's feast day and I could hear somebody fiddling at the lock. I was a bit startled and called out, but nobody replied. When I opened the door I found a flower had been stuck in the keyhole, and I saw the figure of Padre Pio slowly disappearing at the end of the corridor ... He loved each one of us in a very individual way. That was how he was, and how I always remember him."

On my way from San Giovanni Rotondo I went up to Monte Sant'Angelo to visit the site of the Archangel Michael's fifth-century apparition. The day was bleak and windy and a funeral was passing silently through the town.

Over the facade of the church that houses the shrine was the legend: *"Terribilis est locus iste hic domus dei est et porta coeli."* ["Terrible is this place: this is the house of God and the Gate of Heaven."] The vestibule was decayed, weed-ridden, abandoned. There was no sign of human life save for two Italian youths practicing karate kicks at each other beneath the portico.

Five great flights of stairs plunged down into the bowels of the mountain. In the final cavern brimstone exuded from the living rock as if the visitation of the angel had gouged and scorched the interior like a white-hot meteorite. A ridiculous fifteenth-century hermaphrodite of a statue representing the mighty Archangel Michael was sited for veneration in a grotto watched over by a squinting monk in a soiled white habit.

The place was dark, humid, and there was indeed, I felt, a sense of something truly terrible having occurred which would leave its stench in mortal nostrils till the end of time. But was it Christian?

This damp cleft, this sticky inner sanctum at the end of the labyrinthine flights of marble steps, was reminiscent of those womb-like Cretan sanctuaries of the Mother Goddess, who belonged to both the mountain and cave; who fostered dream incubation and miracles of healing, and who, according to legend, had given birth to Zeus.

Was Michael a mutant figment of that ancient cave goddess? Or of Apollo? Or Hermes? Or Mercury? The greatest enigma of angels is surely the elusiveness of their evolution, even within the history of Christianity.

When I was a child we said a morning prayer: "Oh my good Angel, whom God has appointed to be my guardian, enlighten and protect me, direct and govern me during this day."

The angels of my childhood were protectors, companions, ministers. Several times in my life I have shared memories with people who saw their angels in infancy, often as a pillar of light; and I carry in my mind a powerful description of a supernatural presence recollected by the naturalist W. H. Hudson. It would appear, said Hudson, at a distance of three or four feet from the head of his bed, in the form of a column five feet high and about four feet in circumference. It was blue in color, and varied in depth and intensity; sometimes it was sky-blue, but usually a "deeper shade, a pure, soft, beautiful blue like that of the morning-glory or wild geranium."

My boyhood in the forties was filled with stories of sightings of angels. As young men and women went off to war, as London crumbled in the blitz, there was a burgeoning of interest in the protective power of angels. And memories of the power of angels in the previous generation were still fresh. An uncle told me how the explorer Sir Ernest Shackelton reported that on a return journey across the Antarctic wastes he and his companions were aware of "one more" who traveled with them. My grandfather, who still kept and polished shell cases from the First World War on his mantel shelf, talked of the army of white figures that had held off the Germans at Ypres. And tales still proliferated of the Angels of Mons, a legend of shining presences that had started with a fictitious account in the London *Evening News,* only to be confirmed by countless soldiers. During the Battle of Britain in the Second World War there were tales of mysterious figures who continued to fly the planes when the Royal Air Force pilots had been killed.

And looming hugely beyond these recent legends was the dynamic of the war of Christ and the angels against the mighty host of Satan. The received cosmology and history of these superior beings was based on the story that Lucifer and one half of the angel presences had rebelled out of pride against God and had been cast out of Heaven, whence Satan fell "like lightning."

In this alternative cosmology the good and the evil angels are ranged against each other, with Christ and his lieutenant and standard-bearer Michael at the head of one army, and Lucifer at the head of the other, locked in combat over the fate of each individual soul. This is the relentless battle between the Powers of Light and Darkness, the background struggle for each human soul.

Nowadays some scripture scholars tell us that the notion of Satan leading a hostile army against Christ and human souls is due to a fatal misreading of a phrase in Saint Paul, and the misinterpretation of the Greek word *archai* as "hostile super human powers" rather than merely "human rulers."

All the same, the idea of the almost equal nature of the struggle between Heaven and Hell, and hence the drama that surrounds the uncertainty of its outcome, has probably had a most profound influence on Judeo-Christian and Islamic cultures. Eschatological legends and literary masterpieces like *Paradise Lost* are one thing; applying them to the world of human politics and history is another. It is widely believed in evangelical Christian circles that the Second World War is only to be understood in terms of a suspension of the reign of Christ the King which allowed Satan freedom through the medium of Hitler to range about the world for the ruin of souls and the torture and physical destruction of millions. This notion lurks beneath the secular view of Hitler as a dark, superhuman power for evil who prevailed with his followers for a period before the reinstatement of the Light. Insistence on a mythic reading of history leaves little scope for understanding the human mechanisms and failings, the widespread human responsibility for the causes of the Second World War. Variations on such readings of history are shared by Muslim fundamentalists who see the antagonisms between the Middle East and the West in terms of holy wars, or jihads, of Allah and the faithful against Satan and the infidels.

So angels were soldiers. Or messengers and intermediaries. Or invisible ministers. In the fifth century Augustine of Hippo explained that the mission of angels as spokespersons belonged specifically to the Old Testament, and not at all to the new dispensation. The God of the Jews seldom spoke directly to humankind, hence the need for angels. In the New Testament the Lord speaks for himself, and in time the Virgin Mary became the principal Mediatrix, precluding the need of angels as intermediaries. She bridges the Old and the New Testaments, being the last to receive an angelic announcement. The new role of the angels, in the New Testament, is to act as ministers to Christ, and thereby to us all. As Gregory of Nazianzus, a fourth-century Church Father, puts it: "Ministrants of God's will, strong with both inborn and imparted strength, traversing all space, readily present to all at any place through their zeal for ministry and the agility of their nature ... different individuals of them embracing different parts of the world, or appointed over different districts of the universe...."

This is very like the notion of pagan gods, although there is from the outset an absence of erotic desire in these Christian otherworldly spirits. Not surprisingly the notion of "angelic" qualities, thus described, was to provide a powerful impetus for the early Christian ideals of celibacy, monasticism, and priestly ministry.

But who is Michael? What mythic attributions surrounded the little Renaissance statue in this dank grotto in Gargano, the last official site of his appearance to humankind on earth?

Michael is a super-angel who bestrides the legend of heavenly aggression and the ideal of heavenly and earthly ministry. His name means "Who is like God"; Palestine and the synagogue were, in Jewish tradition, his special care.

As we have fallen through sin into the power of Satan, Michael's role is to continue the fight for our deliverance. According to Catholic tradition all our guardian angels are subordinate to him. But he ministers not only to humankind but, in a special way, to God himself. He presides over the worship of adoration rendered to the most High, for he offers to God the prayers of the saints symbolized by incense, the smoke from which rises toward Heaven.

Like the ancient Egyptian god Anubis, Michael was widely depicted in the Middle Ages holding scales of justice, and Christians prayed to him that he should introduce them to Heaven after death. According to the Egyptian mythology, Anubis weighed the human heart against the weight of a feather: only the lightest of hearts would float into paradise. Michael carries on that dread task.

Looking about the gloomy, neglected cave on the top of that remote mountain in Italy, it was difficult to believe that this had once been the greatest shrine in Christendom to his mighty spirit.

Has Michael had his day? It would seem not. According to the twelfth chapter of Daniel, Michael's most magnificent and crucial role is yet to come. He, it seems, will preside over the End Time, the Final Doom, the Apocalypse.

> *At that time shall arise Michael, the great prince who has charge of your people. And there shall be a time of trouble, such as never has been since there was a nation till that time; but at that time your people shall be delivered, every one whose name shall be found written in the book. And many of those who sleep in the dust of the earth shall awake, some to everlasting life, and some to shame and everlasting contempt. And those who are wise shall shine like the brightness of the firmament; and those who turn many to righteousness, like the stars for ever and ever.*

There is a school of scriptural scholars who believe that now, in the 1990s, in the run-up to the third millennium, the dire time is even upon us, and that we shall be hearing much of Michael in the years to come.

Could I ever find it in myself to believe in angels again?

There had been an occasion not many years ago when my family and I took over a rambling apartment in Turin. We thought we had made it child-proof. One Sunday morning as we were sitting in bed drinking coffee, our twelve-month-old boy toddled in with a razor-blade trembling on the end of his tongue. I had a curious feeling that he had been steered toward our bed just in time by angelic propulsion.

On another occasion in Zurich I was about to step off a pavement; I was looking, I thought, in the right direction and began to move out, when something told me to freeze: at that moment a tram car, horrifyingly silent, swept past from the opposite direction an inch from my nose.

We all have those moments, and it's enough to make one think.

21

The Flying Monk

Driving south through Apulia the next day, it struck me as strange that angels were invariably depicted with wings when it was widely attested by trustworthy witnesses that some favored human beings had flown without them.

The thought was provoked by signs to Grottaglie, a scruffy provincial district that lies along both sides of rusty railroad tracks between Brindisi and Taranto. There is nothing nowadays to show for the extraordinary life and antics of the "flying monk" who once lived there, except the existence of some rare and curious hagiographies that a canon in the Duomo of Taranto lent me to satisfy my curiosity.

From the very outset of my journey I had been pursuing rumors and reports of levitation associated with holiness; all the leads had come to nothing. Somehow levitation was an extremely elusive phenomenon. But all those interested in such matters seemed to agree that the most well-attested, and astounding, instance of the prodigy on reliable record was the case of the "flying monk" of Copertino. I had first come across Joseph of Copertino in a chapter on levitation in Father Herbert Thurston's *Physical Phenomena of Mysticism*. The discussion was intriguing, for it seemed to me that this, of all prodigies, supported the contention of paranormal activity. I was prepared to accept that small metal objects defied gravity through what some people call telekinesis; of rising tables in séance conditions I was less certain. But for a human body to float unaided was something yet again. Even a small exhibition would indicate the presence of a considerable mystery.

As Father Thurston sensibly commented: "So far as regards the law of gravitation in itself, it does not greatly matter whether an ecstatic is raised above the ground three inches or thirty feet, and we have as much reason to be impressed if such an incident happens once as if it happened fifty times."

The problem was capturing a subject in the act without the possibility of hypnosis, illusion, or fraud; no easy matter in the twentieth century, it seemed. In a list of "levitating" saints, Father Thurston makes mention of at least fifty, from Andrew Salus in the ninth century to J. B. Cottolengo in 1842. Would I be prepared to accept the affidavits of reliable witnesses who were confident that they had observed scores of instances of such a phenomenon in the case of a single person?

Joseph of Copertino (modern Grottaglie), born in 1603, presents us with a major challenge. Nothing I had previously read about him in Father Thurston, nor in the most recent edition of *Butler's Lives of the Saints,* prepared me for the details reported in the eighteenth-century Italian hagiographies published after Joseph's canonization in 1767. I refer principally to the *Vita di S. Giuseppe di Copertino sacerdote professo dell'Ordine de' Minori Conventuali di S. Francesco,* published in Florence in 1768, the year after Joseph's canonization. (Some of this material can also be found in Norman Douglas's *Old Calabria.*)

Joseph was brought up near Taranto in a land of large skies, clear southern light, and the distant prospect of the shimmering Ionian sea. This is the country of wild dances: the *villanella* and the *tarantella,* the wild leaping dance that was believed to be the only antidote to the bite of the European wolf-spider, the tarantula. He grew up in the repressive post-Tredentine era of the counter-Reformation, when traditional local dances and wakes of all kinds were officially thwarted by diocesan law.

His parents were destitute. He was born (like Saint Francis of Assisi, and, naturally, his Savior) in a stable. His childhood was miserable, over-disciplined, and prone to painful disease. At the age of seven he developed an abscess which became gangrenous and spread in the form of ulcers so that he had to be treated with "iron and fire." For four years he was plagued by this sickness until he was cured miraculously by the application of some oil from the lamp of the Virgin of Galatone.

He grew up an absent-minded youth and was considered an imbecile, incapable even "of discriminating between brown bread and white," it was said. He acquired the nickname of "Bocaperta" —"gaping mouth." He dropped anything that he carried, especially anything breakable. Given to sudden tantrums, he was equally capable of long trances and deeply religious expressions of piety and self-discipline.

After failing to acquire any sort of schooling or trade he was taken into the Franciscans, and despite difficulties with his studies was ordained a priest in 1628. By dint of a miracle, so it was reckoned, he managed to learn by heart the only question he was asked in his faculty examination. He was by all accounts virtually illiterate, but his religious life was to become a succession of amazing ecstasies, miracles, and prodigies, probably unparalleled—according to Thurston—in the life of any other saint in the history of Christendom.

He multiplied bread and wine, drove out devils, healed the lame and the blind, and even quelled storms and tornadoes. He enjoyed the charism of "continuous prophecy" and could literally sniff out evil and witchcraft from a great distance. In his ecstasies it was noticed that hosts of flies would enter his mouth and rest on his open eyes without his seeming to notice. Like Saint Francis he had a special way with animals, and he referred to himself as *asinello*—"the little ass."

As he matured Joseph was described as "tall, with fresh complexion, large-boned and athletic ... tough, strong and capable of withstanding excessive pain ... His beard was long and thick, his shining eyes were constantly raised to heaven." His superiors confined him in remote friaries around Italy; but wherever he went his fame quickly followed. His self-denials were extravagant even for that era of harsh discipline and reform. He wore a hairshirt, deprived himself of bread and meat, and sprinkled bitter substances, known as *death powders,* on his meagre diet of herbs and roots. Others who tried these powders fell violently ill. He slept on bare boards in a robe that he changed seldom. All the same, it was said that every place he inhabited was filled with a heavenly odor. Like Catherine of Sienna, he sometimes ate leaves filled with pus produced by lepers' sores. Twice a week he beat himself so severely that thirty years after his death the walls of his cell were still caked with blood. In between times a single impure or vain thought would prompt him to scourge himself with skewered needles and lumps of metal which gouged his flesh until the blood flowed and he would collapse in a faint. He also persuaded others to flog him until he was senseless. Removing his clothes one day under the rules of obedience, it was discovered that he had attached a quantity of chains and lumps of iron to his bare skin. He was, in the words of the witnesses, "one great open sore."

But the prodigy that made him famous was the exercise of his *"ratto,"* an astounding leap or flight through the air accompanied by blood-curdling shrieks and cries. According to the official eighteenth-century *Vita,* containing affidavits taken under oath, some seventy separate flights were observed during his lifetime. It is noteworthy, moreover, that Prosper Lambertini, the future Benedict XV, who was Devil's Advocate in Joseph's cause for canonization, delivered himself of the following verdict in his disquisition on sainthood, *De Servorum dei Beatificatione:* "Whilst I discharged the office of Promotor of the Faith the cause of the Venerable Servant of God, Joseph of Copertino came up for discussion in the Congregation of Sacred Rites, which after my retirement was brought to a favorable conclusion, and in this eye-witnesses of unchallengeable integrity gave evidence of the famous upliftings from the ground and prolonged flights of the aforesaid Servant of God when rapt in ecstasy."

An early, somewhat modest example occurred shortly after his ordination when shepherds came to the church to play music: "When they began to play their instruments, he started to dance in the nave like David before the ark. Then he sighed and with a cry flew up like a bird above the main altar, a height of over six feet, and embraced the tabernacle with his arms." His biographer comments that the "prodigiousness of this spectacle filled the pious shepherds with holy terror."

As the years passed the feats became more complicated, more astounding. One involved a curious combination of flying and paranormal lightness of bodily weight: "He flew up into an olive tree where he remained in a kneeling posture for the space of half an hour. A marvelous thing it was to see the branch which sustained him swaying lightly, as though a bird had alighted upon it."

On another occasion he performed a flight combined with an

extraordinary feat of weight-lifting, when a calvary was being erected at Grottaglie: "Two crosses were already in position, but ten persons together could not lift the third which was about thirty-six feet high and very heavy. On seeing this, Joseph flew about seventy yards from the door of the friary to the cross, lifted it as easily as if it were a straw, and placed it in the hole prepared for it."

On other occasions Joseph would sweep others along on his flights. Once, while the monks were at prayer, he sailed over to the father guardian: "grabbing him by the hand, he raised him from the ground by supernatural force, and with a joyful cry dragged him along, spinning him round and round in a violent dance, the priest being moved by Joseph, and Joseph by God." On another occasion he snatched a sick man by the hair and flew into the air drawing the man with him; on reaching the ground the man found that he had been cured of a "severe nervous malady." Once he threw a lamb into the air and took flight after it to the height of the trees where he "remained kneeling in an ecstasy with extended arms for more than two hours."

In the course of his life Joseph was to perform astounding *"ratti"* in various parts of Italy, including Grottaglie, Copertino, Fossombrone, Naples, Rome, and Assisi. These "flights" occurred as much in the presence of the sophisticated and educated as the credulous and ignorant. He counted among his admirers Prince Casimir of Poland, Prince Leopold of Tuscany, the Duke of Bouillon, Isabella of Austria, the Infanta Maria of Savoy, and various cardinals. The Duke of Brunswick was instantly converted from Protestantism on witnessing one of his flights.

The *Vita,* again, describes a typical exhibition. While the Lord High Admiral of Castille, Ambassador of Spain to the Vatican, was passing through Assisi in the year 1645, the father guardian at the Franciscan monastery commanded Joseph to descend from his cell into the church, where the Lord High Admiral's lady was waiting for him. "As he entered the church and gazed on the statue above the altar, he threw himself into a flight of twelve paces passing over the heads of the congregation. After staying there some time he flew back over them with his familiar cry, and returned immediately to his cell. The Admiral was stunned, his wife fainted, and the spectators were filled with holy awe."

But his most awe-inspiring flight, perhaps, occurred at Fossombrone, where, "detaching himself in swiftest manner from the altar with a roar like thunder, he went, like lightning, gyrating hither and thither about the chapel, and with such force that he made all the cells of the dormitory shake, so that the monks rushed out in fear, crying, 'Earthquake! Earthquake!' "

After an extraordinary life of wanderings, alternating with periods of virtual confinement in enclosed monasteries, Joseph was finally sent to Osimo, where he suffered his final illness. When the surgeon came to bleed him, he observed that Joseph was raised almost a whole "palm" in the air. A fly had alighted in the middle of the pupil of Joseph's eye, and the surgeon tried to chase it away to no avail.

This same surgeon certified that after the saint's death on August 10, 1663, Joseph's heart and ventricles were empty, "devoid of any blood, indeed the heart itself was dry and desiccated." As the hagiographer commented, this was "not through the natural burning of a fever, but through the supernatural flame of Divine Love." After his death the miracles associated with him continued for a century as consistently as they had done during his lifetime.

He was canonized one hundred years later, in 1767. His life and amazing prodigies were thus unabashedly proclaimed during the first full flush of European skepticism and empiricism.

So what are we to make of these extraordinary claims, witnessed by so many people over a period of almost forty years?

One thing seems certain: his style of "flight" bears little resemblance to the much-vaunted, yet seldom-witnessed, cross-legged "levitations" of Eastern yogis. Nor was it dependent on the sort of low-lit, illusory effects that obtained when D. D. Home, in the presence of witnesses, was said to have floated out of a third-floor window in London in 1868. Joseph's feats were performed before large numbers of educated witnesses, indoors and out, and in the searching light of day.

Could Joseph of Copertino's witnesses have been, in any sense, hypnotized? The description of his flight from *behind* the distinguished visitors at Assisi in 1645 seems to preclude such a possibility. And yet, a sense of illusion combined with an extraordinary, acrobatic athleticism might provide a rational explanation for the phenomena. We are told that he had unusual strength and that he was amazingly disinhibited; his *ratto,* like the currently fashionable cinematic performances of Ninja martial arts, was always preceded by a loud cry denoting huge and sudden effort. Is it not possible that he had developed fierce leaps and jumps well within the capacities of a modern ballet dancer, or a high-jumper, but which seemed preternatural in Joseph's era, and especially in the context of a church, or a monastery orchard? His "flights," and spinning dances, his noisy gyrations, are reminiscent of the boys of Illfurt and the girls at Garabandal, suggesting the possibility of almost pathological bursts of energy; yet, as I suggested earlier, such feats seem normal nowadays to the exponents of break-dancing techniques.

Reading the testimonies of the details of Joseph's life, I wondered too whether his behavior might be linked with his habit of indulging in long fasts alternating with unusual foods and additives. Ever since I arrived in Italy I had been carrying around with me an absorbing book called *Il Pane Selvaggio* (published in English as *The Bread of Dreams*) by the controversial Italian historian, Piero Camporesi. Camporesi, whose work has acquired something of a cult status in Italy, believed that there was a link between the use of seeds and herbs in time of famine and the incidence of altered mental states, trances, and convulsive dancing.

Camporesi was convinced that many of these alternative substances were hallucinogenic and explained the extraordinary powers of many of the wandering jugglers, acrobats, and tricksters who wandered the country during this period. By the same token he believed that the relationship between fasting and ascetic diets might shed some light on the tales of visionary experiences, the spiritual crises, and the physical phenomena of mysticism associated with many saints of this and earlier periods.

Camporesi's central argument, however, was concerned with the use of alternatives to wheat in the making of bread in rural Italy during the seventeenth century, and the curious divide between white bread eaters, and dark bread eaters, known throughout Italy as *matta panes* ("bread-crazies"). The significance of the description of Joseph as one who did not discriminate between dark and white bread made sense against this background, as did the account of his peculiar diet of herbs and roots, and the *death powder,* which made others ill, but upon which he thrived.

But what *were* these substances, and how, precisely, would they have affected him? The hagiographers give no clue; but Camporesi's free-wheeling exposition puts Joseph's diet and behavior into a rather more intelligible context than that of routine religious asceticism.

Among the flour substitutes for wheat bread he lists water brambles, acorns, turnips, dog grass, lupins, gus, hazelnuts, sorb-apples, pumpkins, elm leaves, broad beans, various pulses, millet, "panic grass," rye, barley, vetch, sorghum, and a variety of "tasty roots."

"Among the most common and popular foodstuffs," writes Camporesi, "was . . . a bread disguised and flavored, and in addition spiced with coriander seeds, anise, cumin sesame seed, and all the possible delectable additives available in the 'vegetable kingdom' . . . even the flour of hemp-seeds." The ingestion of hallucinogenic seeds and herbs by people who were chronically malnourished may help to explain, he argues, the incidence of trance and sudden explosions of choreal dancing.

Then there was "darnel," a wild grass that formed the basis of what Italians called "dazed bread." According to a seventeenth-century apothecary quoted by Camporesi, bread made in this way gave rise to "every pernicious adventure possible"; the "evil darnel" causes people "to beat their heads against walls."

Another commonly used herb was ergot (nowadays the basis of the modern drug lysurgic acid, or LSD), which was probably responsible for the motor crises and neuroses of St. Vitus's Dance.

In a telling discourse on the combined effects of protein and vitamin deficiency, Camporesi evokes some of the leading characteristics of common diseases in seventeenth-century Italy: poor wretches, "tormented by shingles, subjected to sudden attacks of convulsions and epilepsy, the deliria of fevers, the festering of wounds, ulcers which ate away at the tissues, unrelenting gangrene and disgusting scrofula, the crazed patterns of 'St. Vitus's Dance' and other choreographic epidemics. . . ." All of which are reminiscent of the symptoms of Joseph of Copertino, to which we might add self-inflicted punishments, fastings, and vigils. Is it surprising that he took screaming leaps and thought that he was flying?

The Church, mercifully, no longer holds up the likes of Joseph as a model of heroic sanctity, so a reductive interpretation of his life is of little consequence to the modern faithful. On the other hand, he is cited by people of all faiths, and none, even to this day, as evidence of the possibility of "levitation." My own guess, in the light of Camporesi, is that he never flew, nor did he levitate. In the surrealistic settings of sanctuaries and monastery gardens, his immense reputation for sanctity and asceticism were fueled by his noisy, energetic acrobatics.

There is nothing so very unusual about leaping a height of six feet, nor a distance of twelve paces: it seldom happens in a church, however, accompanied by a scream. As for sitting on light branches, or lifting heavy weights, this is the stock in trade of activities on the margins of the paranormal, but it is not hard evidence of levitation as such. On the other hand, there is little doubt that Joseph himself, intoxicated, half-starved, and yet amazingly athletic, was quite convinced that he was capable of taking to the air.

But perhaps Father Thurston should be allowed a last word on the question of flying and angels. At the end of his discussion on levitation, he says this: "Assuming, then, that we have reasonable ground for crediting the fact of levitation, there remains the question of its possible explanation. Theologians for the most part offer the rough and ready solution that in the case of holy people it is a manifestation of divine power, effected perhaps through the ministry of angels; but that in such cases as those of Simon Magus, sorcerers, and spiritualistic mediums, it is the work of the devil. Without venturing to reject this explanation outright, I found certain difficulties, too complex to summarize here, which suggest that it would be wise to suspend our judgment."

With which I, for one, heartily concur.

22

The Weeping Statue of Syracuse

Lt had been a year of jumping, shaking, winking, bleeding, weeping statues. Every since my encounter with the stigmatic effigy of the child Jesus in the Bronx, I had been noting parallels across the world.

At Denia near Alicante in Spain, a bust of Christ crowned with thorns wept tears the color of blood for ten days on end in the home of one Antonia Alvarez and in the presence of assembled villagers.

In Granada, Spain, an estimated 130,000 people flocked to the Basilica of Saint John of God; four streaks of blood-red tears had appeared overnight on a plaster statue of Christ and the liquid had also seeped into a handkerchief that had miraculously materialized in the statue's hand.

At Sezze in the province of Latina between Rome and Naples the faces of both the Virgin and Christ were seen to weep tears and blood in the local church.

At Caltanisetta in central Sicily villagers witnessed a red-colored liquid several inches long issuing from a ceramic statuette of the Virgin in the possession of a local woman.

At Ballinspittle in Ireland, a wayside statue of the Virgin rocked to and fro. Up to 10,000 pilgrims were gathered each day for a month from every part of the country. And the prodigy seemed to be catching. In the neighboring parish of Courtmachsherry the Virgin's statue swung so vigorously one day at lunch time that the parish priest had to hold on to it for more than an hour. In Asdee, County Kerry, a group of children claimed to have seen a statue of the Virgin open its eyes and move its hands. And in Castleblaney in County Monaghan, clergy were appealing to the faithful not to give credence to paranormal phenomena after several hundred people attended an all-night vigil at the church of All Saints where a statue of the Virgin appeared to have shifted its location.

Throughout the summer, sightings of moving statues had been claimed in fifteen of the Irish republic's twenty-six counties.

In the church of the Holy Trinity in Pittsburg, Pennsylvania, Franciscan pastor Father Vincent Cvitkovic, along with at least one hundred parishioners, declared that the eyes of a life-size statue of the crucified Christ closed during a prayer meeting. "I am still in shock!" said the artist who had recently redecorated the eyes with acrylic paint.

In Akita, Japan, Bishop John Shojiro Ito was rejoicing at the news that Rome had officially ratified the miracle of a weeping wooden statue of a Virgin in a convent of nuns. Over a period of six years some 500 Japanese Christians and non-Christians had reported the phenomenon in 101 separate incidents. The eyewitnesses included the mayor, Keiji Takada, who is a Buddhist.

I was pondering the significance of these prodigies when I arrived in Syracuse, Sicily, to visit the Shrine of Our Lady of the Tears, perhaps the most acclaimed weeping Virgin in modern times, and, until the Akita decision, the only phenomenon of its sort approved by a local bishop.

The old quarter of this ancient seaport town is separated by a bridge from the mainland; the locals refer to it as the "island." It is a warren of narrow streets and flights of steps, with sudden piazzas lined with orange trees, and glimpses of the sea at every corner. Syracuse was once the pivot of Eastern and Western sea-lanes where pagan pieties merged with early Christianity. The decaying Duomo with its Baroque additions was once a temple to Athena, and there are ancient catacombs alongside sacred caves and ruins of a Greek theater; a fountain in a chasm below the seawall is said to be the transformed nymph Arethusa, chastely bubbling for all eternity so as to escape the unwelcome attentions of Alpheus, who himself was transmogrified into a river.

Nowadays the economy of the region is dependent on the vast

petrochemical plants that straddle the coastline north of the town, although not so long ago, in the immediate postwar period, poverty seemed endemic and the Italian Communist Party was fiercely contesting the power of the Mafia, the Church, and the Christian Democrats.

It was in 1953, during a period of austerity, and political strife, that a recently married young woman named Antonina Giusto, aged twenty, witnessed a curious phenomenon in her bedroom that was to stimulate an upsurge of piety in the region. Above the matrimonial bed she had hung a plaque of the Virgin made of glass, ceramic, and plaster. Nothing special, it was a trifle sentimental and of no artistic or commercial value. On the morning of August 29 Antonina was lying in bed after her husband had gone to work; she had been suffering from "pregnancy toxemia" with episodes of blindness. She looked up at the plaque above her and saw that the face of the Virgin was suffused with tears.

She called her sister-in-law, then her aunt, and within an hour crowds were gathering outside the house. By the time Angelo Giusto, her husband, returned from work, the town was in an uproar and police were patrolling the street. According to hundreds of sworn testimonies the plaque wept profusely. People stood in line all day to wipe away the tears with cotton wool and handkerchiefs; the quantity of liquid was prodigious and inexplicable. They put the object in a box, and then into a drawer; they took it out and it continued to weep. It wept by day and by night. Thousands came and went in the bedroom, soaking cotton wool and handkerchiefs in the liquid; they tasted it with their fingers and declared that it was indeed "salty" just like human tears. The plaque was paraded in the main square of the town in the glare of the midday sun and it wept without ceasing. Priests and monsignori turned up, and eventually the bishop. On the fourth day of the prodigy scientists were summoned by the Episcopal Curia of Syracuse. Immediately after they had taken their samples, the weeping stopped abruptly, and it has never resumed.

I heard this tale from the mouth of the shrine's director, a rotund, sweating gentleman called Signor Carmelo Maconda, as he sat in his office next to the vast concrete basilica that is still being built at a cost of $32 million, twenty-six years after the event.

He leaned across his desk and handed me a paper.

"You should know," he said, mopping his brow, "the full details of what the doctors think."

The document was signed by a team of officials, including six medical doctors, a chemist, and a professor of pathology, along with police officers and two lieutenant colonels from the local garrison. It told how these gentlemen had squeezed into the narrow bedroom of the young couple to gather a decent quantity of the liquid on September, 1953.

The young wife kept the object covered with a cloth in a locked drawer. The plaque was clearly wet in many places on the face and bust and the scientists had to struggle in competition with hysterical devotees to collect a cubic centimeter of the liquid in a glass tube.

The document concluded: "An examination with a magnifying glass of the inside corners of the eyes did not show up any pore or irregularity in the surface of the enamel. The part of the plaque apparently made of maiolica was taken off the black glass that supported it, and it was noticed the image was made of a layer of chalk of about 1 to 2 centimeters thick, painted with different colors on the outside and left uncolored on the inside, where there was an irregular white surface that at the moment of the examination was completely dry."

After I had digested this information, Signor Maconda handed over the details of the scientific analysis. First they wanted to see whether the two elements from which the picture was made were present in the "miraculous" tears. Then the scientists compared the plaque's liquid with the real tears of an adult and of a child.

Real tears, according to these Italian experts, contain sodium chloride, plus very small particles of protein or analogous substances formed of carbon, hydrogen, oxygen, and nitrogen. "In the Virgin's 'tears,'" they said, "we noticed the presence of sodium and chlorine and also some black amorphous nodules. The same elements were found in the tears taken from the adult and the child present. No trace was found of the substances from which the plaque was made, indicating that the liquid had not come from inside the object."

In conclusion, they asserted that the alkalinity and the composition of the weeping plaque indicated that the liquid was of analogous composition to "human lachrymal secretion."

This final affirmation was signed by Drs. Michele Cassola, Francesco Cotzia, Leopoldo La Rosa, and Mario Marletta, on September 9, 1953.

Signor Maconda now took me on a tour of the unfinished basilica, which was being completed with the financial assistance of the local province. We clambered over duckboards, up ladders, and along gangways supported by scaffolding; there were piles of sand and cement and girders, but all was silent and deserted. The works had come to a standstill.

If it is ever completed, the immense basilica, designed to hold 20,000 pilgrims at a time, will look like a giant upside-down witch's hat. There are to be twenty-two chapels in the crypt; there will be reception areas, parking lots, and hostels to house tens of thousands of pilgrims at a time. And yet, there is some doubt as to whether the shrine will ever again attract a significant number of pilgrims. The cult of Our Lady of the Tears, while not exactly dead on the vine, is suffering from proliferating rival cults throughout Italy and elsewhere.

We ended up in an office where a team of nuns was sitting at tables making up relic cards for distribution around the world. Each card showed the image of the original plaque and contained a tiny piece of cotton displayed within a see-through envelope, above which was written: "This has been rubbed on the miraculous image."

Signor Maconda now introduced me to a wizened man who turned out to be Antonina's husband Angelo, who was responsible in some way for handling the relic and running errands.

With considerable ceremony he withdrew the silver and gold reliquarium from a safe, holding it by the hand-grip with a white cloth. In the center of this elaborate monstrance was a phial in which one could see a small portion of limpid liquid, faintly blue in color.

After viewing the miraculous plague, which struck me as cheap and sentimental, I asked Angelo how he felt about the miracle after all these years. Did he have any regrets? Had he been happy?

Angelo looked worn and distracted. His brow was furrowed and he shook slightly. He had bloodshot eyes and a smoker's cough.

"Well," he muttered, "the problem is that everybody said I was a Communist. But that wasn't true. They also said we weren't married. But that wasn't true either . . . of course we were married!"

"What do you think of the relic?" the director asked me, as if to forestall further conversation with Angelo.

I realized that I had been staring at the relic glumly, as if waiting for something to happen. The sight of the phial, which few people ever saw at close quarters, did nothing for me.

Signor Maconda was looking at me curiously. "It's not getting through to you, is it?" he murmured.

"I'm afraid not."

With this, he clapped a hand on my shoulder and said: "Come with me: I'm going to show you something else!"

Outside in the parking lot was an ancient Lancia. Signor Maconda ordered me into the front passenger seat and we lurched off with screeching tires into the traffic of Syracuse. After a fifteen-minute drive we pulled up outside an unkempt modern public building on the outskirts of the town.

Signor Maconda marched up a sweeping marble staircase gesturing that I should follow. At the top he ushered me through swinging doors into a convention hall where there was a film screen in front of a stage. Two young people were sitting at the far end talking.

He clapped his hands. "The film!" he shouted. "Now we show the film." Turning to me he said: "Listen, mister, I am going to show you something that not even the cardinals and the bishops see. This film is very old and in bad condition. But because you are a writer ..."

After some delay in the projection room above, the lights went down and an ancient black-and-white home-movie flickered into life on the screen.

There was some pious music and an urgent commentary; scenes of Syracuse, forty years ago, still war-damaged, poverty stricken. The young couple, Antonina and Angelo, were introduced, smiling, standing in the doorway of their house; then the famous plaque, at this stage dry-eyed.

The story was being told with some embellishments, including the antagonism of the Communists to the local Church; then, suddenly, we were out in the main square. The plaque was placed on a black velvet catafalque, raised above the heads of a vast crowd so that it could be seen by all.

The camera zoomed in on Mary's face, and there were the tears clearly to be seen, welling in the eyes of the plaque, and rolling down the cheeks.

Now the camera panned to the crowd, showing the faces of the people. There was wonder, devotion, joy; a sort of common expression of dazed happiness. Next, the camera showed a street off the square where sick and elderly men and women were attempting to hasten with painful steps toward the gathering crowds.

Once again the camera focused on the plaque and the rolling tears, and I began to understand the importance of the immediacy of a living prodigy of this sort, the sense of presence, the importance of the moment. No basilica, no silvered reliquarium, no dabs of cotton wool could substitute for the special atmosphere of a miracle in progress. The faces of the crowds were truly pathetic, gripped with a sort of common stamp of possession.

I heard a snuffle; I looked at my three companions. They were all shedding tears. And I must confess that it was as much as I could do to keep back my own.

Before leaving Syracuse I walked into the offices of the Communist Party off the main square where I found four men wearing dark blue open-necked shirts. One wore a black, shaggy beard; he invited me to speak.

I explained that I had come to visit the Shrine of the Tears. I said I wondering what the impact of the miracle had been on the fortunes of the Communists in the town.

"Do you think the miracle was an anti-Communist plot?" I asked.

Blackbeard shrugged: "It was a lot of nonsense," he said.

Then he looked at the others and said something in dialect at which they burst into laughter.

The man gurgled a little. "I was saying that the miracle happened in August, and it's bloody hot here: even the statues sweat.

"Look, Signore," he went on, "I could think of a lot of psychological, or sociological reasons for the miracle, but, no, it wasn't a plot."

At this point the others started talking and laughing, swapping private jokes.

Blackbeard talked over them. "There were rumors at the time about Communists trying to undermine the miracle, but the truth is that there is no distinction between Catholicism and Communism, especially in the South. The distinction is between Communists and Capitalists, and that cuts through religion as well. We have a saying in this part of the country: 'The Communists carry the Virgin on their backs'—you know, at the processions—'and the Capitalists carry the Devil.'

"In somma," he said, "what can one say? The Virgin started to produce drops of water and some scientists said that they were real tears. So now they're going to produce that horrible monstrosity of a basilica. It's no concern of this party office."

With this he shook my hand, and the others followed suit.

As I drove back north toward Messina and the ferry to Reggio di Calabria I found myself meditating on the possible meaning of the language of tears of the Virgin of Syracuse.

All the principal apparitions that I had studied on my journey had featured the sorrowing Virgin, and I was aware that she was a convention of Marian visions over hundreds of years, as well as a subject of countless icons in the East. The idea of a weeping Mary ultimately derived from the "Stabat Mater"—or Mary at the foot of the Cross, the moment at which the Mother of God and the passion and death of Christ come together in a single image. Mary's tears express the sorrow of the human race for the death of Christ, but they are also a symbol of mediation, for what son can refuse the tears of a mother?

And the religious metaphor runs even deeper. From my boyhood I remember the collects in the Mass *pro petitione lacrymarum,* asking God for the gift of tears out of the hardness of our hearts, just as in Ezekial, He drew from the desert rock a fountain of living water for His thirsty people.

I remembered, too, the outstanding example of the "charism of tears" displayed by the medieval mystic Margery Kempe of Lynn, who wept so copiously and noisily that one priest of her acquaintance banished her to the crypt of the church during his sermons.

Margery had consulted another mystic, Juliana of Norwich, about the matter of weeping, who advised her that when God visits a creature with tears of compunction, devotion, and compassion, one ought to believe that the Holy Spirit is present in the soul. Juliana added that no evil spirit could grant the gift of tears, for, according to Saint Jerome, "tears torment more the devil than do the pains of hell."

The tears of Syracuse had left me mystified, and a little humbled. My suspicion that the phenomenon was merely a hoax, perpetrated to confound the Communists and to attract tourism to the region, were probably wide of the mark. I did not set much store by the scientific data, nor did I rule out the possibility of freak condensation, but I felt that as long as I concentrated on authenticity, rather than the meaning of the cult itself, I was missing the point.

While watching the film of the miracle in action, I felt moved and touched, almost on the point of understanding. Yet I was tempted to wonder whether the wider theme of all this secreting, bleeding, lactating, liquefying, weeping, and sweating, so widespread in Mediterranean folk religion, might not signify some very simple and obvious psychological mechanism.

I was headed for Naples and the most famous phenomenon of secretion of them all: the liquefaction of the blood of Saint Januarius in the cathedral, which I had planned to witness on the saint's feast day.

Saint Januarius is believed to have been thrown to the bears and decapitated in the amphitheater of Pozzuoli during the Diocletian persecution of A.D. 305. According to legend a certain Eusebia scooped up the martyr's blood from the dirt and placed it in a sealed *ampolla* such as contained embalming ointment; this blood relic then accompanied the rest of his remains on a tour of the crypts of Campania to Capodimonte, Benevento, Monte Virgine, and who knows where else, before being carried to its final resting place in the *Tesoro* of the Cathedral of Naples in 1497. The earliest documented report of the "miracle," however, is suspiciously late: 1389, during a period of unparalleled relic fakery.

But Naples boasts not only the liquefaction of the blood of Saint Januarius: it has been blessed with no less than sixteen other liquefaction miracles including the milk of the Virgin Mary (in the church of Saint Louis), the blood of Saint Alfonsus Ligouri (collected by an enterprising dentist), and no less than two liquefying heads of John the Baptist. Is it something in the air of the Bay of Naples? Or was some mixture accidentally (or not so accidentally) discovered which hardens when enclosed in the dark, but liquefies when exposed to warmth and the light? How else should we explain the incidence of so many liquefaction prodigies within a ten-mile radius of this city, the majority of them appearing in the late sixteenth century?

Whatever the case, when the dried blood of Saint Januarius is placed close to his skull and bone relics on his feast day, it is said to liquefy. What is more, tradition has it that if the blood remains dry in these circumstances, dire consequences for the people of Naples may ensue: earthquake, revolution, outbreaks of cholera, the eruption of Mount Vesuvius, the death of the archbishop. A band of women, known as the *zie di San Gennaro*—literally the "aunts of Saint Januarius"—take up their position before the altar steps. If it looks as if the relic may fail to do its stuff they scream insults at the saint in unrestrained dialect.

I passed through Naples on the eve of the saint's feast, September 18. And so it was that after a restless night in a hotel near the station (some ten youngsters were sleeping in cardboard boxes beneath my window) I walked through streets reeking with mountains of uncollected refuse to the Via del Duomo. In the shadow of the cathedral vast crowds had gathered, among whom mingled bands of child gypsies, transvestite male prostitutes, vague-eyed down-at-heel conscripts, and phalanxes of ill-dressed, undernourished, hard-faced teenagers.

What dire consequence, one wondered, could be visited upon this city worse than what it was suffering already: the marauding hooded bands of Cammorra bandits, unemployment, the black market, the sweatshop labor, protection rackets, drugs, the homeless tens of thousands, the North African migrant problem, violence (some 130 murders a year), the water shortage, hunger, the polluted air. And yet, a walk across this city to the cathedral on the feast day of its favorite saint indicated that Neapolitans looked anything but defeated.

A monsignor in the Vatican had furnished me with a letter of introduction which I duly presented at nine o'clock at the door of the cavernous sacristy whence issued, mysteriously, a delicious smell of coffee and sweetmeats. A fussy young priest then led me to the sanctuary through the packed congregation to join a group of privileged dignitaries within a roped-off section bordered by banks of orange gladioli. There were a dozen coquettish Neapolitan ladies fashionably dressed in large hats, and as many males, local politicos and *padroni* it seemed, in pale blue suits and dark glasses.

One of the women was praying the rosary with deep fervor while her companion, who had a sinister bulge in his jacket, was scanning the stock market listings in the *Messaggero.* I took my place among them and sat in wait for the ritualized miracle, listening to the approach of drumbeats like thunder in the air.

At length the congregation burst into applause as a file of altar boys and ecclesiastics began to make its way up the nave to the accompaniment of two or three steel bands, at odds with each other and the full-throttled organ. Banners, flags, gonfalons, and cloth of gold umbrellas were held aloft at all angles; loutish, unshaven seminarians in grubby dog-collars carried smoking candles and glittering incense thuribles. There were monks, friars, canons, monsignori, sword-bearing carabinieri in cockaded hats and high boots, brillianteened fops in tails and decorated sashes, and gun-toting policemen. Following up the rear was the Cardinal Archbishop of Naples, Monsignor Giordano, a humble-looking little man in glasses who looked as if he would rather have been elsewhere. Then the bearers brought in the blood reliquarium and the silver bust of Saint Januarius, adorned with a cloth of gold cope and mitre. The saint's skull, I understood, lay beneath the silver mask.

Standing out from among prelates was an immensely tall archpriest with a long craggy face the color of parchment. He was strutting about, casting complacent looks from side to side, his aquiline nose at an imperious angle. As he approached the altar some of the men in dark glasses sprang forward and kissed his outthrust ringed hand.

When the members of the procession were ensconced in the choir stalls, and the bust and the blood phial had been placed on their stands on the left side of the altar, the cardinal came forward to a lectern to begin his sermon. At this point a line of women in black dresses closed in on the rails below; these were the formidable *zie di San Gennaro,* and they looked in no mood to be messed with.

The cardinal began to speak in a small, tired voice. I guessed that he was not a Neapolitan nor even a southerner. And within a few minutes it seemed abundantly clear that he did not care too much for miracles of the sort he was about to preside over here. Incredibly, he was lecturing the five or six thousand faithful in the church on the need to believe without seeing.

And as he continued it became clear that he was not carrying his congregation with him, and especially not the prelates and priests on the altar. The complacent-looking fellow was chatting and chortling in pleasant vein with two elderly canons who sat on either side of him. One or two of the younger priests were yawning extravagantly and looking at their watches, while the Master of Ceremonies, whose surplice contained enough lace to make a bridal train, was assiduously picking his nose.

Finally, when the sermon came to a conclusion, a gasp of anticipation rushed through the vast cathedral like a passing express train.

Now to the important business. The miracle!

The cardinal took hold of the blood reliquarium and held it up while the priests began to intone a litany to the saints. Two phials were contained within the reliquarium. One was empty and seemed to contain no more than a few dust stains; the other, which was slightly larger, being about four inches high and four inches across, contained the "blood," a solid mass of black stuff which filled half the phial.

When the litany had finished the cardinal turned the reliquarium around several times, but the substance within remained a solid and immoveable lump. A *credo* followed the litany; then the rosary; then another litany. And every so often the cardinal would turn the monstrance around and around. To no avail.

Things were getting a little tense down at the altar rails. The *zie* were looking fidgety; there was a discernible note of hysteria in their responses and supplications. The complacent prelate came forward and whispered something in the cardinal's ear, whereupon his Eminence began to blow hard on the glass phial as if he were trying to breath life into a dying fire. The moment was reminiscent of another, supposed miracle, although widely deemed of dubious authenticity, namely, the "spontaneous" kindling of the holy fire in the Greek Orthodox rite at the Church of the Holy Sepulchre in Jerusalem.

Suddenly the cardinal stopped blowing. He blinked once or twice, then his face was suffused with intense relief. Something was happening. The prelate came forward and inspected the phial closely. He was smiling, his complacency now knew no bounds. He summoned a decorated fop in scarlet sash and tails, who took out an enormous white handkerchief, shook it once or twice, then held it aloft.

With this the cathedral shook to the rafters with cheers and shouts. The blood of Saint Januarius had once again liquefied. The city would not, after all, fall to pieces. The city was safe for at least another year!

The cardinal was turning the reliquarium this way and that. He came forward to the pen where the dignitaries were standing and showed the phial to each of us in turn. As he thrust it toward my face he managed to clout me on the nose with it.

The solid, dry looking lump was now shiny and viscous; the edges had turned dark brown. Fine grainy specks were suspended in muddy liquid and the mass inside the phial was swimming about like a lump of lamb's liver.

Yet what did I feel at that moment?

The organ was surging and the bells of the cathedral were pealing; I was immensely impressed, for the original mass had seemed as dry, as solid, as a lump of stone. And yet, the "prodigy" failed to exert the slightest sense of moral or spiritual power for me personally, at least, not at that moment. At the very second that the evidence of the "miracle" was presented incontrovertibly before my eyes, I could only wonder whether I was observing an exhibition of magic, a clever material trick developed by some smart aleck in the fourteenth century and surviving to the present day? And what if I were witnessing a marvelous manifestation of God's intervention? The significance, as far as I was concerned, had less to do with God's mercy, his action in the world, than with procurable and primitive emotions of superstition, propitiation, and manipulation.

Was the congregation inhibited by such scruples? Not a bit of it. The crowd was ecstatic, roaring, threatening to take the roof off the Duomo. Some serious-looking foreigners—Swiss, Scandinavians, Germans, perhaps—were peering forward with puzzled looks, much as I had done, as if they were examining some baffling chemistry experiment. Others were reacting to the unbridled jubilance with a faintly disdainful Protestant air.

Even as I entertained these thoughts, the phial of the saint had been placed back on its stand on the side of the altar. Members of the congregation were embracing and kissing each other, turning their backs—so soon—on the relics and making for the wide-open cathedral doors and the sun-lit city streets beyond; meanwhile the prelates and priests and altar servers were charging down the nave in a motley scramble, hastening, I imagined, toward the treat of nougat and doughnuts and sweet black coffee that awaited them in the sacristy.

The whole point, it occurred to me suddenly, was, surely, the sense of resurrection, triumph, re-awakening, in those cheers. And the noise was now stupendous. It was as if the city's team had scored the winning goal in soccer's Supercup. Except that it was the city itself, along with its ancient, its local pieties that had somehow "scored," resurrected, overcome its perennial miseries, its disadvantages, its demoralization. The spontaneous combustion of Easter fire; the arrival of spring rain; the flow of milk and honey, the blending of Christian and pre-Christian sacramentals and emblems, each and all seemed to blossom, ignite, flow, in the culmination of this extraordinary ritual. And seen in this light, it mattered not a jot whether the phenomenon was "authentic" or fake.

PART SIX

POWERS OF DARKNESS

23

Archbishop Milingo

O n my return to Rome I spent some time in the library of the Venerable English College reading around the liquefaction phenomenon.

I discovered that my own reaction had been typical of non-Neapolitans for hundreds of years. Writing in 1785, a Spanish prelate, one Abate Don Juan Andres, commented on the "discordant shrieking" of the "common people," and the "contemptuous amusement of the foreigners."

"In no single instant," he continued, "could I perceive anything of that devout and respectful impression of awe which ought, one would think, to be the natural effect of a miracle . . . a manifestation of the divine omnipotence in overriding the laws of nature."

The view seemed to support my contention that the mere fact of an inexplicable prodigy carried no power to change people's hearts and lives, to move them morally or spiritually; and yet there was evidently a huge cultural gap, both in what might be considered a spiritual stimulus and an appropriate reaction, between northerners and Italian southerners. The miracle of Naples belonged to the people who lived there. Maybe, I reflected, a little cynically, God has another miracle for the likes of us northerners!

Working through scattered materials on Neapolitan devotions, one evening I came across a report by a Jesuit priest called Father Putignani on the liquefaction of the "milk of the Mother of God."

Writing in 1725, Father Putignani described the veneration of the substance as: "fine grain, whitish in color, like dried up milk but rather of hard texture, until the vigil is reached of Our Lady's Assumption into Heaven. For on that day in a solemn procession of the Fathers it is carried from its shrine to the High Altar, and at that same hour it liquefies. The veneration of it is attended with much pomp, nor is one day sufficient to content the devotion of the people in regard to this prodigy of the Mother of God. The celebration is continued for a whole octave."

Suddenly I was filled with disgust at the description of the obnoxious ritual. I shut the book with a bang.

I felt that I had reached the end of a cycle in my quest, and I had no wish to go any further with such prodigies. Even if a liquefaction, or a lactation, or a shedding of tears, were to have been reliably occurring in the next room, I would not have taken three steps to observe it. I left the library and went back to my room.

That night I found it hard to relax. I felt that I had reached an impasse; I had no idea how I was going to proceed, and it was worrying me.

Going over the various phenomena I had seen, and people I had met, in Yugoslavia, Spain, the United States, Canada, and now Italy, nothing had truly impressed me purely for its "paranormal," or inexplicable, quality. What was more, I was now quite convinced that if I were to be hit on the head by a "miracle," as I nearly had been in Naples, it would make not the slightest difference to me.

The mystery of my original dream remained, but the more I traveled and the more I saw, the less I was convinced by the simplistic notion of supernatural "intervention" with which I had started out. The strongest impression seemed to come from the journey itself: the search, a sense of hunger, of dissatisfaction, and the feeling that something would eventually be resolved. But what? And where would I go next?

At last, when I fell asleep, I had a vivid dream. I was in an unfamiliar, dismal church attending mass. A prelate was dispensing communion and I found myself standing back from the congregation, unable to receive the sacrament because I was not in a state of grace. After the last person had left the altar steps the priest came forward and presented the host to me. I lowered my head and shut my mouth tight, refusing to take the host. With this he pushed the host viciously into the side of my face, shouting: "Take it! Take it!"

At last I gave in and opened my mouth, almost with a sense of relief at the prospect of reconciliation, but at that moment I realized that the bread was not the body of Christ: it was the body and spirit of the devil, and I woke in terror with a shout that must have awakened everybody on my corridor.

As I lay in the darkness wondering about the significance of the dream, I began to see that I had yet to address a path of my journey that I had avoided confronting ever since the beginning. And I acknowledged that for all my years of agnosticism, which included, of course, a confident rejection of a personal focus of Evil, I was nevertheless afraid of coming in contact with anything to do with demonology or possession.

And yet, I felt that I was obliged to take stock of the Christian claims for the reality of the powers of darkness before I could say that I had brought my journey to a conclusion. But how should I do this? Where should I begin?

Ever since my childhood experience of the "Evil Eternity" I had maintained a healthy trepidation for the Satanic. And I had remembered all my life a remark made by one of our seminary professors: "You start by dabbling in demonology; and in the end demonology dabbles with you!"

The precise focus of my fears as a boy was to do with the casual, vindictive way in which the devil was said to chose his victims. We were once given a retreat at St. Wilfred's by a cadaverous-looking Jesuit who told the story of a seminarian in Rome who was suddenly seized by the devil. "The youth in his frenzy laid his hand on the oak panel of the refectory," said the priest, "and immediately a perfect burn-mark of his hand appeared on the wood.

"If you do not believe this story," he added, "the burn-mark is there for all to see to this day."

That night we quaked in our beds.

It seemed curious more than thirty years on, to be back in a seminary, lying awake in the early hours, mulling over Catholic teaching on the devil.

Traditional Catholic teaching holds that the Evil One is not merely a notion of negation; he is an effective agent, a living, spiritual being, perverted and perverting, a mysterious and terrible reality.

It is contrary to the teaching of the Bible and the Church to refuse to accept the existence of Satan, or to dismiss him as a pseudo-reality, a convenient fantasy for the unknown cause of suffering, violence, and misfortune in the world.

Satan is described by Christ as "the Father of Lies," the "Murderer from the very beginning." Satan launches insidious attacks on humankind. Not all sins are directly attributable to diabolical action, but a lack of moral strictness exposes souls to the influence of what Paul calls the *"mysterium iniquitatis,"* "the mystery of evil," and runs the risk of being damned.

Christian demons are the fallen angels who under Satan seek to drag humans souls into a state of rebellion against God (thus forcing us to identify with their own situation). In this struggle the point of death is all decisive; for the doomed souls will be dragged at that moment into eternal loss.

But what had this mythic stuff to do with the alleged realities of Satanism, possession, and exorcism?

The next morning I brought up the subject at breakfast with a college member of the staff, who promptly suggested that as far as contemporary phenomena were concerned the case of Archbishop Emanuel Milingo deserved careful consideration and investigation.

Milingo, who now lived in Rome in an apartment owned by the Vatican, had been accused of witchcraft by his fellow bishops in Zambia where he had been head of the hierarchy since 1969.

He was summoned to see the pope in 1982 and allegedly was confined in the Augustinian monastery close to the Vatican City, where he was obliged to undergo various inquisitions and psychological tests. Despite these humiliations he had remained loyal to the Church and his priesthood. Relieved of his diocese, he had been given a job at the Vatican commission for tourism and immigrants, which he used as a base to continue his controversial mission involving the casting out of devils and the castigation of Freemasons.

Assuming that it would be difficult to approach him through official channels I called a friend who worked for the BBC in Rome, and he provided me with the archbishop's home address and directions.

Archbishop Milingo's apartment was situated in a palazzo immediately opposite the Porta Sant'Anna, the entrance to the "business" sector of the Vatican City. Without an appointment I set off to attempt to meet the archbishop one afternoon in mid-siesta when most prelates could be expected to be at home.

Inside the lobby of his apartment there was a line of young black men and women sitting as if in a doctor's office. There was an impression of lassitude and deep resignation.

A door opened and a girl in African costume emerged carrying a plate of fried sausages and bacon; she disappeared through another door further down the corridor. Distantly I could hear the sound of a ranting high-pitched voice through closed doors.

Another girl appeared wearing the same costume; seeing that I had nowhere to sit she ushered me into a spacious parlor with comfortable modern sofas and armchairs. On the walls were various African artifacts: leopardskin shields, clubs, sticks with hairy tops. They were hung alongside pictures of the pope, the Sacred Heart, and the Madonna and Child. A figure of a dancing straw fetish shared the sideboard with a plastic statue of the Virgin Mary.

I waited for an hour, which hour stretched to two. Outside I could hear the people in the corridor chatting as if they belonged there permanently. At last I fell asleep.

I woke to the sight of a wide, black, glistening face peering down at me. There was a flash of purple, a gleam of gold and amethyst. It was Archbishop Emanuel Milingo.

"Have you an appointment?" he cried in a high-pitched, strangulated voice.

"Of course," I lied.

I saw that he held in his hand a copy of the Jerusalem edition of the Bible.

"Who are you? British? I have no time."

He seemed about to withdraw, when I said: "I came to ask you about Satan, Your Grace."

Quickly the archbishop pulled forward an easy chair and sat down so close to me that he was practically in my lap. He gave off a heady stench of incense and musk. Holding me by the arm he cried out:

"O Holy Michael Archangel, defend us in the day of battle! Be our safeguard against the wickedness and snares of the devil!

"That prayer," he now whispered huskily, "was written by the good Pope Leo XIII, one hundred years ago. He promulgated that it should be read in all churches throughout the world at the end of every Mass. And why? In the year 1890 Christ Our Savior appeared to Pope Leo and told him that he had given Satan to the world for exactly one hundred years."

The archbishop's eyes stretched wide. "We are now in the last days of Satan's reign, and he is working overtime through his agents to complete the takeover of the world. His agents are nothing less than the Freemasons who have penetrated to the very heart of Christ's Church.

"It is the task of the Freemasons to lull Christians into believing that the devil and his demons don't exist, especially priests. Satan plays with priests like toys when they don't believe in him.

"After the last war bright young Freemasons were placed in seminaries around the world. These agents of Satan were waiting for their time to come. That time was the Second Vatican Council. Many of these brilliant men were by now the leading experts who advised the Council Fathers. And what did they do? They had the rite of exorcism taken out of the sacrament of baptism; they eliminated exorcism from the orders leading to the priesthood; they banned the prayer to Michael the Archangel; they took the devil out of the Catechism. They left Christ's Church defenseless against the wiles of the devil. Above all they succeeded in making Christians think that the DEVIL DOES NOT EXIST! The Freemason Anti-Christs became priests for this purpose. They aim to take religious power throughout the world, just as they have taken economic and political power."

The archbishop was crying out in an incantatory, piping voice, his lips blowing out the words with an explosion of musky breath and saliva.

I interrupted him to say, "Archbishop, are people influenced or possessed by Satan himself, or by numbers of devils?"

"By both! I have delivered a young girl of twenty-five devils including Satan himself!" he bellowed. "Twenty-five! The hospital could do nothing for her, so they brought her to me, this sixteen-year-old girl. Her body was stiff and dry as a stick and she could not talk. I called the parents and some relatives and we gathered around her. Her mother began to speak to the spirits. It was *terrifying!* The spirit voice came out of the girl, a different voice from her own. Her body was frozen, with no evidence of blood circulation. The voice said: 'Go and bring her elder sister, then we shall discuss matters.' This sister was eighty miles away, and so we summoned her.

"The background to this case was that both these sisters had decided to become nuns. The spirits were revenging both girls by disturbing them. When the other sister arrived we discovered all this. Then I exorcised her; but as the spirits left they said that they would wait for her at home and reenter her. And this is precisely what happened on several occasions. Sometimes she fell at the door of her parents' home just as she was about to go into the house. These were very difficult devils. I tried everything. I even left her all night in the church before the exposed blessed sacrament. I felt that my powers had been exhausted.

"One day in the chapel I managed to speak to the spirits and by the authority of Christ Our Lord I ordered them to answer the questions: How many are you? What are your names? Why do you not obey the Lord? They answered that there were now only three remaining: Satan, an evil spirit taking the name of the grandmother, and a nameless spirit.

"Satan then told us that the girl was a pledge. The spirits had healed her mother of a mysterious illness. In her misery she took an oath that if Satan healed her she would give him her daughter for seven years. Satan said that it would not be possible for them to leave her for another five years. But we used the authority of the Lord to destroy this pact, and the girl was healed."

"People say that you are practicing witchcraft," I said. "Is there any truth in this?"

"Why do they say that I am making false doctrines? I do nothing but teach by the Scriptures. Christ spent his entire mission casting out devils. And now they say that the Devil doesn't exist!

"Why ... don't ... they ... read ... the ... Scriptures! Read Saint Paul to the Ephesians: 'Put God's armor on so as to be able to resist the devil's tactics. For it is not against the human enemies that we have to struggle, but against the Sovereignties and the Powers who originate in the darkness in this world, the spiritual army of evil in the heavens.'

"Then Saint Peter: 'Be sober and watch because your adversary the Devil goes about like a lion seeking whom he may devour ...' The devil plays with the unguarded like toys! Remember Acts, Chapter Nineteen, the seven sons of Sceva, the Jewish exorcists. The evil spirit said: 'Jesus I recognize, and I know who Paul is, but who are *you?'* And the man with evil spirit hurled himself at them and overpowered first one and then another and handled them so violently that they fled from that house naked and badly mauled.

"Read Apocalypse, Chapter Twelve, of Our Blessed Lady and the Dragon, and of the war that broke out in Heaven and how Michael with his angels attacked the dragon, and the dragon fought back with his angels, but they were defeated and driven out of Heaven . . . It is for this reason that when the devil was disappointed he came to the earth to fight the generations of Jesus and he tortures and destroys them.

"Now Satanism is at its strongest throughout the world. These are the years of the devil, Black Masses, and blaspheming God, and Judas priests . . . Before he died Pope Paul VI knew what he had done. He knew it! He had let Satan free within the Church. He said he could smell the stench of smoke around the sanctuary. He said the truth!

"I was in Holland two weeks ago! I was praying in Amsterdam from seven in the morning to half-past-two, and the priests were falling like corpses before me. The devil congratulated me for calling him a liar. A witch came to me and said: 'How dare you!' I received a letter from the devil telling me that I should never dare to speak to the demons like that. It said the devils are more powerful than me and they'll be watching for their chance. But this isn't true, you see."

As the Archbishop continued to rant in my face I suddenly felt faint. I felt as if I was losing control, that I was somehow ready to surrender myself to this chanting, ranting prelate.

I rose and started backing out of the room, and he followed, still ranting and banging his well-thumbed Bible.

"Come to my service! Come to my service! At the Ergiffe Hotel . . . out on the bypass."

I stumbled out of the front door and, abandoning the idea of waiting for the elevator, I leapt down the marble staircase three steps at a time, still pursued by his strange smells and echoing incantations.

"Come to my service . . ."

Archbishop Milingo's "service," I gathered on inquiry, was nothing less than a session of exorcism conducted in the conference hall of a hotel on the Rome Autostrada. I had every intention of attending this spectacle at the next opportunity, although I felt that I was in need of some preparation by discussion and reading.

That very evening I was to receive some unexpected guidance.

I had arranged to have dinner in a restaurant on the Campo de Fiori with the Jesuit historian Father Philip Caraman, who was doing research in Rome for a new biography of Ignatius Loyola. In his time Father Caraman had been the personal confessor of a circle of famous literary figures in England, including Graham Greene, Evelyn Waugh, and Edith Sitwell, and had been much in demand for more than half a century as a wise and scholarly spiritual director.

Nearly eighty, Father Caraman was the very picture of the Jesuit of mythology. Emaciated, with skin like ancient parchment, his dark, intelligent eyes scrutinized me through heavy horn-rimmed spectacles.

After listening to my story about Milingo, he began to heave his shoulders with hilarity.

"One has to be extremely cautious," he said eventually. "Evelyn Waugh once thought he was possessed by demons and asked me to exorcise him." Toying with his wine glass, Father Caraman leaned back and launched into his story.

In January of 1954 Evelyn Waugh had traveled alone by ship to Ceylon in an attempt to throw off a bout of depressive illness. In the course of the voyage he was disturbed by the sound of voices which he thought at first to be the result of defective ventilation pipes in the vessel. Eventually he became convinced that the entire crew and passengers were plotting against him. He believed that someone on board had been murdered and buried at sea; he tried to send radiograms back to England, but he discovered evidence, so he thought, that these messages were being distributed among the passengers. The voices in his cabin plagued him by day and by night and he suspected that the BBC was somehow involved in the plot. In a letter home from Cairo he described the plotters as a party of "existentialists" who were practicing a form of long-range telepathy to persecute him.

As soon as he reached Colombo, Waugh took a plane back to England. On arriving in London he installed himself at the Hyde Park Hotel and sent for his wife, Laura.

Father Caraman, who was living at Farm Street at that time, was invited to join the Waughs for dinner at the hotel. Laura met him in the lobby and hustled him straight into the dining room.

Waugh leaned across the table and said: "I have invited you to dinner here this evening, Father, because it is imperative that you exorcise me! I am possessed by devils; and they are telling me that you have the priestly power to put them to flight."

"I thought this was one of Evelyn's elaborate practical jokes," went on Father Caraman. "But he so persisted with his demands for exorcism that I began to wonder whether he was not in earnest. He left the table for a few minutes to go to the lavatory, and only then did I gather from Laura how serious matters were. When Evelyn came back I told him that I had no objection to exorcising his presumed demons but that I would like first as a matter of precaution to get a doctor to take a look at him. I had a friend who was one of the top psychiatrists of the day and a specialist at the Maudsley Hospital. He was also a Catholic and certainly would not have dismissed out of hand the notion of demon possession.

"The doctor joined us by the time we had withdrawn for coffee and he immediately asked Evelyn some very direct questions, avoiding all but purely medical matters. Evelyn answered in a very humble, childlike manner. When asked for details of his medication, Evelyn described his habitual sleeping draught, which was a potent cocktail of alcohol and barbiturates.

"At length the doctor got out a pad and pen and said, 'Instead of taking your usual draught tonight I want you take a dose of something else to help you sleep. Perhaps Mrs. Waugh could fetch it from the all-night chemist at Piccadilly Circus.'

"As things turned out Strauss pinpointed the problem, which was alcohol and barbiturate poisoning. I later discovered that Evelyn's voices had disappeared by the following morning. There was no more mention of demons or exorcism."

For the rest of his life Waugh apparently remained free of persecutory voices.

In the conversation that followed, Father Caraman seemed to be of the opinion that in the ancient world possession by demons was a common description of a very wide range of illnesses. Hence the emphasis on exorcism in the New Testament. While not ruling out entirely the idea of possession it was important to approach the whole question, both in scripture and in subsequent times, with great caution.

"Discernment is enormously important," he went on, "not only in the matter of ascertaining the presence of supernatural phenomena, but in attempting to distinguish whether these derive from the good or the bad."

"Saint Ignatius," he said, "had been prone to voices, ecstasies, and revelations, but was convinced that such promptings could as well come from his own imagination, as from God or indeed the devil.

"Ignatius insisted that the grace of discernment is aided by man's activity, especially his prudence and learning. You should read Ignatius on the 'Rules for the Discernment of Spirits,' which you'll find set out in his *Spiritual Exercises.*"

Back in the English College that evening I found a copy of the *Exercises* in the library. This famous treatise, which I had not dipped into since my youth, is the key to the spiritual life of all Jesuits; it is short, dry, and formulaic, not unlike a military drill book. The spiritual life is seen as a battle ground in which one is called to follow the standard of Christ, or the standard of Satan.

For all its brevity and slavish adherence to categorizing, the *Exercise* can become an imaginative stimulus in the hands of a skilled spiritual director or preacher:

"Smell the indescribable fragance, and taste the boundless sweetness of the divinity . . . Touch by kissing and clinging to the places where those persons walk or sit . . . Hear in the imagination the shrieks and groans and the blasphemous shouts . . . smell in the imagination the fumes of sulphur and stench of filth . . ."

Ignatius's imagination, during prayer and while saying Mass, frequently ran riot. He saw demons as black dogs and glittering snake's eyes, the Trinity as a burning ball of fire, the Godhead as a powerful flash of lightning, the Virgin Mary as a lady bathed in white light. There were voices and lights and heavenly music. He often found it difficult to distinguish the products of his imagination from supernatural encounters, and he was further assailed by scruples as to the possible supernatural origins. Were they from God, or from the devil?

Ignatius's method of discrimination set out in the chapter entitled "Rules for the Discernment of Spirits" proceeds from an obvious distinction between "spiritual consolation" and "spiritual desolation." It is a development of the idea that "by their fruits you shall know them." Good spirits fill us with tranquility and peace and happiness; bad spirits leave us ultimately disturbed, agitated, and unhappy. The problem is, however, that the evil spirit may begin by appearing in the guise of a good spirit. "It belongs to the bad angel," says Ignatius, "transfiguring himself into an angel of light, to enter with the devout soul, and to come out his own way; that is to say, to begin by inspiring good and holy thoughts in conformity with dispositions of the just soul, and afterwards gradually to endeavor to gain his end, by drawing the soul into his secret snares and perverse intentions."

The evil spirit is like a "military chief" who examines the "citadel" for its weak points; he is alike a "false lover" who wishes to hide his true desires from a woman's "honest father" or "honest husband." Less flattering to women, Ignatius likens the evil spirit to a "woman, inasmuch as he is weak in spite of himself, but strong in will; for as it is in the nature of a woman, quarreling with a man, to lose courage and to take to flight when he shows himself undaunted . . . if the man begin to take flight and to lose courage, the rage, the spite and the ferocity of the woman become very great, and altogether without bounds."

It is clear that for long periods of his life Ignatius longed to find incontestable evidence of the supernatural, and was at pains to develop a system of verification. Leafing through J. C. Aveling's excellent study of the Jesuits I learned that Ignatius was so desperate at times to establish direct communication with the supernatural that he even tried to test whether God was contacting him by a code. At one time he carefully noted the passages in the Mass when he felt ineffable feelings coming on.

Yet I gathered that in his cooler moments Ignatius wondered whether many of his apparitions, voices, and visitations might not be the result of illness, eyestrain, or merely an "overheated imagination." "To the end," wrote Aveling, "he remained quite undecided whether his visions and sensations were a spiritual help or a hindrance." Authentic or otherwise, it appears that he granted that "sensible" phenomena might be an aid to beginners in the spiritual life, but that "progressives" should wean themselves from all interest or encouragement of voices, visions, and extraordinary feelings.

If Ignatius was, as Father Caraman had assured me, an expert in the matter of discernment of good and evil spirits, it struck me that he had ended his life, nevertheless, little wiser than the rest of us.

24

Casting Out Demons

took a taxi out to Archbishop Milingo's Mass at the Ergiffe Hotel on the Rome bypass. I had already gathered from a Vatican contact that the archbishop was obliged to conduct his services in a hotel because he had been forbidden the use of any church in the diocese of Rome. It was not simply that the pope did not approve of what went on at these services; Milingo could not find a single parish priest in a city of a thousand parish churches that would allow him to celebrate his unusual Mass.

The sun had set and the service had already started by the time I arrived. I had to push my way into the crowded hall with some difficulty so as to get in a position where I could see the makeshift altar.

Milingo was dressed in a red silk vestment; six priests in white robes stood on either side of him. All seven celebrants were spreading their arms forward in a hieratic gesture, as if warding off evil. Many of the congregation had also adopted the same gesture.

It was an early stage in the Mass, but the room, which held about six hundred people, was already stifling and permeated by the heady, musky stench that I had noticed in Milingo's presence in his apartment. The secular atmosphere of the venue, the absence of all the familiar emblems and sacramentals of a Roman church, lent an atmosphere of illegality and strangeness to the proceedings.

There was a preponderance of Italians in the congregation, and most of them were women; there were just a few black faces. The devotees looked for the most part like manual workers; many of the younger women were dressed in jeans and some of them had taken their shoes off. There was a mood of nervous tension, and people seemed wild-eyed with expectation. It was as if each person was wondering whether the proceedings would evoke an evil spirit from the depths of his or her own soul.

Having met Milingo face to face, I have to confess that I was wondering about myself. Not that I gave the slightest credence to the belief in possession by demons, but I was convinced that Milingo had considerable powers, perhaps of hypnotism, and I wondered whether I should have enough strength to withstand his ability to evoke unwelcome, hysterical emotions.

The homily was short; Milingo spoke in rapid but poor Italian, his voice shrill, insistent. He spoke about Christ's healing ministry, about the demons of ill health, about Christ's casting out of demons. There was more than a hint of paranoia in his drift as he spoke of his "enemies" and ranted about the evils of the Church of the Spirits.

As the Mass resumed, I began to hear odd sounds, here and there, not at all the sort of sounds one expected to hear in a congregation at Mass; now somebody would murmur, then there would be a whimper and a little cry. People looked petrified. Why, I asked myself, should people come to these proceedings in order to be scared out of their wits? Was it the sort of thrill that attracted people to horror films?

After the communion, which was distributed speedily by the concelebrant priests on the altar, Milingo came forward with a holy water stoup and sprinkler. People were pressing forward. He told them that when they had been touched by the water some people would begin to tremble and cry out but they were not to be afraid.

At the very mention of the word fear—*paura*—the congregation seemed to stir with a renewed sense of terror. Then he began to sprinkle about him on all sides with the holy water.

The shock of the first series of shrieks was so awe-inspiring that it took me a few seconds to regain my breath. A young woman, just five yards from me, had gone into a paroxysm of screaming, her eyes rising so that only the whites were visible, and she had collapsed into the arms of those about her. The room had become

extremely hot and airless; I guessed it might be as high as 100°
Fahrenhcit.

Milingo was being brought forward to the woman, hands
stretched out and praying in a strange tongue; the sweat was rolling
from his face. But within a space of five or six seconds, shrieks were
coming from several different parts of the room, and one or two
people had passed out and fallen to the floor.

The priests were praying on the altar, some of them with their
eyes shut tight, others in a distracted terror-stricken manner; the
congregation was weeping, offering supplications, and clutching
rosaries all at once in a babble of voices. Milingo was going from
one screaming person to the next, talking rapidly, and shrilly, in a
language that I could not understand. He seemed to be expending
an extraordinary energy.

Just when it appeared that seizures and paroxysms had reached
their height I saw a middle-aged woman go down and start to writhe
and shake in a fashion that was quite obscene. She seemed to be
having an orgasm before our eyes. But even as I looked away, a
young man went down on the floor almost in front of me and began
to paw and scrape the floor, barking and whining like a dog.

Meanwhile Milingo seemed to have had success with one of
his "exorcisms." A woman had got back to her feet and was looking
about her sheepishly; her friends were clapping and cheering and
praising God.

One by one Milingo was standing over each afflicted person,
and, as far as I could tell, he was entreating the demons to depart.
From time to time he seemed to enter into a trance. One by one
the demons were obliging.

I pushed my way to the doors of the conference hall and took
a deep breath of fresh air. I had no desire to witness the session
for another moment.

As I was driven back to Rome by taxi I noticed, as did the driver,
that the whole of the interior of the vehicle was permeated with a
strange musky stench that I had noticed in Milingo's apartment. It
was on my hands and in my clothes.

Milingo had frightened me, not so much with an impression
of evil as a threat of loss of control. I was also filled with a sense
of foreboding at witnessing the intrusion of "pagan" rites into the

Mass. My feelings reminded me of the discomfort I had experienced in my dream in Dubrovnik in which I had seen prelates cavorting in the sanctuary; and I reflected wryly that some sort of vestigial feeling for the integrity of the Church had survived in my nature.

At the same time, it reinforced my view that Milingo's cosmology of demons against the powers of light encouraged a dualistic, fundamentalist approach to the world. If every misfortune in life, from a lost purse to the measles, can be put down to the presence and activity of demons, there was little room for alternative interpretations of the world's ills. In the meantime, routine public exorcisms and sprinklings with holy water only served to strengthen the view that fear and the powers of darkness hold the center stage of life, rather than the love and mercy of God.

On the evening of the following day I made my way to a Jesuit community house in Via dei Penitenzieri, to talk with an expert on the subject of exorcism and possession.

A frail, scholarly-looking man with silver hair met me at the porter's lodge. I shall call him Father Stephen. He was dressed in black and I guessed that he was in his sixties. He looked highly intelligent and alert; but he moved slowly as if in delicate health.

He led me upstairs to a spacious room, bleak and bereft of creature comforts. There was a desk near the windows, which had been thrown wide open to the raw autumnal evening air. There was a black crucifix on the wall and an icon of Our Lady of Pity. The only cheerful feature was a bookcase filled with scholarly editions. His breviary lay open on the table.

Mild-mannered and quiet spoken, he asked me to sit down opposite him. He had agreed to answer my questions in a formal interview, but he warned me that he might not be able to talk about specific cases or persons.

He started by saying that there had been a resurgence of interest in possession and exorcism partly as a result of a resurgence of Pentecostalism in the Churches.

"People are rediscovering the long neglected gifts of the Holy Spirit. They are fascinated by the idea of being able to exercise the charism of good and evil spirits; but most of them are out of their depth and they are hooked on the idea of the *power* that's involved."

"But is Satan a reality, as a person?" I asked.

"Yes," said the priest quietly. "Saint Ignatius calls him 'the enemy of human nature.' Scripture presents him as a personal being, without a body, but with intelligence and freedom.' But we mustn't make the mistake of thinking of him as someone capable of confronting God as an equal."

"But don't the majority of Christians play down the idea of Satan in the twentieth century?" I inquired. "People don't really believe in him any more than they believe in Santa Claus."

Even as I said it, I was conscious of being crassly journalistic.

The priest was gazing patiently into his lap.

"It would be a great mistake to dismiss Satan," he murmured. "You should remember that Christ encountered him in the wilderness at the very beginning of his public life. We find it easy to accept the presence of evil in the world. We see it all around us. Evil phenomena are not entirely the work of Satan. There is the sense of natural evil we find everywhere in nature like genetic handicaps, cancer, droughts, earthquakes, pain. These are privations of good which are part of the mystery of God's creation. We recognize as Christians that nature is *fallen,* and we human beings have shared in that fall. But there is also the evil that is caused by deliberate acts of will, by individuals and groups of individuals. Satan was the first to establish *injustice* in creation by his pride and disobedience, and we humans are similarly capable of evil by free and responsible acts of wickedness. Personal, responsible evil is an inward closing of our will against God, like a closed fist. It is saying 'no' to God."

"But do we ever sense Satan's actual presence? How do we tell whether Satan is actually present, in *possession* of a human being?"

The priest was leaning forward intently as if hearing a confession. He was silent for a few moments, as if trying to control my impatience.

"One tends to gather confidence in one's diagnosis in retrospect, where ritual has succeeded after medical means have failed."

"Tell me about *that.*"

"There is exorcism, of course, and then there is deliverance. In exorcism we address the devil in person so as to force him to leave a situation or release a person who is in his power. Exorcism often involves a direct address of Satan or an evil spirit, and the exorcist may even attempt to encourage the devil to reveal his identity. On the other hand in the rite of deliverance we call upon Christ or God to order the devil to depart. Deliverance is much more common, and although the presence of a priest is not necessarily required, it is better that it should be done with the knowledge of the local bishop and in the presence of a priest. Exorcism is very rare indeed, and ideally should involve two exorcists working together at the specific request of the bishop. There are certain dangers for exorcists."

As if by way of an afterthought the priest added: ". . . and also for those who are engaged in deliverance."

"Is there a danger that an exorcist can become possessed himself?"

The priest smiled.

"You don't catch the devil in the same way as you catch flu," he went on. "Possession is a state of affairs that develops in stages, and a person's will is involved. The possessed person has *invited* the evil spirit in. You have to distinguish between *temptation* which can amount to an obsession with demonic interference, and demonic *oppression* which often comes in the form of dreams. In both these latter cases a person should still be capable of praying on his own behalf for deliverance. But possession is different; this state is brought about by that person's deliberate courting of the powers of darkness, and the common circumstance in which this happens is membership or contact with Satanist groups."

"Can you describe, Father, some of the common characteristics of possession?"

"I have to repeat the reservations I made earlier," he said evenly. "Any of the symptoms of oppression or possession may just as well be the result of psychosis, depression, or auto-suggestion, but the symptoms are cumulative. They would include a hatred of the sacred, including holy objects, or reading matter, prayers, and even the mere presence of Christians. Constant fear, paranoia, restlessness, lying, foul language, and obscene and murderous thoughts would be present. The possessed person often gives way to cursing, violence, and unbridled lust. He or she cannot go into church without vomiting and laughing and jeering out loud. They are prone to frightening grimaces, cramps, and wasting of the body; raving, screaming, unnatural voices, the speaking of unknown languages, the display of incredible strength and rage in the presence of an exorcist; clairvoyance, psychic and poltergeist activity in the immediate vicinity; visions of abhorrent and threatening figures. When all these things come together in a unique circumstance, and when medical help has repeatedly failed, we would be advised to consider deliverance, and then exorcism."

"From what you say, Father, the practice of Satanism is to be taken seriously."

"It's a bit like drugs," said the priest. "You start by experimenting, and in the end it controls *you.*"

"Do you think," I asked, "that Archbishop Milingo is dabbling with powers that are dangerous?"

"I can't comment on an individual case," said the priest abruptly. "But I can say this: I've witnessed the Archbishop dealing successfully with a very difficult case of presumed possession. . . . And now we really must end this conversation."

Before I left, the priest handed me a prayer card. "Keep this by you," he said. "It's known as the breastplate of Saint Patrick."

As I stood to go, he took me by the forearms and to my astonishment began to recite the prayer over me, and as he did so my blood ran cold:

> *Christ be with me, Christ within me,*
> *Christ behind me, Christ before me,*
> *Christ beside me, Christ to win me,*
> *Christ to comfort and restore me.*
> *Christ beneath me, Christ above me,*
> *Christ in quiet, Christ in danger,*
> *Christ in hearts of all that love me,*
> *Christ in mouth of friend and stranger.*

25

Satanism and the New Age

Before leaving Rome I had ar-
ranged to meet with a young man back in London who had suffered
from "oppression" and had been helped and rehabilitated with
"deliverance" prayers.

Before this encounter, and on my arrival in England, I took
the opportunity of reviewing a quantity of research material I had
gathered on the vexed subject of modern Satanic cults.

Rumors of Satanic activity seemed to be proliferating throughout the United States, Britain, and many parts of Western Europe,
and yet there were disputes over the exact nature of the "abuses"
that were involved. Allegations by social workers that Satanists used
young girls as "brood mares" to acquire fetuses for ritual sacrifice,
and that children had been sexually abused and even murdered,
were being challenged both by the press and the police in a number
of countries.

What was the nature and the extent of this spread of Satanism?
Was it merely an excuse for deviant sex? Or did it contain a sinister
demonic content? And what did that mean?

The current rise in Satanism appears to have developed on the
periphery of the hippy, flower-power movements of the late 1960s
and early 1970s. Mind-expanding drug usage, the free love ethic,
and the quest for alternative life-styles extensively promoted in the
popular music culture preceded a significant shift toward experi-

enced-based psuedo-religion and intuitive philosophies of life. There was a renewed interest in Eastern religions, spiritualism, and guru-driven cults, accompanied by a rediscovery of the occult, witchcraft, astrology, "channeling," and voodoo. Everything and anything, including the "darker" regions of belief, seemed to provide a possible idea or theme in the quest for do-it-yourself rituals and alternative religions. And the quest, like the promotion and commerce of popular music, was marked by an ethos of consumer choice; people were shopping around, procuring and discarding their latest cult fads, just like any other commodity in the pop-culture.

By the mid-1970s these proliferating expressions of religious counterculture were increasingly associated with the loose alliance of spiritual quests known as "New Ageism." New Ageism is a focus for the view that human beings are approaching a new stage of evolution by discovering alternative powers within themselves, the planet, and the cosmos. New Ageism seeks to heal the perceived social malaise of modern life, the drastic effects of Western civilization, by promoting a "rebirth" into a new stage of power, consciousness, and control over one's destiny.

New Ageists believe that the planet earth moves through the zodiac every 26,000 years; our entry into Aquarius, the New Age, started in the 1960s. Humanity is returning to nature, and we have the opportunity to become "autonomous individuals" in a decentralized society, stewards of our own resources and heirs to new riches and powers far beyond our present state.

In the coming new civilization we shall inherit beauty, love, and creativity beyond our wildest dreams, provided that we can learn to stand firmly centered between the "Earthly Mother and the Heavenly Father." Meditation is crucial; our prayers are answered by the "celestial figures," the "teaching presences of the universe," as well as by God, the total living force of the universe.

A central concept of the movement is holism, the notion that mind, body, and spirit, along with all the systems of the planet and cosmos, must be seen as a whole in terms of multi-relationships. In this sense the insights and efficacies of Eastern philosophies, alternative technologies, and healing arts are deemed superior to most "reductionist," "Western" science and medicine.

Dogma is frowned upon. The movement finds room within its boundaries for such diverse convictions as belief in UFOs, visitors from outer space, Gaia science, astrological speculations, and ESP.

Healers, prophets, and seers abound, as do their methods of operation, which range from immersion in rebirth capsules to the application of crystals: one "directory" that came into my hands listed no less than 4,000 resident healers in Britain alone. And the myriad movements incorporate and overlap with enthusiasm for ecology, self-sufficiency, herbalism, vegetarianism, and the quaffing of distilled water.

The New Ageists regard Christ as merely another "evolved master," along with Krishna, Mohammad, Buddha, other gurus, and major and minor prophets of the various world religions. Moreover, by the discovery of the "divine spark" within us, we can ourselves become prophets, or create our own gods and goddesses. In this general drift Christianity has not been condemned as such, but is looked upon as one of many means to achieve the promise of a wholly new approach to spiritual consciousness and practice.

Against this background of widespread fragmentation of mainline religious systems, the appearance of Satanic cultism is hardly surprising. The ethos of choice and privatization, the tendency to dabble and experiment, naturally led to a peripheral interest in the darker side of the spectrum of spiritual possibilities. The quest for a means to control the powers of light naturally found a corresponding tendency in the opposite direction. The quest for wholeness, peace, beauty, sensitivity, and joy has found a corresponding, if minority, desire to celebrate evil, violence, ugliness, coarseness, and hatred. The splintering of religious authority, the process of voluntarism, relativism and pluralism-run-riot, made it inevitable that Satan would be on offer in the supermarket of cultic options. By all accounts the emergence of Satanism was not so much the expansion of an existing line of tradition as the proliferation of new and transient experimentation dependent on the interests and personalities of the individuals involved and their reading matter.

Secrecy is paramount. Groups have tended to flourish and die away with the bewildering rapidity of childhood make-believe, making it difficult to study the phenomenon with any degree of accuracy or detail.

In many cases the experimentations have been no more (or less) harmful than the effect of films such as *Rosemary's Baby, The Exorcist,* and *The Omen,* the novels of Dennis Wheatley, or student Halloween japes. And overt expressions of Satanism in the late 1960s and early 1970s seemed in most cases as frivolous as they were ephemeral. A church of Satan was founded on the U.S. West Coast by one Anton Szandor LaVey in 1966, which was to spawn in turn a splinter group known as the Temple of Seth. These sects studied and disseminated a so-called *Satanic Bible,* an anthology of occult mumbo jumbo and permissive platitudes. LaVey and his followers proclaimed the cult of the ancient Egyptian god Seth associated with creative and sexual freedom. Satan, the devotees insisted, was a much maligned, much misunderstood spiritual entity.

Yet during this same period there was at least a hint of more sinister influences at work. Charles Manson's millennialistic "Family" cult, which culminated in a series of multiple killings, was influenced by a local neo-Nazi Satanic organization known as the Ordo Temple. Many of the characteristics of charismatic cults were discovered in Manson's relationships with his devotees as inversions of traditional norms of spiritual values. Self-sacrifice, obedience, austerity, discipline, surrender to a higher power, the rejection of "negative feedback" of society, parents, and prevailing culture, culminated not in spiritual growth but in hatred, violence, paranoia, destruction, and murder. The Manson killings, the Moors Murders in England, the mass suicides of nearly one thousand devotees in Guyana's "Jonestown," were stark reminders of the dark potential of do-it-yourself ritualism in a permissive society.

But does this add up to a thriving, dangerous, worldwide system of Satanic abuse? One of the principal problems of assessing the nature and the danger of criminal Satanic practice is the absence of firm evidence of the sort that would get through a court of law. The Christian Exorcism Study Group based in Marylebone Road in London have built up a composite picture of occultism and Satanism in Britain and other parts of the world. Whenever priests or parish workers are alerted to Satanic practices in the locality, they are asked to provide the Study Group with details.

Recruitment, they say, often begins at universities, and even at earlier schools, among the sexually deviant, the lonely, and those with a propensity or fascination for the weird, the terrifying, and the "gothic." The "softer" occult interest groups, like palmistry, tantric yoga, and astrology, are also targets for recruitment, as are covens for "white" witchcraft. Drug pushers gravitate toward Satanic groups because of the obvious opportunities they afford. Secrecy is of the essence and the path from early introduction to full initiation into the hard-core practices is apparently conducted with elaborate caution. If some of the practices are indeed abhorrent and involve drugs, pedophilia, and techniques of mind-manipulation, it is not surprising that Satanist ringleaders wish to keep their activities secret. Initiation ceremonies are said to be sexually compromising, and they can lead to blackmail when members attempt to leave a group.

Yet what is it that these various independent groups believe in common? According to the Christian Exorcism Study Group, Satanists hold that the Creator God has withdrawn from his world and does not intervene in its affairs. Satan is the true Son of God and is locked in a struggle with Christ for control of the world, and the outcome of the contest is uncertain.

My own research, derived from sources in Britain, Holland, Italy, and the United States, indicated that many Satanist groups are principally fascinated with blasphemy and sacrilege for its own sake. And it is for this reason that the alleged rites are based on an inversion of Christian prayer and liturgy, and a deliberate distortion of Christian beliefs. Stimulus for ideas for rituals, which are constantly revised, is derived from sources such as the *Malleus Maleficarum,* the seventeenth-century inquisitional handbook by the Dominican Fathers Kramer and Sprenger, and the *Compendium Maleficarum* by Francesco Maria Guazzo. Repeated translations and reprintings of such books have ensured the continued spread of interest in, and experimentation with, ideas and rituals, which are described in their pages. Descriptions of the supposed beliefs and practices of seventeenth-century witches thus find their echoes in alleged reports of the more excessive current Satanic rituals.

In one of the largest child abuse cases of this century, more than a hundred children from sixty-three families were alleged to have been subjected to sadistic sexual abuse associated with Satanic ritual at Pekela, Holland, in 1987. The events came to light when a local doctor examined a four-year-old boy suffering with anal bleeding without apparent cause. Further investigation led to allegations that a wide circle of Satanic ritual had routinely involved children in horrifying sexual abuse. The doctor, Frederich Jonker, said: "The children spoke of being in church, of having to lie down on a table naked ... They also mentioned the presence of babies ... of them being 'strapped up,' of having to cut the babies loose, and of having to cut crosses in their backs. There was also a baby put in a plastic bag. They spoke of a black baby which they were forced to hit with sticks, but they told us that this wasn't bad because black babies don't have a heart or blood anyway. We asked them, 'Was the black baby a doll then?' The children told us that dolls don't cry or crawl." According to Jonker the children were obliged to kill animals with shovels and forced to watch the "execution" of a cat with a chain saw.

The police conducted a year-long investigation in Pekela, and there were a number of arrests, but due to lack of hard evidence there were no convictions. The press in Holland eventually dismissed the allegations as "mass hysteria"; yet stories of a similar nature have continued to come in from various parts of the world. Organizations in London, such as the National Society for the Prevention of Cruelty to Children, have reported recent case histories of child abuse linked with Satanic ritual in various parts of Britain and especially in the North East and the East Midlands. Yet, despite extensive police investigations, no conclusive evidence has yet been produced to bring charges, and academic and media skeptics continue to associate the accusations with a lack of objectivity and the tendency to seek confirmation of a prejudice rather than the truth.

The tension between the skeptics and the convinced is all the more intriguing in the light of historical research in the 1970s into the witch hunts of the seventeenth century. Norman Cohn's *Europe's Inner Demons* (1975) conclusively demonstrated that witchcraft and Satanism existed purely in the minds of the inquisitors who were seeking it out. He claims that he has not found a single case of alleged witchcraft or sorcery in which the documents are not tainted. The "confessions" of so-called witnesses were the victims of the fanciful projections of Church officials. And beneath the urge to engage in mass witch-hunts Cohn speculates that the phenomenon of Satanism was "seen as an incarnation of apostasy, a living proof of the power wielded by the Devil in his battle against the Christian God." The collective obsession with witches, he suggests, arose out of a need for scapegoats on the part of those who had an unconscious urge to apostasize during a period of widespread skepticism in Europe.

For my own part, I was inclined to remember the life and example of the seventeenth-century Jesuit, Father Friederich von Spee. In 1627 the Bishop of Würzburg appointed Spee as confessor to those condemned to the stake during a period when tens of

272 THE HIDING PLACES OF GOD

thousands were dying as a result of the witch trials. Spee attempted to console more than 260 victims of these pogroms; the majority of them were women, and many were girls aged under ten years. Sickened by all that he had seen and heard, Spee wrote a book, without leave of his superiors, which he published anonymously in Latin in 1631. The book exposed the injustice, the false confessions, the brutal stupidity of trial by ordeal, the wickedness, the insanity of the witch craze. It was the act of a brave man, certainly comparable to the courage of those isolated Germans who attempted to speak out about Nazi atrocities from the inside. He was, of course, dismissed, and he ended his days writing mournful nature poetry in exile.

But one of the great ironies of the *Cautio* is that despite its sanity and deep humanity nobody has bothered to translate it or to provide us with a scholarly modern edition of the work. In the meantime the bloodthirsty fantasies of the *Malleus Maleficarum* continue to go through countless reprintings in dozens of languages.

26

Victim

Aman I'll call Philip Tudor lives in a cramped apartment high above the Elephant and Castle district of South London. He met me as I came out of the elevator on the eleventh floor. He was in his mid-thirties, I guessed, tall and broad in the shoulder. He wore his hair almost shoulder length at the back, but it was receding at the front, giving his head a dome-like, intellectual appearance. He was dressed in black corduroys and a black sweater, and it was quite obvious that he was wearing makeup, which gave his long, oval face a pallid, effeminate look.

He offered me some Scotch. When I declined he poured himself a third of a tumbler and topped the glass up to the brim with water.

There were several crucifixes on the walls, a holy water stoup and a print of Millais's painting, "Christ the Light of the World."

He sat opposite me in a battered armchair, leaning forward, glass in one hand, a lit cigarette in the other. He was shaking slightly as if he were cold.

"You've heard of phrases like 'his hair stood on end,' " he said, "or 'he jumped out of his skin,' or my 'blood froze' . . . I can tell you that when you get mixed up with Satanism those phrases become a literal reality. But it's not what people think . . .

"Let me tell you the whole thing from the beginning . . . I'm going to be frank with you, and you're going to be shocked; but people have got to understand what they have to be afraid of."

He paused a moment as if to gather his thoughts.

"Three years or so ago," he began, "I joined an amateur theater group; I can't tell you where ... it wasn't around here. The bloke that ran the thing, let's call him Michael H., was a very forceful type; people tended to get involved with him. He was bisexual and seemed to be able to attract men or women as it suited him. I admit that I was quite attracted to him myself ... If you haven't guessed already, I'm gay.

"Michael H. had a strong presence and a very quick tongue. He made me feel inadequate; yet the more he put people down the more they got infatuated with him. He had terrific self-confidence and appeal.

"I'm not sure what his background was; he gave the impression he'd dropped out from something like medicine or law. He was well-educated; he knew a lot of people and was on the fringes of the art world.

"I realized that he had an inner circle and it irritated me that I didn't belong to the favored few. He would come and have a drink with some of us occasionally as if he was doing us a favor, but he was always rather cool socially, and sort of knowing, as if he had you taped.

"Then one day, out of the blue, he rang me in a friendly way and asked if I'd like to take part in a sort of theater workshop; he said it was hush-hush and involved some experimental work. 'I think it might appeal to you,' he hinted. I was flattered, and I agreed to go along; in fact, I was fetched by car and driven with several other members of the group to a house.

"As soon as I arrived I guessed what was going to happen. There were twelve of us including myself and Michael H. It was a large room at the back of the house and a table had been set up to look like an altar; we were asked to take our clothes off and put on long blue robes. At first I thought it was rather pathetic, a bit of a cliché. But when we got started I realized that the whole point of it was to give vent to a stream of blasphemy. The idea was to outdo each other, take it to the ultimate extreme.

"By upbringing I am Church of England, but I hadn't been to church for years and I wasn't particularly interested in religion. But somehow you retain a basic feeling of reverence for it. Michael H.

told us that the point of the exercise was to release ourselves from the stranglehold of subconscious ties, to make ourselves free and thereby powerful.

"He would begin to recite a prayer, asking us to repeat it reverently with him; then he would suddenly say something obscene and make us repeat it. At one point two or three of the group started to giggle, but each time this happened he stopped and made us do it again. He kept saying: 'Come on! Enter into it!'

"The next stage was the ritual. There was a chalice filled with wine on the altar and some communion breads, and after saying reverent prayers like a priest he spat into the chalice and started cursing. Then somebody turned the light out so that there was only one candle, and everything started to degenerate.

"In the end there were people copulating, or at least they were going through the motions, like realistic improvising; then one of them started masturbating for real and came all over the altar; people were making obscene gestures with the chalice and the crucifix, and Michael H. was urging everybody on with a stream of filth, getting everyone worked up. In the middle of all this he got one of the girls to lie on the altar and he started fondling her, then he took one of the communion breads and pushed it up her vagina, saying 'Fuck Christ! Fuck Christ!' It sounds pathetic, a bit comic, just to talk about now, but at the time it started to make me feel really weird. I was taking pleasure in the blasphemy. But he still hadn't reached the really scary part.

"Toward the end he put his arm around me and he looked into my eyes. He said to me: 'How would you like to make a pact with the devil, Philip?' Then he kept coaxing me to ask out loud for the devil to take possession of me. He kept on and on and on; he wouldn't let me go. The others were all joining in. In the end I gave way, and said what he wanted me to say . . ."

At this point Philip was pressing the whiskey glass to his head; his shoulders were heaving slightly and the tears were rolling down his face.

"He said to me, 'Philip, if you want to see the devil just look into the corner of the room . . .' I was petrified, and I didn't want to look, but he just kept coaxing me, saying, 'Come on, Philip, don't be frightened. He's over there and he wants you to look at him.' All the others were standing round me and saying, 'Come on Philip . . . come on . . .' In the end I looked into the corner . . . and I saw this thing. I don't know how it got there. It looked as real as anything else in the room, like a sort of monstrous filthy crow, as big as a man standing up, and the longer I looked at it the clearer it became. It was *horrendous*. Its wings were covered in shit and slime, and when it opened its beak a huge bloody penis came out and made this dreadful retching sound ...

"I ended up in complete hysterics screaming my head off. I don't know how it ended, or how I got home. I suppose they took me. Anyway I eventually got to bed and fell asleep and I woke up at about four o'clock in a state of unbelievable terror. It's difficult to describe; it was as if from moment to moment I was about to be swallowed up in a sickening total abyss. I never thought such fear was possible. I felt as if the bird was at my shoulder. It was as if the ground kept disappearing from under me. Somehow we all take our security for granted, but once you've had the experience of losing it nothing is the same again. My mind seemed to be invaded by an endless stream of filth and obscenity and disgust that had nothing to do with my willpower. It was like being controlled. I was so frightened I thought I was going to have a heart attack. Then at about five in the morning the phone rang. It was Michael H. He just said one thing to me: 'Hello Philip, are you enjoying the feeling?' Then he started to laugh, and I could hear some other people laughing with him. Then he shouted 'Say hello to Satan for me!' and slammed the phone down.

"The following days and weeks were a nightmare of purest hell. I felt as if my personality wasn't my own, as if I was outside of myself in some way. My head was filled with involuntary obscene ideas like an echo chamber, and I had a constant battle with myself not to scream out obscenities in public. The strangest thing of all was that I couldn't stand the sight of a flower, or anything nice or beautiful, or the sound of pleasant music ... And it seemed that whenever I was getting a bit of a grip on myself Michael H. would ring and it would start all over again. The frightening thing was that he seemed to know exactly what I was feeling. It was as if I was completely in his control and that he had a malignant power over me.

"I never went to the drama club again, and I stopped going to work. I went to the doctor, but somehow I couldn't tell him or anybody else the whole story, partly because I was frightened of Michael. The doctor gave me some pills which didn't touch me; in fact they seemed to make things worse. When I wasn't thinking of vile ways in which I could kill people, especially little children, I was thinking of killing myself—all day long. I'd be walking along the street and all the time I'd be thinking, 'I'll throw myself under the next bus!' It was like a constant struggle not to actually do it.

"In the end I confided in a friend of mine who told somebody else who was a keen member of a local church. It turned out to be the worst thing I could have done. This person came round one evening. She was a young woman with a really crazy look in her eye; she asked me lots of questions and I could see that she was getting more and more worked up. She kept saying, 'Yes, I know . . . yes, I know . . . I know all about this . . .' Then she went off saying that she'd be back later.

"When she returned she had about eight people with her. They charged into the apartment and took over the place taking down pictures off the wall and moving furniture. Next they put me down on the floor and started reciting prayers and chants and throwing water all over me. They kept shouting out, commanding the devil inside me to identify himself and holding crucifixes in front of my face and slapping me. Eventually I started to struggle and they began pummelling and punching me and kicking me. When they left I was drenched to the skin and black and blue all over. But they didn't do the slightest bit of good.

"They came back quite a number of times and I was convinced for a time that I really was possessed, which only made matters worse.

"One night I was so restless that I couldn't stay in the house. I thought I'd go and throw myself under a train. You've got to laugh, I suppose . . . there just weren't any trains running. I kept bumping into all these weird down-and-out people . . . they're up all night, talking weird stuff. I walked with this old girl for about two hours and she didn't stop talking . . . And I kept thinking, 'This is how I've ended up!'

"In the early morning she disappeared and I was by myself walking along a road . . . I was passing a church with the priest house next to it. The door of the house opened and a young priest came out and started walking across toward the church, I suppose he was going to say early morning Mass or something. I just ran straight up to him and asked him to help me. It turned out to be the best thing that could have happened. He took me back into his house. He was a very gentle person; he sat me down and coaxed the story out of me.

"We must have sat together for two or three hours; I was in a terrible state, shaking and crying, and he just kept saying the Lord's prayer over and over again, especially the part which goes: 'but deliver us from evil' ... He put a little silver chain with a cross around my neck and he took me to see a doctor who gave me some sleeping pills.

"I saw a lot of the priest after that and he became a friend. He helped me to get grounded again and to realize that I'd been under the psychological domination of Michael, not the devil. I believe in the power of evil, I've experienced it and it's terrible; and I believe that I've been helped by Christianity, but I don't believe in demons and all that stuff. The sort of thing I experienced is much more frightening than any demon."

As we said goodbye he said: "I'll never understand why they do it, that's one of the most frightening things, it's the sheer pointlessness of it. I was lucky to escape ..."

As I reflected in the following days on Philip Tudor's story and the widespread rumors of "Satanic" child abuse, it struck me that it would be tragic to rule out the possibility of such deadly activities for the simple reason that there was an absense of tangible evidence. How would Philip Tudor, an intelligent adult, have proved anything against his tormenters? His experiences were real, and yet there was nothing to show except his fear. And it appears to be the same with mounting numbers of children who have been subjected, by their own accounts, to extremes of "Satanic" terror. Nobody would want to argue that convictions should be brought on the evidence of the children's stories alone. Yet there is a danger in the chorus of skepticism and mockery aimed at these children and their social workers.

The predicament is somewhat analogous to the gulf that separates benign religious experience and normal criteria of empirical verification. Just as we find it difficult to measure holiness, the power of prayer, or a sense of spiritual presence, scientific, forensic evidence is largely useless when it comes to matters of psychological influence, mental cruelty, oppression, and evil intent; absence of evidence does not mean that such things are not real, it simply means that it is difficult to nail the alleged culprits.

What convinced me, in the end, that these children and their protectors deserve careful consideration was the effect of my encounter with Philip Tudor. For several days I found myself haunted by his story, and strangely undermined in myself; I understood something of what he had felt; I empathized with his experience to a point of entering into it, and I was frightened. In consequence I felt compassion for both the child victims of these alleged attacks, and for those who are attempting to care for them. They, too, will have been more deeply affected than we can ever understand.

I learned, too, the value, the importance of being *grounded,* and something of the power of religious sacramentals and prayer in achieving this. Yet how was one to regard the efficacy of Christian objects such as crucifixes, holy water, and prayers without slipping into the dangers of the religion of fetishes and magic?

Yet one night as I lay, in the small hours, unable to sleep, I was grateful for the presence of Briege's small Celtic cross next to me on the bedside table.

27

The Gift of Tears

I had brought my travels to an end. But I could point to no specific, objective phenomenon that demonstrated "supernatural" intervention that contravened the laws of nature. And I was convinced that if I were to journey "ten thousand days and nights," until, like John Donne's rider, age snowed "white hairs" on me, I should still bring back nothing in the way of "proof."

The mystery of my dream persisted, as did a sense of having been "led"; but this remained a private, subjective riddle, which continued to tantalize without promise of conclusion or meaning.

I tried to turn my mind to other things, to prepare myself for a return to journalism and publishing, but I was restless, hungry, in a way that I could not describe. I could not say that I had found God, nor that I had been encouraged to believe in him again. Yet I had been making, for the first time in my life, some complex distinctions between religion's dark and benign faces. I had begun to cherish the *grounding* of religious belief. My regard for those who could believe and practice a non-judgmental respect had developed almost to the point of envy.

One day I found an echo of the peculiar quality of my mood while attending the funeral of a friend who had remained a loyal and pious Christian to the very end. At an early point in the service a Psalm was sung that I had not heard for thirty years:

Like the deer that yearns
for running streams,
so my soul is yearning
for you my God.

My soul is thirsting for God
the God of my life;
when can I enter and see
the face of God?

I could not subscribe to the full meaning of the words and yet I experienced a sense of dependence, an acknowledgment of the existence of a creator on the horizon of my life and consciousness.

Not long after this I accepted an invitation to go to Dublin to see Briege McKenna once more. I flew to Ireland in a state of confusion.

On the evening of my arrival at All Hallows, Barbara, the retreat administrator, came to fetch me after supper and took me to Briege.

She was waiting in a ground floor parlor at the back of the building. There were a dozen armchairs set in a circle, as if for a conference. She did not get up when I entered the room; instead she asked me to come and sit next to her.

She looked tired; there was a weary edge to her voice. Chatting amiably for a while, she told me about a recent trip to Nigeria. I was wondering, once again (unworthy thought!) what she would do if she fell in love with one of her priests. But she unnerved me suddenly by stopping and looking at me curiously.

I said almost without thinking: "How do you get through life loving Christ, a figment of history?"

Even as I said it, I hated the superficial question and was bracing myself for a pious answer. I should, by now, have known her better. She merely laughed.

Then she said gently: "The only way any of us are going to discover God's love in life is through the love of human beings. Christ's love comes through you and me as a loving people."

Suddenly she leaned forward, and before I could utter a word or resist, she took my hand and said:

"Just before we go, John, I'd like to say a prayer with you . . ."

To my embarrassment she immediately began to pray out loud, in short impromptu sentences, as if she were seeking guidance as she went along. I had seen evangelicals praying in this way on American television. There were occasional pauses for a breathless "praise you Jesus . . . Praise you . . ." She was thanking God for the opportunity to talk with me, praising Jesus, asking for guidance and grace.

I was seized with a mixture of outrage and curiosity. I wanted to tear my hand away and tell her to stop, but fascination kept me rooted to the chair. Every so often she paused again, as if inviting me to praise Jesus.

I could not. I would not.

Then she stopped suddenly. I stole a look at her face; her eyes were shut tight with concentration and her lips were pursed. She seemed to hold on to me tighter, with both hands. Then she said: "I see an image, John. You are sitting in a chapel. You are all by yourself, in complete solitude. On the chair next to you is a Bible. You pick it up and open on a certain page . . . I see that page open . . ."

I had heard this tone of voice before, the lull of the fortune teller gazing into the palm of the credulous client. I wanted to laugh, and yet I wanted to know what she was going to say next.

Briege's eyes were still shut tight. Her concentration seemed immense, her face almost in pain.

"I can see the heading of the Book of Wisdom, Chapter Nine, . . . I feel that the Lord has a special word for you in Wisdom, Chapter Nine . . ."

She was finished. Smiling and pulling me to my feet, she said, "God bless you, John, and now let me kiss you."

With this she gave me a tight hug and kissed me on both cheeks.

As I left her at the door, I asked: "Sister, what's in this Wisdom, Chapter Nine?"

"I've no idea," she replied. "I don't ever recollect reading it."

A snack of biscuits and tea was provided for the retreatant priests at ten o'clock. I escaped the jovial clerical throng and went out of the grounds in search of a pub.

The "Cat and the Fiddle" on the Drumcondra Road welcomed me into its roaring bosom with an hour to closing time. I was standing, sipping a glass of Guinness, trying to put my thoughts in order, when I felt a finger on my shoulder.

I turned to find a stocky little man with pale thinning hair and spectacles. I recognized him as one of the priests from All Hallows.

"So you've escaped, too," he said, toasting me with his glass.

We sat ourselves down in a corner.

"So what do you make of Briege, Father?" he said.

He was surprised to discover that I was not a priest.

"She's great, but a bit manipulative."

"Rubbish!" exclaimed the priest. "If you had an inkling of the problems she's sorting out among those priests you wouldn't say that."

"So?"

"For some of the priests she's the only answer. Take me. I'm a chaplain in the Irish Army: my milieu is the NCO's mess, not a nun's apron strings. I was out in Beirut, being shelled ... There's not an ounce of sentimentality in me, I can tell you. That woman put a finger on a deep-rooted problem I've had for ten years. She shocked the life out of me ... She knew the effect she had, too, she's been keeping an eye on me. Several times she's looked across at me; just the eye contact is enough."

"Do you believe that she has special powers?" I said.

"I do."

"But why *her?*"

"I don't know."

"And how does it work?"

"I don't know. It's a mystery ... and I'll tell you another thing ..."

He was looking me directly in the eye. "You're coming here is no idle coincidence in your life; when you get mixed up with Briege it's for a reason ..."

I awoke with a start and saw by my watch that it was two in the morning. I had fallen asleep on the bed after returning from the pub, and I was still fully dressed.

I wondered if I might find some biscuits in the room where the priests had gathered for their night collation. On tiptoe I went down the granite staircase to the ground floor. But everything had been cleared away in the common room and there wasn't a crumb to be found.

On the way back I stopped at the oratory door. It was open and a light was still on. I went in and sat down in sight of the Blessed Sacrament tabernacle.

I must have sat there for thirty minutes in the stillness of the night, thinking about faith and its relationship with evidence. Could faith be acquired by a skeptic who had merely been granted a small shred of evidence? Or did faith only feed on faith?

Sitting in the oratory gazing at the flickering sanctuary lamp, I began to wonder again whether it was possible to pray without faith. Did it make sense for an agnostic to seek guidance and help from God? Surely it was no more unreasonable, I thought, than the act of someone adrift at night on the ocean, who cries for help or fires a signal that may never be seen. What was the prayer of the agnostic, if it wasn't a cry for help?

Just at that point I noticed a Bible on the chair next to me, and I remembered Sister Briege's "vision" over me that afternoon. "I see you sitting in solitude in a chapel," she had said.

I picked it up and turned to Wisdom, Chapter Nine. It began with the passage:

> *O God of my fathers and Lord of Mercy,*
> *Who has made all things by your word . . .*
> *Give me the wisdom that sits by your throne,*
> *And do not reject me from among your children;*
> *For I am your servant and the son of your handmaid . . .*
> *Weak and shortlived with little understanding of judgment . . .*
> *For who can learn the counsel of God?*
> *We can hardly guess at what is on earth,*
> *And what is at hand we find with labor;*
> *But who has traced out what is in the heavens?*
> *Who has learned thy counsel, unless*
> *You have given wisdom*
> *And sent the holy spirit from on high?*

Had I been made especially susceptible by my mood, by an indefinable sense of hunger and restlessness? Or was it one or two drinks too many in the "Cat and the Fiddle" on the Drumcondra Road?

Whatever the case, in the solitude and silence of the oratory the words opened my mind and my heart, and the phrase "do not cast me off from among your children" echoed the yearnings I had felt when face to face with the rejected religion of my childhood and youth in my American dream. I wanted to believe this, and I was moved to tears by the force of the appropriateness of the sentiments expressed in the passage.

Sitting in the oratory I lost all sense of time, until the tall windows captured the first pale light of day.

I felt that I had found an acceptable prayer to pray, and in the silence and stillness I was even, for a moment, prepared to believe it possible that my tears were a token of the "loving-kindness of the heart of our God," who gives "light to those in darkness."

28

Journey's End

People who knew that I had undertaken a journey in search of the supernatural made visible would ask me: "Have you come across *anything* that was absolutely inexplicable?" My first reaction was to say "no."

That answer is not strictly true.

I have to admit, although it embarrasses me to do so, that I was baffled to the point of mystification by just one phenomenon, namely the tears of the Virgin of Syracuse. After looking at the evidence with some care I simply could not find an explanation as to how it might have happened. What is more, I was impressed by the fact that a similar phenomenon had occurred in Japan over a period of several years, and, even as I write, there are reports of an identical phenomenon in New York City.

My reluctance to admit that I was impressed by this event stemmed from my unhappiness about the implications. For it seemed to me a crude, unaesthetic exhibition, and to focus merely on the lack of explanation was to put the phenomenon within the realm of magic, and at the mercy of some scientific explanation in the future.

And what would be the purpose of such a miracle? To demonstrate the power, the legitimacy of the cult which laid claim to it?

What if I heard of a Hindu or a Buddhist statue that wept, would

I immediately accept that it lent credence to Hinduism or Buddhism? I rather think that I would not. In fact, I would tend to be annoyed at the idea that somebody should attempt to offer "evidence" for a creed or philosophy of the supernatural in this way.

There is, of course, a secondary question, which addresses the meaning of the phenomenon: what is the significance of the Virgin's tears in traditional Mariology? Yet the symbolism of the sorrowing Virgin—in Michelangelo's Pietà, for example—has far more impact, it seems to me, as a product of religious and artistic imagination than as a magic trick on a plastic plaque. So why should the Virgin, or God, or any other supernatural being, take time out of eternity to create an effect that is more successfully achieved by human hands and heart? The obvious, and unsatisfactory, answer brings us back to the suggestion that it is a display of power, an item of "evidence."

And as my journey progressed I became increasingly bored by the idea of physical prodigies: the gold Medjugorje rosaries, the liquefaction of blood in Naples, the jumping of Virgin statues. A token of my disgust with such "miracles" was my disinclination to even walk a few yards to witness such a thing. Crossing Europe on my way back from Italy, I stopped in Nevers in France and found myself deliberately deciding against visiting the "incorrupt" body of Saint Bernadette, which, apparently, is there in the cathedral for all to see. The idea of such an exhibit seemed repellent and irrelevant.

By the time I had reached Syracuse, I had undergone a change. I believe that I had begun to discern more clearly the difference between the apprehension of mystery, on the one hand, and crude magic masquerading as supernatural "evidence" on the other. And this growth in discernment had much to do with a stealthily growing conviction that I was no longer interested in evidence.

After leaving Dublin where, ironically, I had experienced that taste of tears, I was conscious of no great spiritual conversion. I had prayed, in the fashion of that shipwrecked mariner, calling out for help on a dark sea—just in case. But I felt nothing. If anything I felt a sense of dryness, of cynicism even, at the exercise I had put myself through: the journalist in search of God and of one or two good stories to boot on the way.

But the futility of the quest was even more apparent to me than the acknowledgment of those possible layers of self-seeking and self-deceit with which I had exploited my quest for faith. It reminded me of a priest friend who had a dream in which the members of a religious community were searching for God in cupboards, in drawers, under the stairs, on the undersides of their plates.

And yet, regardless of my explicit, and my hidden, motives, I realized that something had happened.

One morning after returning to England I drove up to the West Midlands to visit my old junior seminary. What led me there I have no idea, any more than I had an inkling as to what I should find there.

As I drove down the quiet country lane the building and its church looked much the same, but as I parked the car at the back of the buildings I began to see the extent of the calamity that had befallen the place.

The refectory, the lecture rooms, the libraries, and the cloisters had been looted, vandalized, devastated. The gardens, once beautifully tended, were overrun by weeds; the little cemetery at the head of the valley was completely overgrown. Father Faber's retreat had been demolished by a falling tree, and the church was locked up. St. Wilfred's, which had survived two-hundred years educating countless generations of priests, was an empty, abandoned shell.

It struck me at that moment that I was beginning to understand an inner truth that I had been trying to articulate with difficultly for so many months.

As a boy at St. Wilfred's I had once listened during Easter week to a speaker at a Franciscan retreat talking of the strict vocation to the contemplative life in the silence and austerity of a Carthusian monastery. Afterward I had walked in these same gardens thinking how heroic, how unattainable an ideal that was. How I longed for the courage to love God that much!

And now, thirty years or so later, I was only just beginning to understand that the desert wilderness of spirituality is not to be found exclusively in those convents and houses of prayer where men and women dedicate themselves, externally, to the service of God. The desert may lie at the very heart of a person's life, in the depths of one's being.

Many people who have turned away from religion, even with a sense of hatred, rejecting all its idiosyncratic externals, to embrace skepticism, agnosticism, even militant atheism, are perhaps as much in the desert, in the "dark night of the soul," as any contemplative. What we are fleeing, perhaps, is not God at all, but the false or the inadequate representations of him which hinder any possibility of ever making progress in coming to recognize him or reach out for him. What we are rejecting, even hating, is not God, but the "trash and the tinsel" that passes for him.

And thus it is that "hatred of God may bring the soul to God."

As I walked through the devastated, deserted gardens of St. Wilfred's my younger self seemed to come to meet me: without reproach or condemnation on his part, and without remorse or self-recrimination on mine.

A Postscript:
The Religious Imagination

Consider the striking preliminary vision in *The Revelation to John:*

"I saw . . . one like a Son of man, dressed in a long robe tied at the waist with a belt of gold. His head and his hair were white with a whiteness of wool, like snow, his eyes like a burning flame, his feet like burnished bronze when it has been refined in a furnace, and his voice like the sound of the ocean. In his right hand he was holding seven stars, out of his mouth came a sharp sword, double edged, and his face was like the sun shining with all its force."

To attempt to read the passage literally, applying strictly concrete or rigidly allegorical meanings, would severely diminish its power and significance. The polarities of snow and fire, rushing waters and roaring furnace, the majesty of the sun and stars contrasting with the tactile tensions of brass and wool, combined in the single image of a being both youthful and ancient, human and divine, are the discourse of poetry.

John brings to his writing the history of his own reading of the scriptures, and his skill as a poet; and we, the readers, are invited to respond with an appropriate receptivity. We are aware that he is selecting, shaping, fusing images and allusions to create an imaginative effect. He is "inspired," but he is by no means recording a series of dictated instructions; his inspiration is that of the poet: captivated, yet free.

In drawing together scripture and poetry in this way, I want to prepare the ground for suggesting, in conclusion, that a crucial key to understanding the nature of popular, or folk, mysticism involves an acknowledgment of the power of the imagination. I want to argue that through a deeper understanding of the nature of imagination, both artistic and religious, we may reclaim a wide range of religious experience from scientific debunking and religious fundamentalism.

This is by no means to propose that such mystical experience is purely subjective. It is a plea, rather, to elevate religious imagination above superficial fantasy and make-believe on the one hand, and fundamentalist magic on the other.

It is no easy matter to distinguish fantasy from imagination, for the meanings are subject to alteration from era to era, but an essential distinction involves separating disinterested originality and creativity from shallow, vicarious figments of hallucination and ego-centered daydreaming.

Coleridge describes imagination as a shaping power, that "dissolves, diffuses, dissipates in order to recreate," extending our consciousness by providing a new unity to our perceptions; it is an "echo" of the imagination of God himself in his "eternal creation."

This is an extraordinarily radical notion; for he is suggesting that we can perceive God's action in the world through language, images, nature, and human relationships. He is saying that God is to be apprehended not as an object competing for our attention with other objects in, or outside, the world, but wherever the imagination expresses itself in the opening up of the human heart. In this way, says Coleridge, it is possible to discover "transcendence" in "the incidents and situations of common life."

Coleridge's favorite image of transcendence in nature ("counterfeit infinity" he sometimes called it) was the waterfall or the fountain: "What a sight it is ... the wheels, that circumvolve in it— the leaping up and plunging forward of that infinity of pearls and glass bulbs—the continual *change* of the *Matter,* the perpetual *Sameness* of the *Form*—it is an awful Image and Shadow of God and the world."

This notion of the meeting of finite and infinite in a single image prepares us for the idea of symbol as something that, in Coleridge's words, "partakes of the reality which it renders intelligible," as something that shares in the power, the mystery, the presence even, of what it represents.

Symbolism in this sense is not so much true or false, accurate or inaccurate, nor is it amenable to any of the measurements we would expect to bring to material phenomena. Symbols are weak or strong, depending on the extent to which they participate in the reality they exemplify.

At the same time, symbolism yields not to probing and measurement, but to sensitivity, tact, and acquiescence; as Jacques Maritain puts it, we should "listen to the interiority . . . , to the poetic sense, be open to what it conveys, let ourselves be attracted by the magnetic ring . . . and this requires a sort of previous, tentative *consent.*"

For the theologian Karl Rahner, this tentative consent is a "pre-apprehensive openness in a person's nature to the mystery of being."

It is clear that imagination, symbolism, in this sense plays a crucial role in many forms of religious practice and experience: in the reading of scripture, in prayer, in acts of faith, in liturgy; and in the highest mystical states, as widely endorsed by contemplatives such as John of the Cross, Teresa of Avila, and Ignatius Loyola.

In the milieu of popular mysticism, however, there is a tendency to ignore the role of the imagination and to emphasize literalism. And yet, in the context of a Marian apparition, a prophecy, a miracle of healing, we surely should be prepared to interpret the externalization of the phenomena—the reported images, the iconography, the narrative and theatrical elements—as forms of interior and transcendental truth rather than as concrete descriptions. The intention should be to *understand,* as we would understand a poem or a piece of music, rather than to *explain* and *control.*

The Medjugorje and Garabandal apparitions are, as we have seen, unfolding stories in the context of the folk religion of Mediterranean communities. They are about the motherhood of God, the caring presence of her mediation, her assent to God exemplified in the gospel of Luke. To the extent that apparitions symbolize Mary's promised availability, they offer the promise of her living participation in the narrative of the children who see and address her. Such apparitions could be said to be the language, the theater, the liturgy of folk mysticism, the authentic imaginative perceptions of people steeped in traditions of local spirituality.

But fundamentalists will ask: What of the *reality* of Mary's presence? Is she *really* present in a spatio-temporal sense? And if she is not, how are we to distinguish genuine apparitions from make-believe?

This kind of questioning betrays, I believe, a lack of trust in the authenticity of the religious imagination of the child seers, as well as a lack of confidence in the discernment of those pilgrims who have made their journeys and experienced what they believe to be a sense of God's amnesty and mercy. This is not to evade the central question, for at the heart of mystical experience, poetic or religious, there seems to lie a deeply felt impression of *real presence* that goes beyond superficial literalness.

Thomas Merton, the American writer and Trappist monk, once entered into correspondence with Aldous Huxley on the question of genuine and pseudo-mysticism. Merton wrote:

> What I would call a *supernatural and mystical* experience ... has in its very essence some note of a direct spiritual *contact of two liberties,* a kind of flash or spark which ignites an intuition ... plus something much more which I can only describe as "personal," in which God is known not as an "object" or as "Him up there" or "Him in everything" nor as "the All" but as—the biblical expression—*I AM,* or simply *AM* ... this is not the kind of intuition that smacks of anything procurable because it is a presence of a Person and *depends on the liberty of that Person.*

The Medjugorje apparitions, as with those of Lourdes, Fatima, and Garabandal, focus on the person of Mary, who in Catholic belief is the Mother of God. It seems to me that the notion of a child perceiving Mary's presence (which is rooted, in Catholic understanding, in *God's* presence) as a "contact of two liberties," is equally valid. And to interpret the narrative and theater of her visitations as *symbolic,* rather than literal (in a procurable, spatio-temporal, concrete sense), is to enhance that presence rather than to diminish it.

The argument, I am convinced, can be extended across a great many experiential phenomena that have been covered in this book, including visions, divine healing, religious dreams, stigmata, prophecy, even, alas, in a negative and antagonistic sense, oppression and encounters with the so-called powers of darkness.

Such experiences and aptitudes are properly characterized as "private revelation," in that they convey no infallible message from the supernatural to society at large (beyond an endorsement, or revaluation, of religion's traditional truths); yet neither can they be said to be purely subjective or fanciful.

Who are these seers, these stigmatics, the healers and religious dreamers? They are special people, artists of the popular religious imagination, endowed with a more than usual sensitivity to the rhythms and archetypes of the transcendental, who are capable of perceiving a sense of the presence and love of God in vivid images and even physical symptoms.

To this end they may apprehend, exert a mastery over unconscious archetypes (in a Jungian sense) and the physical workings of the body's autonomic and neuronal systems. They are not magicians, nor do they exert power in a dualistic realm of matter versus spirit; they inhabit *our* world of flesh and blood and people and human relationships, and work through *them*.

The principal opposition for such a view will come not from scientists, nor even from theologians, but from the religious fundamentalists who seek to subject "supernatural" encounters to management, exclusive ownership, and manipulation. For the fundamentalist, the religious imagination is too inclusive, too open to religious pluralism, too liberal, too available to rival denominations and religions, and even to agnostics and atheists. It may come in various guises and in various degrees: through love; through poetry, music, art; through nature; through compassion for those who suffer or who are in need; through scripture, prayer, and ritual. For some it may take the prodigies of folk mysticism to kindle, or rekindle, the jaded religious imagination.

The awakening of religious imagination does indeed open the transcendental to all, for it is surely part of what it means to be fully human.

Index